INVISIBILIA DEI

A Collection of Hermetic, Mystical,
and Anti-Magical Works
by
Heinrich Cornelius Agrippa

Translated by Dan Attrell

Introduced by Justin Sledge

Detroit, 2024

Published by Esoterica Publications.

First Edition, 2024.

Cover design by Ashley Street.

"There are more things in Heaven and Earth, Horatio, than are dreamt of in your philosophy."

- Shakespeare, *Hamlet*, Act I Scene V

"For now we see through a glass, darkly; but then face to face: now I know in part; but then shall I know even as also I am known."

- I Corinthians 13:12

Contents

Acknowledgements

The completion of a translation project such as this could not have been possible without the invaluable contributions of numerous researchers, archivists, patrons, friends, and family members. We would like to extend our deepest gratitude to all those whose support and guidance have been instrumental in bringing this work to fruition.

First and foremost, we are profoundly grateful to the many scholars whose decades of tireless research have significantly influenced and enhanced our project. In particular, we wish to thank Vittoria Perrone Compagni for her extensive and insightful research on Heinrich Cornelius Agrippa's life and works. Her critical editions and scholarly analyses, especially on the *Three Books of Occult Philosophy* and the *Threefold Way of Knowing God*, have been indispensable resources that have greatly informed our understanding and interpretation of Agrippa's writings. We also wish to acknowledge Brian P. Copenhaver for his seminal studies and translations of the *Corpus Hermeticum* as well as his more recent work on Giovanni Pico della Mirandola. His various projects have greatly enriched our comprehension of the esoteric and philosophical traditions that underpin Agrippa's thought, providing essential context for this work of Renaissance intellectual history. Moreover, we are also indebted to Wouter J. Hanegraaff from the Centre for History of Hermetic Philosophy and Related Currents at the University of Amsterdam for his paradigm-shifting research into the Hermetic tradition, particularly his

studies on the Christian Hermeticism of Lodovico Lazzarelli and his book *Esotericism in the Academy: Rejected Knowledge in Western Culture* (2012). His demonstration of how Agrippa's chief concerns were with something "better than magic" has provided us with a critical perspective that has significantly shaped the direction of this collection.

Additionally, we are grateful to David Porreca and Brett Bartlett for their assistance in navigating certain particularly challenging passages in the Latin texts. Their expertise and insightful feedback have been instrumental in ensuring the accuracy and fidelity of the translations presented herein. Any remaining inaccuracies, oversights, and infelicities are entirely our own.

Acknowledgement is also due to the Internet Archive and the digitizers at Google Books for providing access to numerous manuscripts and early printed texts. Their extensive collections have been indispensable in the realization of this work, allowing us to consult rare and vital sources that would have otherwise been inaccessible.

Finally, heartfelt thanks go out to our patrons and supporters whose generous donations have made this endeavor possible. Your support has been a source of inspiration and encouragement throughout this journey. Special thanks must also go out to the participants of the Summer 2024 Agrippa seminar. It has been a pleasure learning with you all. Last but not least, we would like to express our deepest gratitude to our families for their unending patience, love, and support. Your

understanding and encouragement have sustained us through the long hours and challenges of this project.

Introduction

Heinrich Cornelius Agrippa von Nettesheim (1486-1535?) is often presented as a paradoxical figure. On the one hand, he was famously the author of the *De occulta philosophia libri tres* (or *The Three Books on Occult Philosophy*), a comprehensive treatise of magical theory and practice oriented towards mystical illumination and unity with the divine, first published in manuscript form in 1510, but not finalized and put into print until 1533. On the other hand, he was also the author of a polemical treatise entitled *De incertitudine et vanitate scientiarum et artium atque excellentia verbi Dei declamatio invectiva* (*On the Uncertainty and Vanity of the Arts and Sciences: An Invective Declamation*), a sustained attack on virtually all domains of human knowledge – including the occult philosophy – composed in 1526 and printed in 1530. Among practicing magicians and occultists, he is hailed as one of the great systematizers of arcane knowledge in the history of Western Esotericism. For anti-occultists, such as the Dutch theologian Martin Del Rio SJ (1551-1608), he was little more than a Faustian character, a necromancer doomed to perdition.[1] In the humanist tradition, his skeptical invectives brought low any pretension of certainly attained either by sense experience or by traditional scholastic dialectic. In light of this mixed

[1] Hanegraaff, *Esotericism and the Academy*, p. 87-88.

reception, one is often forced to choose an Agrippa: either the occultist or the skeptic, while promptly ignoring, or explaining the other away.

Nevertheless, in more recent decades, important scholarship led by Paola Zambelli, Charles Nauert, Vittoria Perrone-Compagni, Marc van der Poel, Wouter Hanegraaff, and others has offered us valuable insights that have served to uncover the deeper unity and continuity within Agrippa's thought, thereby shedding light on this paradox. According to their more nuanced and integrated interpretation, it would appear that Agrippa's mysticism was bound up with a kind of skepticism, and that his skepticism, in turn, was an extension of his mysticism, placing his thought very much in the tradition of apophatic (or 'negative') mystical theology and 'learned ignorance' reaching back through Nicholas of Cusa, Pseudo-Dionysius the Areopagite, and Augustine. Perceptions of this apparent paradox, however, were not merely born out of a lack of modern, reliable editions of his two principal works – and the cursory readings of those that are available – but also from (1) Agrippa's own tendency to obfuscate his actual positions by scattering his true opinions throughout his writings, and (2) a general tendency in his readership of ignoring the handful of philosophically substantial works he composed between 1510 and 1526. It is our hope, therefore, that this volume will serve as a small corrective to this latter issue, chiefly by making some of these texts

available in an English translation for the first time, as well as by making the oft-neglected epilogue to the 1533 *Three Books of Occult Philosophy* available to a modern audience.

Educated at Cologne, Agrippa informs us that he learned astrology from his parents and was exposed to both the Lullian philosophy and the Albertian strand of scholasticism in his early years.[2] This exposure to various Latin philosophical traditions primed him for what would later evolve into a deep interest in a wide range of esoteric topics from alchemy to ceremonial magic. From his earliest correspondence it is evident that Agrippa had managed to find himself a like-minded circle of friends and colleagues interested in natural magic, Jewish mysticism, and Hermetic philosophy. Their excitement was the product of a broader Renaissance trend, sparked only a few decades earlier by the work of Marsilio Ficino (1433-1499) and Giovanni Pico della Mirandola (1463-1494), which centered on a primordial wisdom tradition or *prisca theologia* believed to have originated from the secret teachings of such venerable ancient sages as Moses, Zoroaster, Orpheus, Pythagoras, Plato, and perhaps most importantly, the Egyptian Hermes Trismegistus. According to this perennialist tradition, the philosophy of the Greeks, the Cabala of the ancient Hebrews, and the *Corpus Hermeticum* of the ancient Egyptians were central

---

[2] Agrippa, *Epistolae*, 1.23 (in *Operum pars posterior*, p. 702-3).

to the recovery of the most ancient – and therefore the most pure and true – forms of divine wisdom intuited by all the greatest sages of antiquity. Agrippa's profound insights into these topics eventually led him to lecture on them publicly, transforming him from a mere scholar of the arcane into a kind of zealous missionary for his occult philosophy. Unsurprisingly, like Pico and Ficino before him, he faced resistance from Church authorities. In 1509, his lectures on Johannes Reuchlin's *De verbo mirifico* (*On the Wonder-Working Word*) were met with accusations of judaizing – a damnable heresy – and charges of promoting the "most criminal, condemned, and prohibited art of Cabala."[3] Agrippa defended himself against such accusations with little success, marking the beginning of a pattern that would repeat itself again and again throughout his life.

By this time, however, Agrippa had also begun composing what would become the first draft of his (in)famous *De occulta philosophia libri tres*, the manuscript of which still miraculously survives. In April of 1510 he presented his magical magnum opus to the Benedictine abbot Johannes Trithemius, one of the most learned men north of the Alps, if not in all of Europe. The 1510 draft delves into topics of magic, divine illumination, and the highest achievable state for mankind: supreme, eternal, and unbounded peace and joy (or *felicitas*) via

---

[3] Agrippa, *Oratio in praelectione convivii Platonis* (in *Operum pars posterior*, p. 1073).

union with God. Trithemius praised the young scholar, who was still in his early twenties, but advised him to be cautious, suggesting he focus his energies more on metaphysics than on magic. In the end, Agrippa did not entirely heed this warning. The 1510 draft, however, did call for a general reformation of magical practice along Neoplatonic, Cabalistic, and Hermetic lines – drawing heavily on the Florentine Platonism of his forerunners and on recently rediscovered *Hermetica.*

This reformed magic, according to Agrippa, would ultimately serve the goals of divine illumination and the attainment of that mystical self-annihilation in God so eloquently discussed in Pico della Mirandola's famous 1486 *Oratio* (so-called '*On the Dignity of Man*'). He outlined how this reformed magic would operate across three realms: terrestrial, celestial, and divine (or 'supercelestial'), incorporating a wealth of classical and contemporary wisdom into his vision. Although the three books were uneven in length – with the third book being particularly cursory in the 1510 draft – Agrippa's initial development of his occult philosophy marked a truly innovative and bold moment in Renaissance thought and spirituality. And, despite his so-called 'skeptical turn' by the Summer of 1526, Agrippa greatly expanded the work, nearly doubling its contents before its definitive publication in 1533. This expansion, perhaps influenced by Trithemius' earlier advice, is most evident in Book III, where Agrippa substantially developed both his focus on

practical Cabalistic magic and its underlying philosophy of divine illuminism and eternal *felicitas*.

But it is here that we must sharpen our focus on Agrippa's philosophical and spiritual development. As previously noted, a common understanding of the arc of Agrippa's thought suggests: (1) a youthful fascination with the occult sciences, followed by (2) a mature turn toward skepticism, and then either (3a) a regression back into superstition, or (3b) a pragmatic, properly disclaimed, and financially motivated decision to publish the *Three Books* before an unauthorized edition could appear.[4] The latter was certainly a real possibility, since one only needs to recall how Ficino's unfinished draft of the *Corpus Hermeticum* was pirated and printed without his consent to produce the 1471 Treviso edition, an unauthorized publication with wide reaching consequences. In any case, this arc of Agrippa's intellectual and spiritual development is too simplistic to be entirely accurate. After presenting the *Three Books* to Trithemius in 1510, he only deepened his engagement with arcane topics, particularly those of a Cabalistic and Hermetic nature, during his time in Italy from 1511 to 1518. Two of the six works translated in this volume date from this period. The first is his oration introducing a

---

[4] See, e.g., Blau, *The Christian Interpretation of the Cabala*, p. 85: "Thus, for a brief period in his life the skeptic was uppermost in him; both before and after this period he was the credulous philosopher of magic."

series of lectures on the Hermetic *Pimander* (i.e., the *Corpus Hermeticum*) given at Pavia through 1512 and 1515, which were fatefully cut short by the Battle of Marignano in September 1515.

The extant oration which comes down to us in Agrippa's *Operum pars posterior* (c. 1600) seems at a first glance to be as much an apologia by a blood-stained soldier for lecturing on philosophy and Scripture as it is an exploration of Hermes' historicity. However, Agrippa does here reveal his sustained interest in mystical illumination and a rather radical interpretation of the *Pimander*. He carried forward a long-standing tradition, originating in the Islamicate world and likely passed down through alchemical or astrological works, in which the antediluvian patriarch Enoch was identified with the first of three sages named Hermes. Enoch, along with Elijah, are the only ancient Biblical sages said to have ascended to heaven without experiencing physical death. Moreover, Enoch had long been associated with a vast body of angelic knowledge, both exoteric and esoteric. Throughout the Middle Ages, similar legends had come to surround Hermes, making his identification with Enoch a natural, if not unsurprising revelation. In this way, the venerable Hermes was rescued from paganism and credited with spreading the arts, letters, philosophy, and law to both the Egyptians and the Greeks, and thereby, to the whole world.

Indeed, Agrippa went even further, arguing that the *Corpus Hermeticum* was itself a divine revelation, conveying metaphysical truths, religious piety, and moral law. Drawing closely on the Hermetic Christianity developed by the poet Lodovico Lazzarelli – who was, in fact, the first recorded man in history to refer to himself as a "hermetist/hermeticist"[5] – Agrippa identified the Pimander, or "mind of divine power," with none other than his "crucified Lord JESUS Christ of Nazareth."[6] Thus, not only was Hermes identified with Enoch, but the revelation of Hermetic doctrine was also understood as a kind of pre-incarnational theophany, pre-dating both the Mosaic Law and the Gospel. This identification, more so than any of his other comments on the *Pimander* in the extant lecture, reveal Agrippa's desire to harmonize primeval Hermetic wisdom with orthodox Christian doctrine, presenting them as one continuous, unfolding revelation of God's providence through history. In this view, the *Corpus Hermeticum* was to be conceived as Holy

---

[5] Lazzarelli, *Crater Hermetis*, 4.1 (Hanegraaff and Bouthoorn, Lodovico Lazzarelli, p. 173): "*Christianus ego sum, Pontane, et hermeticum simul esse non pudet: si enim praecepta eius consideraveris, a Christiana confirmabis non abhorrere doctrina*" ["I am a Christian, Pontano, but I am not ashamed to be an hermetist as well. If you would study his teachings, you would find that they do not clash with Christian doctrine"].

[6] Lazzarelli, *Crater Hermetis*, 1.1 and 30.4 (Hanegraaff and Bouthoorn, Lodovico Lazzarelli, p. 167 and 263).

Scripture, pre-dating the Mosaic Old Testament and, at least in part, directly inspired by Christ himself.

In his 1515/6 *Oratio in praelectione convivii Platonis*, Agrippa lectured on the topic of love, a popular subject of Renaissance rhetoric, having been especially influenced by Ficino's *De amore*, a commentary on Plato's *Symposium* written in the wake of his famous translation projects.[7] Therein Agrippa developed a theology of love very much in keeping with an enduring tradition set out by Paul, Augustine, and Bernard of Clairvaux's *Sermones super Cantica canticorum*. In these sometimes aphoristic, even staccato sentiments, the divine, as pure love itself, can only be known through faith, culminating in a mystical union of agapic theosis: "*et haec est summa*

---

[7] For an English translation, see Jayne Sears, *Commentary on Plato's Symposium on Love*. See also Devereux, "The Textual History of Ficino's *De Amore*," 173-82. Also relevant is Pico della Mirandola's vernacular *Commentary on a Poem of Platonic Love*, trans. Douglas Carmichael (Lanham: University Press of America, 1986), large portions of which were reused in composing his 1489 *Heptaplus* which blended Platonic and Cabalistic themes into a single commentary on the creation story contained in the book of Genesis. In this commentary, Pico wrote plainly that: "...la felicità non è altro che pervenire al suo sommo bene e ultimo fine, e quell medesimo è ultimo fine d'ogni cosa che è suo primo principio." ["*Felicitas* is nothing other than reaching one's highest good and ultimate end, and that same ultimate end of all things is their first principle"], an idea that lay at the foundations of Agrippa's mystical philosophy.

hominum foelicitas, Deum scilicet fieri,"[8] Agrippa provocatively concludes. This oration, again rich with historical and scriptural references, reveals Agrippa's deepening exploration of mystical union with the divine as *felicitas*, the same ultimate goal for mankind he had outlined in the 1510 *Three Books of Occult Philosophy*. Agrippa's fragmentary *Dialogus de homine* offers us further insight into his religious anthropology, continuing the themes of humanity's alienation from the divine in the Fall and the need for reunion with God through both exoteric and esoteric avenues. His most systematic work of this period, however, would address precisely how human beings could fully come to know God in this lifetime.

The *De triplici ratione cognoscendi Deum* (*On the Threefold Way of Knowing God*), composed during this Italian period but re-worked and expanded before its publication in 1529, represents the clearest exposition of Agrippa's religious epistemology. In this work, he eloquently built upon the following threefold division of the soul first presented in the *Three Books of Occult Philosophy*:

1. *Mens*: the divine spark and the means by which illumination occurs. This element returns to the divine following death.

[8] I.e., "And this is the supreme happiness of humans, namely, to become God."

2. *Ratio*: the seat of the intellect which becomes either divinely illuminated or corrupted in life by the lower regions of the base sense. It can achieve *felicitas* in this lifetime and can depart for heaven following the death of the body.
3. *Idolum*: the seat of dialectical cognition, imagination, and sense perception. It perishes at death and can doom the *ratio*.

Here, Agrippa sets his theory of the soul into a broader temporal framework in which pure and immediate knowledge of the divine is revealed through the course of world history. To be sure, however, knowledge for Agrippa is not merely 'justified, true belief' but rather an encounter with the divine through the mind's agency ultimately underwritten by a radical trust (*fides*) in God's grace and love. Agrippa's epistemology is one of truth as obtained by spiritual/mental communion with the divine, not by assenting to propositions which correspond to states of affairs. He maintained, therefore, that human history – like all perfect things, which consist of a beginning, middle, and end – could be divided into three phases: a time before the Law, a time governed by Law, and a time in which the Law was fulfilled.

Mankind's earliest attempt to know the divine was through nature, extrapolating knowledge of the Creator from the study of created things. Even in the absence of divine revelation, this method of knowing God was

sufficient enough for man to develop not only a sense of reverence – a core Hermetic virtue – but also a sense of justice and piety. On account of divine grace, even pagan ceremonies and sacrifices offered up to the divine before the coming of the Law were acceptable in the sight of God, like the shadows of a perfect righteousness yet to be revealed. This first epoch was, of course, merely preparatory. The religion of sacrifice had been inscribed into the hearts of men because man was made in the image of God, who would ultimately sacrifice a part of Himself to show His love for all creation.

Nevertheless, this first method of knowing God served only to pave the way for a second and superior way: the Mosaic Law, revealed directly by God to man on Mount Sinai, which itself had both an exoteric and an esoteric dimension. The exoteric aspect was the straightforward practice of the Law revealed to all, while the esoteric was the Cabala, revealed only to the wise. In time, however, this form of knowing God also proved to be inadequate as the Law became fossilized into a series of empty, formal rituals, and its true meaning degenerated under Jewish stewardship. The final and supreme means of knowing God, then, arose only at long last through the revelation of the Gospel, by which God had made Himself known to man through His incarnation, living example, sacrifice, and resurrection in the person of Jesus Christ.

But even this 'way of knowing' had both exoteric and esoteric dimensions. The exoteric dimensions were

represented by creedal orthodoxy and the sacramental life of the Catholic Church, which were unto themselves sufficient for salvation. The esoteric dimensions, however, informed especially by Hermetic and Cabalistic teachings – albeit understood Christologically – opened the way to a spiritual understanding of the Gospel which pointed to the possibility of experiencing divine rapture and *felicitas* not merely following the death of the body, but in this very life. This very much continues Agrippa's project of generating an active mysticism whereby the aspirant reaches for the divine as opposed to a tradition of more passive mysticism whereby the aspirant was a mere recipient of mystical experience.

The Threefold Way of Knowing God is not only Agrippa's most detailed exposition of his philosophy's culminating point, but it also presents Agrippa at his most Hermetic. While virtually every page contains meaningful references to Scripture, they are equally replete with allusions and quotations from the *Corpus Hermeticum*, the *Asclepius*, Ficino's pseudo-Dionysian Platonism, Pico's Cabala, and Lazzarelli's Hermetic Christianity. As such, it would not be an exaggeration to regard it as one of the most explicit works of Renaissance Hermeticism. In spite of all this, in his blistering attacks on dialectical reasoning – specifically the logic-chopping syllogistic machinery associated with scholastic philosophy, which he and other humanists famously critiqued – we can already see the skepticism of Agrippa's 1526 *De*

incertitudine et vanitate scientiarum taking shape throughout the text. Here he spares no invective, heaping scorn upon the "sophists of God" whose attempts to know the divine through logical, syllogistic deduction are not just misguided, but satanic. Agrippa forcefully asserts that the dialectical reasoning of the schoolmen was invented by the devil himself, and that scholastic philosophy – once perhaps useful for combating heresy – has now degenerated into a cacophony of human opinions that ironically undermine religious truth. This skeptical attitude towards dialectical reasoning as a means of knowing God, however, stems from his commitment to a mystical knowledge, made only possible by faith (*fides*) and divine illumination, rather than from a generalized philosophical skepticism, such as the kind associated with Pyrrho and his school.[9] For Agrippa, skepticism and

---

[9] Perrone Compagni, "Heinrich Cornelius Agrippa von Nettesheim," in *The Stanford Encyclopedia of Philosophy* notes: "The usual compilation of discordant opinions of philosophers was partly shaped by texts of the ancient skeptics; but for the most part Agrippa made use of more recent sources: Ficino, Reuchlin, and Francesco Giorgio Veneto. There are no quotations from Gianfrancesco Pico's *Examen vanitatis doctrinae gentium*, the first detailed reading of the work of Sextus Empiricus. This significant omission suggests that Agrippa did not agree with the skeptical fideism expressed by Gianfrancesco. *De vanitate* did not, in fact, question the human ability to know causes. Rather, it questioned the capacity of Aristotelian epistemology to account for the nature of things." Cf. Hanegraaff, *Esotericism and the Academy*, p. 81-82 and Nauert, *Agrippa and the Crisis of Renaissance Thought*, p. 148-152.

mysticism are intertwined in the unity of true knowledge, grounded in trust of the divine and the illumination of the mind and soul by God alone.

Agrippa's distrust of truth derived solely from dialectical reasoning continued to find expression in his 1518 *De originali peccato* (*On Original Sin*), where Adam is said to represent faith, Eve 'free reason' (*ratio libera*), and the snake sensuality. In Agrippa's esoteric interpretation of the Fall narrative in Genesis, the snake uses casuistry to convince Eve to eat of the fruit of sensuality. Eve, in turn, uses similar logic to override Adam's faith, with the original sin being the corruption of sexuality into mere carnal desire, a perversion of divine love into *fornicatio*. Here, Agrippa's emphasis on divine love, as opposed to mere carnal fornication, and on knowing the divine through faith rather than through dialectical reasoning, is made explicit. But it would not be until the summer of 1526, following the fiasco of Agrippa's time at the court of Louise of Savoy in France, that he would compose his *De incertitudine et vanitate scientiarum*.

Before turning to the *De incertitudine*, however, it is worth noticing what is conspicuously absent from Agrippa's works of this period. In the surviving writings from 1510 to 1526 – a span of roughly 16 years – there is a striking silence on the subject of magic. Aside from a single mention in *De triplici ratione*, where it is mentioned in passing alongside Cabala (i.e., "the holy name of Cabala

came into suspicion, just as also happened to the sacred name of magic, both of which have become suspect, both of which have been profaned"), Agrippa says little about magic during this time. While this statement still reflects his 1510 view that the name and practice of magic had been contaminated – implying the existence of a once pure form – Agrippa is otherwise virtually silent on the topic. The reasons for this silence can only be speculated upon. Perhaps under the influence of John Colet, Agrippa downplayed the centrality of magic in his thought. Perhaps he was simply heeding Trithemius' advice to be more circumspect, as much of his output during this period consisted of public orations and lectures. And perhaps, when considered alongside *De incertitudine* and the epistolary evidence of 1527-1528, we might conclude that while Agrippa extended his skeptical critique to magical practice, his final stance fell short of a complete disavowal of the occult arts.

To delve deeper into this speculative vein, we must turn to the *De incertitudine*, particularly the chapters and letters Agrippa ultimately appended as an epilogue to his 1533 *Three Books of Occult Philosophy*. Exactly what inspired Agrippa to publish his *declamatio invectiva* remains unclear. Whether it was driven by a bout of melancholy, an outburst of rage in regards to his failures at court, the broader humanist trend toward skepticism, or a proto-Protestant expression of fideism, the *De incertitudine*, when set against *The Three Books* of 1533,

has long perplexed students of Agrippa. But the paradox between the two texts is more apparent than real. Beneath the skeptical critique lie Agrippa's most fundamental tenets: knowledge derived solely from reason, without divine illumination, is at best deficient and at worst destructive. And, as Agrippa argued in 1526, such unilluminated reason has led to a world where sophistry masquerades as wisdom, the arts and sciences are deployed for human corruption and vice rather than for flourishing and piety, and even Christian salvation has been swallowed up by satanic dialectics, a ceremonial life stripped of spiritual power, and superstitions propped up by demonic trickery. In essence, the *De incertitudine* is simply the negative reflection or shadow cast by much of what Agrippa had already written. It is also Agrippa's singular work of social criticism.

Rather than focusing on the substance, methods, and goals of a Christian life built on trust in the divine (*fides*), which seeks to understand the cosmos in pursuit of illumination and the experience of *felicitas* in this life, Agrippa confronts a world that operates in stark opposition. *De incertitudine* is by no means a disavowal of his core concerns – faith, understanding, illumination, and *felicitas* – but rather an indictment of religion, society, the arts, sciences, and occultism when they function without or against these lofty means and goals. Though often interpreted as a devastating tidal wave of criticism from which only the most naive profession of ignorance

survives, the *De incertitudine* is far more nuanced. Agrippa was neither a Pyrrho nor a proto-Hume. The goal of this sage was not the suspension of judgment resulting in *ataraxia*, nor a radical challenge to the limits of knowledge, whether metaphysical or otherwise. Instead, Agrippa sought to bear witness to the flawed state of the world, society, and religion, with the hope of their reform and restoration. This vision was grounded in the time-honored tradition of *docta ignorantia* ("learned ignorance"), a tradition that was not undermined by the alleged skeptical catastrophe represented by the *De incertitudine*, but rather supported by Agrippa's deeper mystical commitments.

This approach also extends to Agrippa's discussions of the occult arts. Just as he moved from discipline to discipline, diagnosing the sorry state of affairs in each before separating the wheat from the chaff, Agrippa applied the same method to various branches of the occult arts. The Lullian art, divination, astrology, natural magic, witchcraft, goetia, necromancy, alchemy, and Cabala are all more or less subjected to a similar critique: they can be redeemed if built upon a foundation of faithful understanding (*fides* as '*fundamentum rationis*') and practiced with a mind rightly guided by reverence and divine illumination, with the goal of advancing the human flourishing, dignity, and true success. On one hand, arts like goetia, necromancy, and witchcraft (*veneficium*) should be rejected outright given that they only lead to

sinister ends. On the other hand, arts like natural magic, theurgy, alchemy, and Cabala do contain elements which can be salvaged – though admittedly Agrippa focuses little on these elements in the *De incertitudine*. The challenge, as he presents it, is to discern what is living from what is dead within these practices. Often, Agrippa's silence is telling, if we allow it to speak. In the chapter on Cabala, for instance, he heaps scorn on the use of 'arithmancy' (or *notarikon*) to generate metaphysical truths through scriptural manipulation. Yet he passes over – like an angel of death – any discussion Cabala's other dimensions, such as speculative cosmology (e.g., the emanations of the divine in the *sefirot*) or the "higher contemplations of divine and angelic virtues [and] sacred names." Indeed, these are precisely some of the elements Agrippa would later add to the 1533 edition of *De occulta philosophia libri tres* which were largely absent from the 1510 draft.

The totalizing scope and effect of Agrippa's skepticism in *De incertitudine* has, in my view, been misunderstood and overstated. His skeptical assault is grounded in the same core values found in his earlier occult, Hermetic, and mystical works. In fact, it is precisely the magical, Hermetic, and Cabalistic elements that are most expanded from the 1510 to the 1533 editions of the *De occulta philosophia libri tres*. If the *De incertitudine* induces totalizing skepticism in some readers, it clearly did not have that effect on Agrippa himself, whose alchemical practice and expansion of his

occult philosophy continued steadily through the late 1520s.

So what are we to make of 1) the epistles, 2) the selected chapters from the *De incertitudine*, and 3) the famous retraction included as the epilogue to the 1533 edition of *De occulta philosophia libri tres*? These were neither printed in Vittoria Perrone Compagni's critical edition nor included in recent English translations by Eric Purdue and Paul Summers Young.[10] We have, therefore, included a translation of this epilogue in this volume. These texts are important because they provide insight into the perilous context of Agrippa's work and may represent his ultimate intellectual stance on the significance of the occult philosophy as we have them. The context is fairly well known: Agrippa attempted to bring the greatly expanded *De occulta philosophia* to print in late 1532 but was interrupted by the inquisition at Cologne. However, with the intercession of his ally Hermann of Wied, the Archbishop-Elector of Cologne, the complete first edition was finished in July of 1533. Exactly why Agrippa and/or the printer Johannes Soter decided to append the three epistles along with eight chapters from *De incertitudine* is unclear. The obvious function would be to provide both Agrippa and Soter with some degree of plausible deniability, given the inquisition's scrutiny. At a superficial glance, the epilogue

---

[10] They do, however, appear in the unreliable English translation of 1651 by J.F.

may appear to support such subterfuge. Nevertheless, as is evident from the chapters from *De incertitudine*, Agrippa did not cast all the occult arts into the outer darkness of his skepticism.

If Agrippa is somewhat dissimulating about the extent of his rejection of the occult arts in certain chapters of *De incertitudine*, he is far less so in the three epistles. Composed in 1527 and 1528, these letters offer a clearer window into his actual stance on occult philosophy after the skeptical assault of 1526. All three letters reveal a central Agrippan theme: that inner divine illumination is the key to true magic, with magic itself serving as a propaedeutic to the bliss of perfect communion with the divine, or *felicitas*. In his epistle to Father Aurelius, Agrippa states that he would gladly discuss these matters in person, as such secrets are meant to be transmitted orally. He also notes, however, that once his *De occulta philosophia libri tres* are published, the key to its understanding would be reserved for an elite few, a claim he would reiterate in the 1533 edition. This is interesting because in a subsequent letter to the same recipient, dated November 9, 1527, Agrippa sorely admitted that he himself had never experienced such divine illumination and was unlikely to ever do so, having lived a life "consecrated as a soldier by human blood, almost always a courtier, bound by the bond of the flesh to a most dear wife... and wholly driven astray by the flesh." Instead, he tragically presented himself as a doorman, like a common

carnival barker, pointing the way to others but never entering himself.

The final letter, written in Paris on February 13, 1528, finds Agrippa lambasting a would-be German wizard who had gained some degree of favor at court. Here, Agrippa denounced the same magical practices he had opposed 18 years earlier: magical flight, finding buried treasure, divining the future, compelling love, curing disease, and all other manner of feats typically associated with the 'grimoire magic' that Agrippa – following Ficino, Pico, and Reuchlin – had sought a decisive break with. In a preview of his 1533 stance, he offered a damning litany of historical charlatans, false prophets, and diabolical sorcerers. His final warning in the letter is telling: "I think I have now said enough on this matter, for I do not wish to pursue it further, lest perhaps the malice of the subject at hand might push the pen where it ought not to go."

July of 1533 saw the completion of the printing of Agrippa's *De occulta philosophia libri tres*. Small variations in the first edition remain as ghostly scars left by the temporary interdict of the inquisition. After mid-1533, Agrippa's correspondences – one of our few sources for biographical information – dried up, and Heinrich Cornelius Agrippa von Nettesheim passed on into the realm of legend and history. His legacy is decidedly mixed. Misinterpretations of *De incertitudine* made him an inspiration for later humanist skeptics, such as Michel de Montaigne, while misreadings of *De occulta philosophia*

libri tres made him a target for demonologists like the Jesuit theologian Martin del Rio. How widely, let alone how deeply, Agrippa's works were read in the centuries that followed remains debatable. The magical reformation he inherited from Ficino, Pico, Lazzarelli, and Reuchlin ultimately amounted to little in the centuries marked by religious reform and scientific revolution. Spurious works of spirit conjuration were pseudepigraphically attributed to him, and even his *Opera Posthuma* is filled with the very kind of medieval magic that Agrippa sought to discard. The 19th and 20th-century occult revival, spurred by works like Francis Barrett's *The Magus* and culminating with the Hermetic Order of the Golden Dawn, placed his occult philosophy into a magical canon alongside texts like the *Lesser Key of Solomon*, works that likely would have offended him at best. To this day, no modern edition of his complete works has been produced. If, as Wouter Hanegraaff suggests, 'Western Esotericism' is to be understood as the "dustbin of history"[11] – a towering heap of knowledge unceremoniously rejected by Enlightenment *philosophes* – then Agrippa stands as its most exemplary figure.

Thankfully, the tide is turning and the 20th and 21st centuries have seen renewed interest in Agrippa. He is undoubtedly a philosopher who deserves a prominent place in the canon of Western intellectual and spiritual

---

[11] Hanegraaff, *Esotericism and the Academy*, p. 128.

history. This volume was inspired by the interest of participants in my recent seminar on Agrippa's occult philosophy. It serves as an intellectual placeholder for an eventual academic publication of Agrippa's complete works. But, with the publication of the more Hermetic works from the Italian period, along with the epilogue material of the 1533 *De occulta philosophia libri tres*, I hope this volume bears witness to the fundamental unity of Agrippa's thought, and I hope it inspires continued interest in a philosopher whose occult philosophy and deep skepticism were ultimately aimed at magnifying human dignity, illumination, and *felicitas*. May his merit inspire us.

Justin Sledge
Detroit, October 2024

Translator's Notes

The works presented in this volume have been organized in chronological order to help demonstrate the development of Agrippa's thought from about 1515 to 1533, the year in which he published the completed version of his *De occulta philosophia*, albeit not without reservations due to the controversial nature of its content. This period marks a significant phase in Agrippa's intellectual journey, during which his ideas on magic and philosophy evolved, taking on a more skeptical stance towards both magic and scholasticism, coupled with a turn towards a deeper commitment to Christian mystical theology. By presenting his works in this manner, our aim has been to provide a more nuanced understanding of Agrippa's intellectual trajectory from youth to adulthood, highlighting the complexities and shifts that defined his contributions to Renaissance and Reformation-era philosophy.

Although I have transcribed and translated both the Pavian *Oratio de potestate et sapientia Dei* (1515) and the *De triplici ratione cognoscendi Deum* (1515-1516) directly from the c. 1600 *Operum pars posterior* (p. 1073-1083 and p. 480-501 respectively), I have for the sake of consistency introduced the same paragraph divisions devised by Vittoria Perrone Compagni in her 2005 Polistampa edition entitled *Ermetismo e Cristianesimo in Agrippa: Il*

De triplici ratione cognoscendi Deum.[12] I am indebted to her many notes and some of the corrections she made by comparing various printed editions of this text, though I have made no attempt here to reproduce her critical edition. The Latin we present is simply as it appears in the *Operum pars posterior*, with expanded abbreviations and some minor corrections where necessary. Wherever possible I attempted to give all my references to modern English translations rather than Early Modern printed editions, as Perrone Compagni has done. This was done not only to add value for English readers and researchers, but to showcase the recent progress that has been made in the anglosphere regarding the study of Renaissance Hermeticism over the decades since the publication of Dame Frances Yates' *Giordano Bruno and the Hermetic Tradition* (1964).

For the *Epistolae* and the *Censura sive retractatio de magia ex sua declamatione de vanitate scientiarum et excellentia verbi dei*, I transcribed and translated the Latin as it is contained in the 1533 Köln edition of *De Occulta Philosophia libri tres* from the collection of Carl Jung.

In terms of translation style, I have attempted to sail a middle course between the Scylla of slavish literalism and the Charybdis of poetic flights of fancy. My aim has been to produce a translation that faithfully conveys the original meaning and nuances of Agrippa's text while ensuring that it remains accessible and engaging to modern readers, without sinking too deeply into the mire

---

[12] Elsewhere, paragraph divisions are my own.

of archaisms and affectations. I have, to the best of my abilities, avoided taking excessive liberties that could distort the author's intent or introducing interpretations not present in the source material (which we have provided in facing pages). By balancing fidelity with readability, I hope to present Agrippa's works in a way that honors his poetic genius and intellectual legacy, and makes his insight and breadth of learning available to a 21st-century audience.

Where Agrippa relied on the works of other authors, such as Marsilio Ficino, Lodovico Lazzarelli, Paolo Riccio, and Pico della Mirandola, I have supplied references and full quotations in translation to the original works with marginal notes. Given that my own translation of the Hermetic *Asclepius* (in partnership with David Porreca and Brett Bartlett, based on Matteo Stefani's 2019 critical edition) is still forthcoming at the time of this publication in the Fall of 2024, quotations of the Latin *Asclepius* (and the *Corpus Hermeticum*) provided in the footnotes have mostly been drawn from Brian Copenhaver's *Hermetica* (1992). Note, however, that quotations from the *Corpus Hermeticum* provided by Copenhaver are based on Greek texts edited by Arthur Darby Nock (and translated by André Jean Festugière), not on the Latin translations that were available to Agrippa himself. As such, some minor discrepancies may arise between my own translation of Agrippa's Latin in the main body of the text and the English passages cited in the notes, though I believe these variations should not impede the overall coherence and understanding of the work. It is my hope that this

translation opens up new avenues for understanding Renaissance Hermeticism and inspires further exploration into the rich tapestry of Agrippa's esoteric and mystical thought.

Dan Attrell
University of Waterloo, 2024

Oratio, habita Pavia in praelectione Hermetis Trismegisti, de potestate et sapientia Dei, Anno MDXV

Considerans Illustrissime Marchio, praestantissimi Patres, ornatissimique viri, varios humanarum rerum tumultus, simul atque duram novercalis fortunae sortem, qua per integrum nunc triennii curriculum bellorum armorumque im[1074]plicitus negotiis usque fatigatus sum, diu et multum cogitavi argumentaque multa in pectus institui, ac multis modis egomet mecum eam rem disputavi, quanam ratione quove consilio et ope post procellosum illum, utrasque praetergressus Scyllas, sanguinolenti maris transitum feliciorem denuo nancisci possem vitae portum. Occurrebant mihi magnopere necessarium esse fungi munere aliquo, et eo potissimum, quod plurimum honestatis nec minus fungi in se contineat. Atque id repperi nunc tale quidem, quod cum decore peragere possum, quodque a mea professione atque militia non est alienum.

Oration, held in Pavia during the reading of Hermes Trismegistus, On the Power and Wisdom of God (1515)

Considering, O most illustrious Marquis, O most excellent Fathers, O most distinguished men, the various tumults of human affairs, and the harsh lot of a malevolent fortune, by which I have been worn out for the whole course of a three year period, tangled up in the business of wars and arms, I have long and deeply reflected and devised many arguments within my heart, and I have debated this matter with myself in many ways, by what means or with what plan and work, after passing through that stormy, bloody sea, and having escaped both Scyllas, I might again obtain a more fortunate port of life.[13] It occurred to me that it was greatly necessary to perform some duty, and chiefly that which contains in itself the most honor and no less duty. And I found it to be something indeed, which I can perform with decorum, and which is not alien to my profession and military service.

---

[13] Here Agrippa opens his oration in good humanist style with a metaphor drawn from Book 12 of Homer's *Odyssey*, wherein Odysseus and his crew are forced to navigate between Scylla, a six-headed monster, and Charybdis, a deadly whirlpool. By referring to "both Scyllas," Agrippa likens his struggles as a soldier to the perilous wanderings of Odysseus on his return from the Trojan War, and the "fortunate port of life" to Odysseus' long-awaited return to Ithaca, symbolizing his hoped-for peace in God (*felicitas*).

Abditiora videlicet sublimioris divinaeque Philosophiae mysteria in florentissimo hoc Gymnasio vobis et reserare et interpretari. Nam cum ab ineunte aetate multijugis literis eruditus, coelestium influxu divinoque genio ab ingenio naturali corroboratus rerum secretissimarum naturam, ipsiusque naturae ordinem spectaculum omnium amoenissimum contemplatus sim, nihil magis ad me attinere arbitror, quam ut sacrosanctam hanc amplexus Philosophiam, ducem me praestem iis, qui ea maxime eruditione sunt digni, ut in Tycinensi Gymnasio optimi quique adolescentes nostro munere atque opera, depromptis ex nostris thesauris novis atque veteribus sacrae illius Philosophiae fructus intellectuque consequantur.

Sed vereor hic (consummatissimi adjutores) ne qua fortassis animum vestrum subeat indignatio ac me non modo arrogantiae, praesumptionis ac insolentiae, verum, etiam temeritatis vitio arguatis, quod ipse ego ut homo sic in natione barbarus, exercitio hactenus miles, habitu exotico, hanc Cathedram conscendere, atque in tam cruda et immatura aetate tanta vobis et ea praesertim polliceri audeam, quae prae rerum magnitudine gravissimum alias ac maturum inveteratumque Doctorem expectant.

Namely, to unlock and interpret for you the more hidden mysteries of the higher and divine philosophy in this most flourishing school. For, having been educated from my youth in all kinds of literature, strengthened by the influence of the heavens and by a divine genius from an innate talent, I have contemplated the nature of the most secret matters, and the order of nature itself, the most beautiful spectacle of all. I consider nothing more pertinent to me than to embrace this sacred philosophy, to put myself forward as a guide to those who are especially worthy of this education, so that every noble youth in the Ticinian school might, through our service and work, attain the fruits of that sacred philosophy, drawn out from our treasures, new and old, and from our understanding.

But I fear here (most accomplished assistants) that perhaps some indignation might arise in your minds, and that you may accuse me not only of arrogance, presumption, and insolence, but even of the vice of rashness, because I, as a man who is thus a barbarian by origin, a soldier by practice up till now, with a foreign appearance, dare to ascend this chair and promise you such great things – especially at such an unripe and immature age[14] – things which, due to their greatness, usually demand a most serious, mature, and inveterate doctor.

---

[14] Agrippa was born on September 14, 1486, making him around 29 years of age at the time he composed this oration.

Verum cum ad vestri intellectus perspicaciam et promptitudinem, et ad vestram erga studia optima diligentiam atque constantiam me converto, meamque haud ignaviter alias exercitatam et legendi et interpretandi consuetudinem cum his confero, nihil prorsus erit quod in hac re vel de capacitate vestra, vel de ingenio meo diffidam. Neque vero junior ipsa aetas prohibet, quin possemus aeque bene vel meliuscule interdum quam seniores aliquid discernere: siquidem non aetate sed ingenio inspirationeque provenit intelligentia: neque enim numerus annorum et multitudo dierum dant scientiam, sed ingenium coelitus infusum, ac spiritus Domini sapientiam praestat etiam parvulis quod in libro Job ple[1075]risque rationibus attestatur Helius filius Barachielis Buzitius. Quod si exempla quaeritis, Samuel cum esset pusillus, accepit Spiritum Domini; Salomon quoque et Josias in juventute acceperunt sapientiam, et Daniel per duodecim annorum, Spiritu S. repletus est, et Paulus Apostolus non vult Timothei juventutem contemni. Et Jeremias audivit a Domino, noli dicere quia juvenis sum ego.

However, when I turn to the clarity and promptness of your intellect, and to your diligence and constancy in the finest pursuits, and compare my not idly exercised habit of reading and interpreting with these, there will be nothing at all in this matter that I might distrust either about your capacity, or about my talent. Nor indeed does youth itself prevent us from being able to discern something equally well or sometimes a little better than the elders: since intelligence comes not from age but from talent and inspiration[15]: for neither the number of years and the multitude of days give knowledge, but talent poured down from heaven, and the spirit of the Lord grants wisdom even to little ones, as testified in the book of Job in many ways by Elihu, the son of Barachel the Buzite.[16] But if you seek examples, Samuel when he was small, received the Spirit of the Lord; Solomon and Josiah also in their youth received wisdom; and Daniel was filled with the Holy Spirit at the age of twelve; and the Apostle Paul does not wish the youth of Timothy to be despised.[17] And Jeremiah heard from the Lord, "do not

---

[15] Agrippa's focus on the topic of heavenly illumination here echoes sentiments already found in the 1510 juvenile draft of the *Three Books of Occult Philosophy.*

[16] Job 32:7-9: "For I hoped that greater age would speak, and that a multitude of years would teach wisdom. But, as I see, there is a spirit in men, and the inspiration of the Almighty giveth understanding. They that are aged are not the wise men, neither do the ancients understand judgment."

[17] I Samuel 3:10; I Kings 3:7; 2 Chronicles 34:1-2; Daniel 1:17; I Timothy 4:12.

Et Ignatius ad Magnesianam Ecclesiam scribens ait, non longi temporis sunt sapientes neque senes sciunt prudentiam, sed spiritus ipse, qui est in hominibus.

Neque etiam mireris Marchio Illustris Joannes Gonzaga strenuissimus militum Dux, quod cum me proximis his annis foelicissimis Caesareis castris militibus praefectum cognosceres, nunc me sacrarum literarum praepositum pulpito cernas. Neque etiam vos candidissimi auditores deterreat ipsum militis cruentum nomen, eo quod Plato ipse ethnicus et Dionysius Christianus severiter praecipiant, sacra nonnisi a sacris viris contrectari debere. Unde me quispiam tanquam humano sanguine, in quo juxta Mose verbum, jam non semel manus nostras consecravimus, pollutum, iccirco perinde ac prophanum respuendum fore existimet. Nulla vos tam sinistra infensaque opinio vel fascinet vel seducat. An nescitis apud veteres poetas ac philosophos Palladem atque Bellonam unam ac eandem literarum militiaeque deam extitisse?

say that I am a child."[18] And Ignatius, writing to the Magnesian Church, said: "It is not they that are aged who are wise, nor do old men know prudence, but the spirit itself, which is in men."[19]

Nor indeed, most illustrious Marquis John Gonzaga, most valiant leader of soldiers, should you wonder that, although in recent years you knew me as a prefect of soldiers in our most fortunate imperial camp, you now see me presiding over sacred literature from the pulpit. Nor indeed should the very reputation of a blood-stained soldier deter you, most fair listeners, given that Plato – himself a pagan – and Dionysius the Christian, strictly command that sacred things ought to be handled only by sacred men.[20] Hence, let no one consider me, polluted as I am with human blood, in which, according to the word of Moses, we have consecrated our hands more than once, to be rejected as profane for this reason.[21] Let no such sinister and hostile opinion fascinate or seduce you. Do you not know that among the ancient poets and philosophers, Pallas and Bellona were regarded as one and the same goddess of letters and war? We have examples

---

[18] Jeremiah 1:7.

[19] Cf. Job 32:7-9.

[20] Prior to holding his post at the University of Pavia, Agrippa had been working in Italy primarily as a diplomat in the service of Maximilian I. He did, however, see combat in the mysterious Spanish expedition of 1508 where he and some friends successfully extracted peasants who had taken a fortified position near Barcelona. The details of this adventure remain unknown.

[21] Cf. Numbers 31:19-24.

Habemus praestantissimorum virorum exempla, qui ob hoc ipsum divinis laudibus praecipue celebrata sunt, quod utrisque et militiae et literarum studiis claruerunt. Non dico nunc Demosthenem illum, qui ut extitit strenuus orator, tam erat ignavus miles. Vix enim conspectis hostibus abjecto clypeo in fugam se turpiter convertit: sed invictos Catones, Curios, Fabios, Decios, Scipiones, innumerosque alios tam Latinorum quam Graecorum Duces: Prae ceteris vero Julium illum Caesarem et Christianae Reipublicae augustum, Carolum cognomento Magnum: qui utrique utrisque sic operam navarunt, ut discerni non queat, utro magis valuerint.

Possem hujuscemodi multos adducere, sed cum non sit praesentis intentionis meae velle laudare militiam, satis erit si hoc vos commoneam, Christum ipsum Centurionem militum sic extulisse, ut diceret, se non invenisse majorem fidem in Israël. Et Propheta ipse ob hoc singulares Deo agit gratias: Quia docet manus ejus ad praelium et digitos ejus ad bellum. Jacob item Patriarcha benedicens filio suo Judae, ajebat:

of the most outstanding men, who for this very reason have been especially celebrated with divine praises, because they distinguished themselves in both military and literary pursuits. Now I speak not of that Demosthenes, who, as much as he was a vigorous orator, was also a cowardly soldier.[22] For, scarcely having seen his enemies, he shamefully turned to flight after throwing away his shield: rather, I speak of the invincible Catos, Curii, Fabii, Decii, Scipios, and countless others, as much of the leaders of the Latins as of the Greeks. Above all, however, I speak of that Julius Caesar and the Augustus of the Christian Republic, Charlemagne by name: both of whom so devoted themselves to both pursuits, that it cannot be discerned in which they excelled more.

I could bring forth many more examples of this kind, but since it is not the intention of my present purpose to praise the military, it will suffice if I remind you of this: Christ Himself so extolled a centurion of soldiers that he said he had not found greater faith in Israel.[23] And the Prophet himself gives special thanks to God for this: because He teaches his hands to fight and his fingers to war.[24] Jacob likewise, blessing his son Judah, said:

---

[22] Here in bringing up the Greek orator Demosthenes, Agrippa makes use of a classic rhetorical device known as *praeteritio* (or *paralipsis*, 'omission'). While claiming he will not speak of Demosthenes' military failure, he effectively highlights it, thus contrasting him with the more heroic figures from Roman myth and history.

[23] Matthew 8:10; Luke 7:9.

[24] Psalm 144:1 (Vulg. 143:1).

Manus tuae in cervicibus inimicorum tuorum. Est enim militia divina benedictio divinumque institutum, ut in Machabaeorum hi[1076]storia sacrae nobis literae tradunt. Ubi Jeremias Propheta Domini visus est extendisse dexteram suam, strenuoque militi Judae Machabaeo aureum gladium porrexisse inquiens: Accipe gladium sanctum, munus a Deo, in quo concides adversarios populi mei. Quo verbo et me consecravit invictissimus Imperator meus, dum adolescentior et quasi puer adhuc accepto e manu sua gladio, haud sine foelici fortunatoque Martis successu miles insigniebar.

Sed ut semel finiam et ad animi institutum redeam. Augustinus in libro de verbo Domini, et Gregorius scribens universis Neapolitanorum militibus, ipseque Decretorum Compilator Gratianus, ex illorum aliorumque sanctorum Patrum testimoniis unamiter concludunt, Militiam nulli imputari in peccatum, neminemque propter militiam a sacris Ordinibus debere repelli. Nec refert cui quis militet, etiamsi infideli, dum modo fidem et reverentiam impleat militia; nam et David militavit Achis Regi Philistinorum, et multi fideles atque sancti Diocletiano et Juliano aliisque

"Your hands will be on the necks of your enemies."[25] For the military is a divine blessing and a divine institution, as the sacred letters tell us in the history of the Maccabees. Where Jeremiah, the Prophet of the Lord, was seen to extend his right hand and present a golden sword to the valiant soldier Judas Maccabeus, saying: "Take this holy sword, a gift from God, with which you will strike down the adversaries of my people."[26] With these words my most invincible Emperor also consecrated me, when, as a younger man and almost still a boy, having received a sword from his hand, I was marked as a soldier not without the happy and fortunate ascension of Mars.

But to finish and return to my intention: Augustine in the book on the word of the Lord, and Gregory writing to all the soldiers of Naples, and Gratian himself, compiler of the *Decretum*, from the testimonies of these and other holy Fathers, unanimously conclude that military service should be imputed to no one as a sin, and no one should be rejected from holy orders on account of military service.[27] Nor does it matter whom one serves, even if it be an infidel, as long as one maintains faith and reverence in their military service; for David also served King Achish of the Philistines, and many faithful men are read to have served Diocletian, Julian, and other

---

[25] Genesis 49:8.

[26] II Maccabees 15:16.

[27] Augustine, *De civitate Dei*, 19.12-15 argues that wars can be just under certain circumstances, and military service is not inherently sinful.

ethnicis Caesaribus militiasse leguntur, fide semper incolumi et laudata. Ne itaque nos inter prophanos connumeremur, catholica Canonum sanctio, divinumque militiae institutum, sacrarumque attrectatio literarum nos excusant: Siquidem et Lactantio Firmiano placet eos qui sacras literas docent, haud secus atque quibus Antistitum manus impositae sunt Sacerdotes sacros existimari debere. Quin et milites ipsi a Psalmista sancti dicuntur, inquiente: Utique gloria haec est omnibus sanctis ejus. Exultationes Dei in gutture eorum, et gladii ancipites in manibus eorum, ad faciendam vindictam in nationibus, increpationes in populis. Ad alligandos reges eorum in compedibus, et nobiles eorum in manicis ferreis.

Quod si quem vestrum scandalizet, barbarum hominem in Lizeto gymnasio bonas literas interpretari, is sciat barbaros etiam homines esse rationales, et frui coelo, atque linguae nostrae Mercurium, pectorique nostro Saturnum, quorum ille interpretandi, hic arcanae contemplationis autor, foelici coelorum dono non defuisse. Quod si quem insuetum scholis militare sagum transversum agit, respondet illi Plutarchus. Non, inquiens, Philosophum facit promissior barba et vestis pertrita, nec idem Isiacos linostoliae: et quod vulgo dicitur proverbium:

pagan Caesars, always with unblemished and praised faith.[28] Therefore, let us not be numbered among the profane; the sanction of Catholic canons, the divine institution of the military, and the handling of sacred letters excuse us: since Lactantius Firmianus also agrees that those who teach sacred letters ought to be regarded as sacred priests, just as those upon whom the hands of bishops have been laid. Indeed, even soldiers themselves are called saints by the Psalmist, who says: "This is the glory of all his saints. The high praises of God shall be in their throats, and two-edged swords in their hands, to execute vengeance upon the nations, chastisements among the peoples. To bind their kings in fetters, and their nobles in manacles of iron."[29]

But if any of you are scandalized that a barbarian man interprets good literature in the Lizeto school, let him know that barbarian men are also rational, enjoy the blessings of heaven, and have Mercury for our tongue and Saturn for our heart, of whom the former is the author of interpretation, the latter of arcane contemplation, and that the fortunate gift of the heavens has not been lacking to them. But if the military cloak is unsettling to anyone unfamiliar with the schools, Plutarch responds to him. "A longer beard and worn-out clothes do not make a philosopher," he says, "nor do linen garments make a worshipper of Isis."[30] And as the proverb commonly

---

[28] I Samuel 27:1-12.

[29] Psalm 149:5-8.

[30] Plutarch, *De Iside et Osiride*, 3.

Habitus Monachum non perficit: neque enim plantam cortex facit, sed vegetalis natura: neque jumenta corium, sed sensibilis anima: nec humani corporis habitus sapientem, sed coelestis ratio spiritalisque intelligentia. Aedepol multa sunt auditores, quae efficacissimis rationibus [1077] ad susceptam provinciam prosequendam nos adhortantur, et admonent adjuvantque Amici scilicet qui innumeris in me collatis beneficiis, magnum mihi ad coepta prosequenda stimulum adhibent, quibus eo ipso morem gerendum duximus.

Compellit me etiam Evangelica religio, ne erga Deum hominesque ingratus esse convincar, talentum quoque mihi concreditum suffodere videar, atque lumen sub modio abscondere, ne denique mihi, quae ficulneae, maledictio contingat, quae fructum suum non dedit in tempore suo. Itaque juxta verbum libri Sapientiae, quae sine fictione didici, sine invidia communico, et honestatem eorum non abscondo.

says: "The habit does not make the monk." For it is not the bark that makes the plant, but the vegetable nature; nor the hide that makes the beasts of burden, but the animal and sensitive soul; nor is it the habit of the human body that makes the wise man, but the heavenly reason and spiritual intelligence.[31] By Pollux, there are many things, listeners, which, with the most compelling reasons, encourage, advise, and assist us in pursuing the task we have undertaken – namely my friends, who, through countless benefits bestowed upon me, give me great incentive to pursue my undertakings, to whom we have thought it proper to show deference in this very manner.

The evangelical religion also compels me, lest I be convicted of ingratitude towards God and men, lest I appear to bury the talent entrusted to me, and to hide the light under a bushel, and lest finally the curse of the fig tree that did not give its fruit in its own time befall me. Therefore, according to the word of the book of *Wisdom*, what I have learned without deceit, I share without envy, and their riches I do not hide.[32]

---

[31] Cf. Pico della Mirandola, *Oratio* (Copenhaver, *Oration*, p. 86-87): "For it is not the bark that makes a plant but dull and unfeeling nature; not the hide that makes a beast of burden but a brutal and sensual soul; not a spherical body but right reason that makes a heavenly orb; not removing the body but spiritual intelligence that makes an angel." Note, however, how Agrippa modifies this quote to make his own point about man rather than angels and heavenly orbs.

[32] Wisdom 7:13.

Alliciunt me insuper haud parum patria, urbs, locus, tempus, otium, tranquillitas, atque post tot bella, pax atque libertas, quae omnia nobis Illustrissimus atque invictissimus de hostibus triumphator Hercules Maximilianus Sforita Mediolani Dux octavus, singulari sua virtute ac sapientia conciliat, continet et adauget. Qua de re Deum immortalem oramus, ut cum perpetuo foelicem fortunatum faciat, egregiasque ejus laudes Celsitudinis, fortunae, virtutis, ingenii, rerum gestarum gerendarumque in memoriam seculorum omnium conservet et augmentet, ut omnia denique ei ex desiderio optimi animi sui, quo nocere nemini, prodesse vero omnibus velit, prospere glorioseque succedant. Deberem etiam nunc splendidiss. Joannes Gonzaga, tuis amplissimis virtutibus congruenter congratulari, atque condignas meritasque illis contribuere laudes: Tua strenue gesta, sapientissime consulta, promptissime ad inventa in medium denarrare, si sermonum unda sensuumque flamma mihi hi suppeteret: in aliud autem tempus haec reservabimus, nullaque unquam abolebit oblivio.

Atque nunc unde digressus sum redibo, et quod propositum meum sit in hanc suscepta provincia id paucis verbis aperiam. Animus est, Hermetis Trismegisti Dialogos de Sapientia et potestate divina inscriptos, interpretari: quocirca prius nunc de Hermete ipso Trismegisto, cujus testimoniorum prae caeteris uti institutum est, ut quis quantusque fuerit, et quo

Moreover, my fatherland, city, place, time, leisure, tranquility, and, after so many wars, peace and liberty entice me greatly, all of which the most illustrious and invincible conqueror of enemies, Hercules Maximilian Sforza, eighth Duke of Milan, by his singular virtue and wisdom, secures, maintains, and augments for us. For this reason, we pray to the immortal God that He make him perpetually happy and fortunate, and preserve and increase the extraordinary praises of his highness, fortune, virtue, talent, and deeds accomplished and to be accomplished, for the memory of all ages, so that finally everything may succeed for him prosperously and gloriously according to the desire of his excellent spirit, by which he wishes to harm no one but to benefit all. I also ought now, most splendid John Gonzaga, to suitably congratulate your most ample virtues and bestow upon them the due and deserved praises: to narrate your vigorous deeds, most wise counsels, and most prompt inventions to the public, if the flood of words and flame of thoughts were at hand for me: but we will reserve these for another time, and no forgetfulness will ever erase them.

And now I will return from where I digressed, and I will reveal in a few words what my purpose is in this undertaken province. My intention is to interpret the dialogues of Hermes Trismegistus entitled *On the Wisdom and Power of God*: therefore, first we will now say a few words about Hermes Trismegistus himself, whose testimony is intended to be used above others, so that it may be known who and how great he was, and in

tempore floruerit, dignoscatur, pauca dicemus: deinde quae in Dialogis, quos explanare intendimus, dogmata contineantur, brevi argumento docebimus. Legimus itaque apud Moysen magnum illum Hebraeorum legislatorem atque Principem, in suo Geneseos libro Abrahamum ipsum Judaeorum Patriarcham mortua uxore sua Sara, plures ex pellicibus filios suscepisse: Inter quos erat nomine Mydan. Is genuit filium Enoch nomine, qui ob interpretandi scien[1078]tiam, qua clarus habebatur, appellatus est Hermes sive Mercurius, quod uterque interprete sonat. Is itaque noster est Hermes, qui apud Hebraeos Enoch vocatus, Abrahae ex Mydan filio nepos. Cujus rei gravis juxta ac fidus testis est autorque peregrinus. Rab Abraham de Avenazre in volumine suo Astrologico. Adstipulatur ei quod scribit Eusebius libro suo de temporibus. Cum esset Isaac Abrahae filius 80 annorum. Jacob vero ex Isaac Abrahae nepos annorum 20. Osyrim apud Graecos inter Deos relatum, eodemque tempore floruisse apud Aegyptios alium Abrahae nepotem Enoch nomine. Accedunt adhaec quae recitat Diodorus Siculus de antiquorum gestis. Praeterea Lactantius et alii plerique antiquitatum scriptores testantur, eo tempore quo vixit Osyris, floruisse Mercurium, qui postea vocatus est Trismegistus: Osyris namque ingenti exercitu orbem peragrans, ut homines ab agresti rudique vita ad cultiorem nitidioremque reduceret, Aegypti regno rerumque omnium cura Isidi uxori relicto, adjunxit ei Mercurium,

what time he flourished; thereafter we will briefly explain the doctrines contained in the dialogues that we intend to expound. Thus, according to Moses in his book of *Genesis*, we read that that great legislator and prince of the Hebrews, Abraham himself, the patriarch of the Jews, after the death of his wife Sarah, had many sons from concubines: among whom one was Midian by name. He begot a son named Enoch, who on account of his knowledge of interpretation, by which he was renowned, was called Hermes or Mercurius, for both names mean interpreter. Thus, our Hermes, who among the Hebrews was called Enoch, was the grandson of Abraham through Midian's son. A serious and reliable witness and author of this matter is the foreign Rabbi Abraham Ibn Ezra in his book on astrology. Eusebius agrees with this in what he writes in his book *De temporibus*. When Isaac, the son of Abraham, was 80 years old, and Jacob, the grandson of Abraham from Isaac, was 20 years old, Osiris was numbered among the gods by the Greeks, and at the same time, another descendant of Abraham, named Enoch, flourished among the Egyptians. They add to this what Diodorus Siculus says in his *De antiquorum gestis* [*fabulosis*]. Moreover, Lactantius and several other writers of antiquities testify that at the time Osiris lived, a Mercurius flourished, who was later called Trismegistus. For Osiris, traveling the world with a huge army to lead men from a rustic and crude life to a more cultivated and refined one, left the kingdom of Egypt and all matters of concern to his wife Isis, and he appointed Mercurius to

cujus consilio in rebus agendis uteretur, quandoquidem prudentia ac sanctitate caeteros mortales antecelleret.

Hunc ferunt interemisse Argum, Aegyptiis leges et literas dedisse, verba in ordinem redegisse, multisque indidisse rebus nomina, isque apud Aegyptios primus astrorum observator, syderum cursus certis numeris descripsit, primusque numerorum, rationum vocumque harmonias adinvenit. Palestrae quoque ad exercendas corporis vires, Medicinae insuper ac lyrae repertore ferunt, atque oleae plantam, non, quod Graeci fabulantur, a Minerva, sed ab eo repertam. Ipse etiam Graecis interpretandi scientiam contulit, ac primus inter philosophos a physicis ac mathematibus disciplinis ad divinorum contemplationem conscendit. Primus qui omnem sapientiae semitam perscrutatus oratione licet modica immensa tamen sententiis de vera sapientia scripsit. Primus omnium de majestate Dei, de ordine spirituum, de animarum naturis sapientissime disseruit. Primus itaque theologiae appellatus est autor et inventor: ferturque universalia sacrorum complexus conscripsisse viginti sex millia, quingenta et viginti quinque librorum volumina, in quibus admiranda arcana, secretissimique mysteria ac stupenda pandit oracula: non enim ut philosophus duntaxat locutus est, verum etiam ut propheta multa praesagivit. Nam priscae religionis ruinam, novae fidei ortum, Christi adventum, futurum judicium, mortuorum resurrectionem, renovationem saeculi,

her, whose counsel she used in her political affairs, since he surpassed other mortals in prudence and holiness.

They say that he killed Argus, gave laws and letters to the Egyptians, arranged words in order, and gave names to many things. He was the first observer of the stars among the Egyptians; he described the courses of the constellations with precise numbers; and he first discovered the harmonies of numbers, proportions, and sounds. They also say he was the inventor of the gymnasium for exercising the strengths of the body, as well as of medicine and the lyre, and that the olive plant was discovered by him, not by Minerva as the Greeks say in their myths. He also conferred his knowledge of interpretation on the Greeks, and he was the first among philosophers to ascend from physical and mathematical disciplines to the contemplation of divine matters. He was the first to explore every path of wisdom and, although with modest speech, he wrote immeasurably profound thoughts about true wisdom. He was the first of all to speak most wisely about the majesty of God, the order of spirits, and the nature of souls. Therefore, he was called the first author and inventor of theology, and it is said that he composed twenty-six thousand five hundred and twenty-five volumes of sacred books, in which he reveals marvelous secrets, the most secret mysteries, and astonishing oracles. For he spoke not only as a philosopher but also presaged many things as a prophet. He foresaw and foretold the ruin of the ancient religion, the rise of a new faith, the coming of Christ, the future judgment, the resurrection of the dead, the renewal of the world,

beatorum gloriam, peccatorum tormenta praevidit atque praedixit. Qua de causa ambigit Augustinus peritiane syderum, an revelatione spirituum illa [1079] cognoverit: Lactantius ipsum inter sybillas ac prophetas connumerare non dubitat.

Hic itaque Mercurius noster, ut acumine intelligentiae philosophos omnes excessit, ita sacerdos perinde constitutus sanctimonia vitae, divinorumque cultu universis sacerdotibus praestitit: Unde in tanta hominum veneratione habitus est, ut post Osyridem ab Aegyptiis Rex appellaretur. Mos enim illis erat, quod et Plato recitat, ex philosophorum numero sacerdotes, ex sacerdotum coetu regem sibi deligere. Regiam itaque dignitatem adeptus Mercurius, constitutione legum, administratione regni ac gestorum magnitudine, caeterorum regum gloriam obscuravit, unde merito Trismegistus, hoc est, ter maximus nuncupatus est, quoniam maximus et sapientissimus philosophus, maximus ac religiosissimus sacerdos, maximus ac gloriosissimus rex extiterit, quapropter pro suae virtutis admiratione divinos honores populus illi consecravit. Tunc pro Deo habitus in coelos relatus, planetarum imus prae caeteris ingenii ac scientiarum largitor,

the glory of the blessed, and the torments of sinners. For this reason, Augustine wavers on whether Hermes knew those things by knowledge of the stars or by the revelation of spirits; and Lactantius has no doubt in counting him among the sibyls and the prophets.

Thus, this Mercurius of ours, as he surpassed all philosophers in the acumen of intelligence, so, being established as a priest, he excelled all priests in the sanctity of his life and in his worship of the divine. Hence, he was held in such great veneration among men that after Osiris, he was called King by the Egyptians. For it was their custom, as Plato also recounts, to choose priests from the number of philosophers, and a king from the assembly of priests. Thus, having attained royal dignity, Mercurius, by the constitution of laws, administration of the kingdom, and the greatness of his deeds, eclipsed the glory of other kings, whence he was rightly called Trismegistus, that is, the thrice-great, since he was the greatest and wisest philosopher, the greatest and most religious priest, and the greatest and most glorious king. Therefore, out of admiration for his virtue, the people consecrated divine honors to him.[33] Then, being regarded as a god, he was taken up into the heavens and was considered the most generous of the planets in ingenuity and the sciences,

---

[33] On the origin of the 'Three Hermes' motif, see Burnett, "The Legend of the Three Hermes," p. 231-234 and van Bladel, "Sources of the Legend of Hermes," p. 285-293 and *The Arabic Hermes*, p. 121-161. See also Campanelli, "Marsilio Ficino's Portrait of Hermes Trismegistus," p. 53-71 for how Ficino (and thereby Agrippa) became familiar with the myth.

illius nomine insignitus, templa numinis sui erecta quam plurima.

Nomen ejus proprium ob reverentiam quandam vulgo ac temere effari vetitum. Primus anni mensis penes Aegyptios suo nomini dedicatus. Oppidum quoque ab eo conditum extat, quod in hunc usque diem Hermopolis, hoc est Mercurii civitas, appellatur. Narrat etiam de ipso Chalcidius moribundum illum astantes his verbis allocutum. Hactenus filii pulsus a patria vixi peregrinus et exul, nunc vero incolumis patriam repeto. Cumque post paulum temporis solutis corporis vinculis a vobis discessero, nequaquam me tanquam mortuum lugeatis, nam ad illam optimam beatamque civitatem regredior, ad quam universi cives per mortis corruptionem venturi sunt. Ibi namque Deus solus est, summus princeps, qui cives suos replet suavitate mirifica. Sed de autore haec hactenus.

De opere illius modo dicamus. Ejus titulus est Pimander, sive de sapientia et potestate Dei. Est autem liber iste elegantia, sermonis refertissimus, copia sententiarum gravissimus, plenus gratiae et decoris, plenus sapientiae et mysteriorum. Continet enim in se vetustissimae Theologiae profundissima mysteria, ac utriusque Philosophiae latentia arcana, quae omnia non tam continet quam explicat: Docet enim nos quis

Many temples were erected in his name to his divine presence.

His proper name was forbidden to be spoken commonly and recklessly out of a certain reverence. The first month of the year among the Egyptians was dedicated to his name. There also exists a city founded by him, which to this day is called Hermopolis, that is, the city of Mercurius.[34] Calcidius also tells about him, that when he was dying, he addressed those standing by with these words: "Up to now, my sons, I have lived as an exile and wanderer, driven from my fatherland; but now unharmed I return to my fatherland. And when after a short time I depart from you, having loosened the bonds of the body, do not mourn for me as if dead, for I return to that most excellent and blessed city, to which all citizens are going to come through the corruption of death. For there alone is God, the highest Prince, who fills his citizens with wondrous sweetness." But thus far about the author.

Let us now speak about his work. Its title is *Pimander*, or *On the Wisdom and Power of God*. Indeed this book is brimming with elegance in speech, rich in weighty thoughts, full of grace and beauty, full of wisdom and mysteries. For it contains within itself the profoundest mysteries of the most ancient theology and the hidden secrets of both philosophies, all of which it not only contains but also explains. For it teaches us who

---

[34] Cf. *Picatrix* 4.3.1 (Attrell and Porreca, *Picatrix*, p. 233) which discusses the founding of the city of Adocentyn (el-Ashmunein or Hermopolis).

Deus, quis mundus, quid mens, quid uterque daemon, quid anima, quis providentiae ordo, quae et unde fati necessitas, quae naturae lex, quod hominum phas, quae religio, quae sacra instituta, ritus, phana, observationes sacraque mysteria, instruit [1080] nos praeterea de cognitione sui ipsius, de ascensu intellectus, de arcanis precibus, de divino connubio, deque regenerationis sacramento, atque ut paucis cuncta complectar, docet nos rite scire atque callere leges divinorum, phas sacrorum, jusque religionum, et quo pacto foelicitatem religione divina debeamus adipisci, quoque pacto mentem nostram, qua sola veritatem apprehendere possumus, rite debeamus excolere.

Ea enim est magorum sapientumque vulgata sententia. Quod nisi mens atque animus bene valuerint, corpus ipsum bene valere non posse: tunc autem hominem vere sanum esse, quando anima et corpus ita copulantur et inter se conveniunt, ut firmitas mentis corporis viribus non sit inferior. Firmam autem robustamque mentem, per quam sine fallacia mirabilia et cognoscimus et operamur, quomodo possimus adipisci, ipse nos Mercurii Pimander edocet. Quae omnia vobis, ut autoris verba id expostulant, partim theologice, partim philosophice, partim dialectico rhetoricoque more enucleabimus, enumerantes scripturas, auctoritates, sententias, opiniones, exempla et experientias ad rem ipsam pertinentes: Sacrorum denique canonum civiliumque legum sanctiones dum dabitur occasio, haud impertinenter adducentes.

God is, what the world is, what the mind is, what each demon is, what the soul is, what the order of providence is, what and whence the necessity of fate is, what the law of nature is, what the divine law of men is, what religion is, what sacred institutions, rites, temples, sacred observances, and mysteries are. It further instructs us about the knowledge of oneself, the ascent of the intellect, the secret prayers, the divine union, and the sacrament of regeneration. And to summarize everything briefly, it teaches us to know rightly and be skilled in the laws of the divine, the obligations of the sacred, the law of religions, and how we ought to obtain happiness through divine religion, and how we ought rightly to cultivate our mind, by which alone we can apprehend the truth.

For it is a commonly held opinion among magicians and sages that, unless the mind and soul are in good health, the body itself cannot be in good health; moreover, a man is truly healthy when the soul and body are so united and in agreement with each other that the firmness of the mind is not inferior to the strength of the body. How we can attain a firm and robust mind, through which without deception we can both know and accomplish marvelous things, Mercurius's Pimander himself teaches us. All these things we will explain to you, as the words of the author require, partly theologically, partly philosophically, partly in a dialectical and rhetorical manner, enumerating scriptures, authorities, aphorisms, opinions, examples, and experiences pertinent to the matter itself: finally, as occasion permits, we will not inappropriately introduce the sanctions of sacred canons

Ignoscat mihi utriusque philosophiae ac medicinarum facultas, ignoscat mihi sacrae theologiae schola, ignoscat mihi veneranda canonum sanctio, legumque reverenda majestas, si quaedam aliquando suorum dogmatum paradoxa interpretari discernereque conabor. Nam etsi scio harum rerum in hoc gymnasio in immensum me excellentiores doctores ordinariosque lectores haberi, nullum illis facturum me arbitror injuriam, sed operam illis accommodaturum, si cum illis hujusmodi doctrinarum fructus in alios divisero: Multa siquidem illorum et scio et intelligo, et memini, polliceorque vobis effecturum me totis viribus, ut nihil sit in suscepta materia tam difficile, tam intricatum, tam obscurum, tamque arduum cuicumque facultati aut scientiae ea traditio consonet, quod me interprete non assequamini omnes, intelligentia, favente nobis ipso ter maximi Mercurii Pimandro mente divinae potentiae Domino videlicet nostro JESU Christo Nazareno crucifixo, qui verus pimander, qui magni consilii Angelus vero mentis lumine illustrat: quem verum Deum et verum hominem, regenerationis autorem confitemur, futurique patrem seculi judicem expectamus.

and civil laws. Let the faculty of both philosophy and medicine forgive me, let the school of sacred theology forgive me, let the venerable sanction of the canons and the revered majesty of the laws forgive me, if at times I attempt to interpret and discern some paradoxes of their teachings. For even though I know that in this school I have far superior doctors and ordinary readers of these subjects, I believe I will do them no injury but will rather accommodate them by distributing the fruits of such teachings among others: for I indeed know, understand, and remember many of them, and I promise you that I will exert myself with all my strength so that there will be nothing in the subject matter undertaken that is so difficult, so intricate, so obscure, or so arduous – regardless of which faculty or science it concerns – that you will not all achieve understanding, with me as your interpreter, by the favor of Pimander himself, the mind of divine power, of the Thrice-Great Mercurius, namely, our crucified Lord JESUS Christ of Nazareth, who is the true Pimander, who, as the Angel of Great Counsel, illuminates with the true light of mind: whom we confess as true God and true man, the author of regeneration, and await as the judge of the future age.[35]

---

[35] This section, and most notably the identification of Pimander with Christ, is an echo of Lodovico Lazzarelli, *Crater Hermetis*, 1.1 and 30.4 (Hanegraaff and Bouthoorn, *Lodovico Lazzarelli*, p. 167 and 263). The identification between Pimander (or in Greek *Poimandres*) with the "mind of divine power" (or "mind of sovereignty") is drawn from *Corpus Hermeticum* 1.2 (Copenhaver, *Hermetica*, p. 1) and 13.15 (Copenhaver, *Hermetica*, p. 52).

Vos igitur illustrissimi candidissimique viri, vos qui virtutem colitis, vos ad mea tantum dicta aures adhibete, animosque inten[1081]dite vestros: Contra, qui sanctas leges contemnitis, hinc vos effugite, et procul hinc miseri, proculite profani. Vos autem qui divina amatis, quiquere rerum arcanarum estis percupidi, et circa abditioris philosophiae symbola, ac mirabilium Dei operum reconditas vires, plenissimaque mysteriorum antiqui seculi traditiones curiosi estis exploratores, vos inquam adeste foeliciter, divinaque Pymandri mysteria attento animo audite. Conabor quippe vobis cum Trismegisto scientiae decorem enunciare, ostendamque vobis quae ratio sit consequendi intelligentiae lumen, sapientiaeque sermones auribus vestris infundam, quod dum abs me agitur, vos quaeso attenti sitis, atque sicut auribus ita et animis verba nostra excipite, nostrosque labores silentio, animadvertentia, diligentia ac constantia vestra remunerate.

Therefore, you most fair and illustrious men, you who cultivate virtue, lend your ears to my words and apply your minds: on the contrary, you who despise the holy laws, flee from here, and far away, O wretches, away ye profane! But you who love the divine, who are desirous of the secrets of things, and who are curious explorers around the symbols of deeper philosophy, and the hidden powers of the wondrous works of God, and the most complete traditions of the mysteries of the ancient world, you, I say, come happily, and listen with attentive mind to the divine mysteries of Pimander. For I will endeavor to explain to you the beauty of knowledge with Trismegistus; I will show you what the reason is for attaining the light of understanding; I will pour the words of wisdom into your ears, which while it is being done by me, I ask that you be attentive, and to receive our words with both ears and minds, and reward our labors with your silence, attention, diligence, and constancy.

PROTESTATIO

Verum quia circa divina saepe solet humana decipi consideratio, et nos quidem non Dii sed homines sumus, nec humani quicquam nobis abesse putamus, nullo pacto vos latere volo, palamque coram te illustrissime Joannes Gonzaga coram vobis venerabilibus ac Deo amabilibus cum scholae tum Ecclesiasticis Patribus, coram omnibus vobis clarissimis auditoribus, coram serpentibus terrae, volatilibus coeli, piscibus maris et universis pecoribus campi, coram coelo terraque protestor, quod quaecunque abs me uspiam dicta scriptave sunt, atque in posterum dicentur scribenturque, his nolo quenquam plus assentiri, quod et ego ipse facio, quam ab Ecclesia Catholica fideliumque choro, ac sacro episcoporum collegio, ejusque capite summo Pontifice comprobatui: quibus omnia dicta mea et dicenda, scripta ac scribenda subjicio, et omnibus ejus negotii censendi et judicandi potestatem habentibus, paratissimus semper ab illis et a quovis melius sentiente, fraterna Christianaque charitate erudiri et corrigi, et stare cujuslibet melius sentientis et intelligentis sententiae. Quae quemadmodum vobis nunc dico, ita in omnibus lectionibus meis ac lectionum partibus, lecturis, dictis, scriptis, dicendis ac scribendis quibusque meis, repetita esse volo, atque ea sic coram Deo et omni creatura protestor.

TESTIMONY

But because human judgment is often deceived concerning divine matters, and we are indeed not gods but men, nor do we think anything human to be foreign to us,[36] I by no means wish to hide anything from you. Publicly, before you, most illustrious John Gonzaga, before you Fathers of both the school and the Church, venerable and beloved by God, before all of you, most distinguished listeners, before the serpents of the earth, the birds of the sky, the fish of the sea, and all the beasts of the field, before heaven and earth, I testify that whatever has been said or written by me anywhere, and whatever will be said or written in the future, I do not wish anyone to assent to more than I do myself, except as approved by the Catholic Church and the assembly of the faithful, and by the sacred college of bishops, and its supreme head, the Pope. To these I submit all my words and writings, past and future, and I am always most willing to be taught and corrected by them or by anyone who has better judgment, in fraternal and Christian love, and to abide by the judgment of anyone who thinks and understands better. Just as I say these things to you now, so I wish them to be repeated in all my lectures and the parts of my lectures, in whatever I have said, written, or will say or write. And this I testify before God and every creature.

---

[36] An allusion to Terence's famous line 77 from the play *The Self-Tormentor*, preserved in Cicero, *De legibus*, 1.33 and *De officiis*, 1.29-30: "*homo sum: humani nil a me alienum puto.*"

CENSURA

Reliquum adhuc superest unum, quod silentio praeterundum minime censeo. Idque diligenter quaeso advertite. [1082] Tria potissimum in usu sunt penes scholasticos differendi genera: Unum a Stoicis ac Peripateticis plurimum exercitatum, qui videlicet proposita re vel quaestione aliqua, alterum aut certam ejus partem disputando defendunt atque adprobant, reliquasque circa hanc opiniones confutantes. Alterum apud Academicos ac Socraticos usitatum, qui in medium adducta reliqua vel quaestione, diversas ad id quod investigatur sententias rationesque adferentes, illisque pluribus praepositis et ad rem ipsam invicem collatis, quod ex his verisimilius probabiliusque visum fuerit, id eligunt atque adfirmant: Hos utroque modos in lectionibus nostris observare intendimus. Tertium vero differendi genus Scepticorum est, quos penes nihil certum est quod sequantur, sed omnia illis indifferentia sunt, ideoque de omnibus in utranque partem disputant, et quae naturae ordine disjuncta distinctaque sunt permiscent atque confundunt. Et perinde ac gigantes montibus montes accumulantes, bellum contra Deos gerere videntur, dum aliquot instructi syllogismis, homines rixosi ac meretriculis loquatiores, incunctanter audent quavis de re cum quovis linguam conferre: litigiosis enim quibusdam altercationum capitiunculis ac sophismatum jaculis armari, omnium disciplinarum etiam sacrarum literarum fores se posse diffringere et penetrare arbitrantur:

CRITIQUE

There remains one further matter, which I think should by no means be passed over in silence. I ask you, therefore, to give me your attention diligently. There are three kinds of disputation chiefly in use among the scholastics: one kind, extensively practiced by the Stoics and Peripatetics, involves proposing a topic or a certain *quaestio*, defending and approving one side or a particular aspect of it through disputation, while refuting the remaining opinions on the subject. The other kind is customary among the Academicians and Socratics, who, when a question or matter is brought forward, present various opinions and reasons regarding the issue under investigation, and after setting these out and comparing them with each other, choose and affirm what seems most plausible and probable from among them. We intend to observe both of these methods in our lectures. The third method of disputation, however, belongs to the Skeptics, who hold nothing as certain in what they follow, and everything is all the same to them. Therefore, they argue on both sides of every issue, and they mix up and confuse things which are distinct and separate by the order of nature. And just as giants who stack mountains upon mountains, they seem to wage war against the gods, while, equipped with a few syllogisms, these quarrelsome men, more talkative than harlots, unhesitatingly dare to argue with anyone about anything. For armed with certain contentious quibbles and the darts of sophisms, they think they can batter down and penetrate the doors of all disciplines, and even Holy Scripture.

atque hi a quibusque consummatis Philosophis ac Theologis aspernantur respuunturque.

Horum scientiam Jacobus Apostolus appellat terrenam, animalem, diabolicam: Paulus segregatus gentium doctor in suis ad Titum, Timotheum Epistolis, stultam et vanam inutiles et contentiosam vocat. Super quo scribens Hieronymus: Dialectici, inquit, solent argumentationibus retia obtendere et vagam rethoricae libertatem syllogismorum spineta concludere, in ea totos dies ac noctes conterentes, ut vel interrogent vel respondeant, vel dent propositionem vel accipiant, assumant, confirment atque concludant, quos quidem contentiosos vocat Apostolus. Haec Hieronymus. Sed et multa contra eos loquuntur Gregorius Nazianzenus in libro secundo de Theologia, et Urbanus Papa scribens: Antiochenis, et beatus Athanasius in epistola quae Encyclion dicitur ad Aegypti et Libyae Episcopos. Divus item Ambrosius in libro de Trinitate, et multi alii sancti patres, quorum verba brevitatis causa adducere obmitto. Ex quorum dictis Gratianus Decretista .XXX[VII].d Nonne [et] Legimus. Et XXIV. quaest. II. cap. Transferunt contra hos argumentatores constituit. [1083] Sed et leges civiles codicis de summa Trinitate lege III, frenum illis injiciunt.

Such people are despised and rejected by all accomplished philosophers and theologians.

The apostle James calls the knowledge of such people earthly, sensual, and diabolical.[37] Paul, the appointed teacher of the Gentiles, in his letters to Titus and Timothy, calls it foolish, vain, useless, and contentious.[38] Writing on this, Jerome says: "The dialecticians are accustomed to set snares with arguments and to confine the free spirit of rhetoric within thickets of syllogisms, spending entire days and nights either asking questions or answering them, whether putting forward propositions or listening to them, assuming, confirming, and drawing conclusions; these are indeed the contentious ones that the Apostle speaks of."[39] So says Jerome. But Gregory Nazianzus, in his second book *On Theology*, and Pope Urban, writing to the Antiochians, and blessed Athanasius in an encyclical letter to the bishops of Egypt and Libya, also speak much against them. St. Ambrose, too, in his book *On the Trinity*, and many other holy Fathers, whose words I omit for the sake of brevity, have spoken against them. From their words, Gratian, the author of the *Decretum*, issues decrees against these arguers in part 1, decree 3[7], c. "Nonne" [and] "Legimus," and in part 2, c. 24, q. 2, c. "Transferunt." But the civil code also puts restraints on them in the third law on the most Holy Trinity.

---

[37] James 3:15.

[38] Titus 3:9 and Timothy 2:16, 23.

[39] Jerome, *On Titus*, 3.9.

Quemadmodum itaque argumentatores isti a quibusque splendidissimis philosophis, sanctissimis theologis ac celeberrimis utriusque iurisperitisis repelluntur, sic etiam illos a nostris lectionibus quam longe abesse volumus: nullius equidem vel argumenta vel quaestiones in cathedra recipere intendimus.

Verum, ne doctorum virorum judicium vereri videar, neque etiam discipulorum meorum ingenio, contra id quod pollicitus sum: non velle satisfacere videar, atque ne quis aestimet nos responsionis penuria declinare certamen, iccirco cuicunque vel circa autoris verba, vel circa testimonia per nos adducta vel aliter recitata seu exposita quippiam exigere vel contradicere libuerit, huic in fine lectionis verbo vel scripto id agere licebit; cui ad singula verba et sententias in subsequenti lectione abunde respondentes satisfaciemus. Quod si incommodum id erit, scripta scriptis referemus. Fecerunt sic veteres theologi, ex Graecis Origenes, Basilius, Athanasius, Cyrillus, Didymus, Eusebius, Chrysostomus, Nazianzenus: ex Latinis Tertullianus, Ruffinus, Hieronymus, Augustinus, et illorum plures aliis qui quidem sancti viri nihil magis odere unquam quam verbosam illam contentionem, in qua plus stomacho quam ratione certatur,

Consequently, just as these arguers are repelled by every one of the most illustrious philosophers, the most blessed theologians, and the most celebrated experts in both civil and canon law, so too do we wish them to keep far away from our lectures. Indeed, we do not intend to admit the arguments or questions of any such person into our lecture hall.[40]

However, lest I appear to disregard the judgment of learned men, or seem unwilling to satisfy the curiosity of my students against what I have promised, or lest anyone think that we are avoiding debate due to an inability to answer, I therefore allow anyone who wishes to question or contradict anything – whether regarding the words of the author, the testimonies we have brought forth, or those otherwise cited or explained – to do so at the end of the lecture, either verbally or in writing. We will then fully address and satisfy these queries in the following lecture, responding satisfactorily to every word and opinion. If that proves inconvenient, we will respond to writings with writings. The ancient theologians did this, such as Origen, Basil, Athanasius, Cyril, Didymus, Eusebius, Chrysostom, and Nazianzus among the Greeks, and Tertullian, Rufinus, Jerome, Augustine, and many others among the Latins. For these holy men loathed nothing more than that verbose contention in which there is more anger than reason,

---

[40] See Van Der Poel, *Cornelius Agrippa: The Humanist Theologian and his Declamations*, p. 65-72 for a discussion of this passage. These last two sentences have been amended in accordance with his n. 20 on p. 66.

plus ad vanam linguae ac memoriae gloriam, quam ad pervestigandam veritatem: neque vere aliud moliuntur disceptatores isti, quam ut Pharisaica hypocrisi circum veniant hominem, donec capiant in verbo. Quod si quis ante istos verbo non labatur, hunc, juxta sententiam Jacobi Apostoli, oportebit esse perfectissimum.

more pursuit of the vain glory of speech and memory than of the truth. For indeed, these disputers aim at nothing other than to ensnare man with Pharisaic hypocrisy until they catch him in his words. Hence, if someone does not falter in their words before them, that man, according to the apostle James, must be perfect.

De triplici ratione cognoscendi Deum

Si genus inquiras verum mortale potentem
Nosse Deum, cuius diceris effigies,
Hoc lege quod mira struxit Cornelius arte,
Cuius et ingenium nobile cudit opus.
Te prius ut noscas, prudens hortatur, et addit
Noscere tu possis qua ratione Deum.

Illustrissimo excellentissimoque sacri Romani imperii principi ac vicario, Guilelmo Palaeologo, Marchioni Montisferrati, domino suo beneficentissimo, Henricus Cornelius Agrippa beatitudinem perpetuam exoptat.

On the Threefold Way of Knowing God (1515-1516)

If thou, mortal race, wouldst seek the truth,

To know the mighty God, of whom thou art said to be an image,

Read what Cornelius constructed with wondrous skill,

And whose noble work his genius forged.

Wisely he urges thee first to know thyself,

And adds by what means thou canst also know God.

To the most illustrious and excellent prince of the Holy Roman Empire and vicar, William Palaeologus, Marquis of Montferrat, his most beneficent lord,
Heinrich Cornelius Agrippa wishes perpetual blessedness.[41]

---

[41] Perrone Compagni, *Ermetismo e Cristianesimo*, p. 5 aptly sets the stage for this text as follows [translated from the Italian]: "After the defeat of the Swiss troops at Marignano (September 13-14, 1515), which had opened the way to Milan for Francis I, Cornelius Agrippa, tied to the imperial party, was forced to abandon his position at the University of Pavia and leave the city. He found a place at the court of the Marquis of Montferrat, William IX Palaeologus. To his new patron, Agrippa promptly dedicated these two works, the dialogue *De homine* and *De triplici ratione cognoscendi Deum*. Both writings were already in circulation by 1516." While this work was dedicated to William Palaeologus in 1516, Perrone Compagni speculates that it was

CAPUT I

Aeternitatis Dominus universorum principium, medium et finis et renovatio, fons pietatis et origo justitiae, pater et bonum, ipse omnipotens Deus, bonissima (ut ita loquar) sua voluntate propter infinitam gloriam suam creavit omnia bona, ut omnia eum glorificent, et sancte incorrupteque agant quae ad illius honorem pertinent, statuitque omnibus praescriptum certis limitibus finem, pulchrumque ordinem, quem transgredi prohibuit. Haec erat voluntas Dei in creatis, creavitque Deus angelos, coelum, stellas, elementa, vegetabilia et animantia quadru[481]pedia, reptilia, aquatica, simul atque volantia, et horum omnium principem et finem,

---

likely composed in large part at an earlier date, and was not published until 1529 in a refined and expanded form.

CHAPTER I

The Lord of Eternity, the beginning, middle, end and renewal of all things, the source of piety and origin of justice, the Father and the Good, the Almighty God, by His most excellent will (if I may say so), created all good things for the sake of His infinite glory, so that all might glorify Him, and do in a holy and incorrupt manner the things that pertain to His honor.[42] He established for all things a prescribed end within certain limits and a beautiful order, which He forbade them to transgress.[43] This was the will of God in creation. He created the angels, the heavens, the stars, the elements, plants, and living creatures – quadrupeds, reptiles, fish, and birds[44] – and the prince and culmination of all these, man, He

---

[42] The work begins with an impressive flourish of rhetoric, filled with references and allusions to a wide range of Hermetic texts. For "The Lord of Eternity," see *Asclepius* 10 (Copenhaver, *Hermetica*, p. 72); for "the beginning, middle, end and renewal of all things," cf. *Corpus Hermeticum* 3.1 (Copenhaver, *Hermetica*, p. 13) and *Asclepius* 30 (Copenhaver, *Hermetica*, p. 85); for the "origin of justice," see Augustine, *Confessiones*, 4.3.4; for "the Father and the Good," see *Corpus Hermeticum* 10.1-2 (Copenhaver, *Hermetica*, p. 30).

[43] Cf. Job 14:5.

[44] *Corpus Hermeticum* 3.3 (Copenhaver, *Hermetica*, p. 13): "Through his own power, each god sent forth what was assigned to him. And the beasts came to be – four-footed, crawling, water-dwelling, winged – and every germinating seed and grass and every flowering plant..."

hominem ad imaginem suam, eique tanquam filio congratulatus est.

Tunc in primis angelica natura non contenta sublimitate sua, ambitiose appetens altiora, ex oppositio se locans contra Deum dixit: In caelum ascendam, super astra Dei exaltabo solium meum, sedebo in monte testamenti, in lateribus aquilonis; ascendam super altitudinem nubium et similis ero altissimo. Hujus ambitionis princeps fuit Satan, hic primus transgressor voluntatis divinae, ob tantam superbiam et injustitiam e coelo pulsus, et deiectus est in hanc vallem contagiosam, ubi ex hinc misere degit cum odioso suo exercitu, omnibus infensus, suamque ipsius iustitiam in creatura Dei propagare non cessat, in tanta superbia pertinaciter subsistens, neque vult proprium peccatum agnoscere, sed Deum ipsum non cessat assidue de peccato suo criminari. Hinc Graece diabolus nuncupatur, hoc est, criminator. Ab hoc incoepit omnis injustitia, iniquitas, malitia, mors, deformitas, et ex eo procedit omne malum, et nihil nisi malum.

Homo autem, creatus in terra et positus in paradyso ut divinae obsequeretur voluntati, ex quo sapientia simul et vita perpetua donatus erat, petitus a diabolo infesta tentatione, quem auscultans, similiter divinae voluntatis transgressor effectus est.

created in His own image.[45] Then He rejoiced over him as a father rejoices over his son.[46]

But at first, the angelic nature, not content with its own exalted status and ambitiously desiring greater heights, opposed itself to God and said: "I will ascend into heaven, I will exalt my throne above the stars of God; I will sit on the mount of the covenant, on the sides of the north; I will ascend above the heights of the clouds; I will be like the Most High."[47] The leader of this ambition was Satan, the first transgressor of divine will. On account of such pride and injustice, he was cast out of heaven and thrown down into this corrupt valley, where he now dwells wretchedly with his hateful army, hostile to all, and he does not cease to spread his own justice within God's creation. Persisting obstinately in such great pride, he refuses to acknowledge his own sin, but instead, never ceases to accuse God Himself of his own sin. Hence, he is called *diabolus* in Greek, that is, "the accuser." From him originated all injustice, iniquity, malice, death, deformity, and from him proceeds every evil, and nothing but evil.

But man, created on earth and placed in paradise that he should obey the divine will – from which he was endowed with both wisdom and eternal life – was assailed by the devil's harmful temptation, and by listening to him,

---

[45] Genesis 1:27.

[46] *Corpus Hermeticum* 1.12 (Copenhaver, *Hermetica*, p. 3): "Mind, the father of all, who is life and light, gave birth to a man like himself whom he loved as his own child."

[47] Isaiah 14:13-14.

Quare etiam ipse pulsus ex hoc delitiarum horto in hanc vallem miseriae, ignorantiae, mortique factus est obnoxius, omni hora moriens, et negligens, cumque neglecta Dei notitia, apertus est fons peccatorum, profluxerunt scelera, elapsi sunt socii tenebrarum, homoque, Deum ignorans, a Deo ignoratus est. Deique notitiam relinquens, a Deo relictus est (ut ait Apostolus Paulus) in propria desideria, in passiones ignominiae, et in reprobum sensum, corruptusque et abominabilis factus est in omnibus studiis suis.

Vides modo quoniam ignorantia Dei omnium malorum fons est, et origo omnium peccatorum, et scelerum radix, ac lignum interitus, summaque impietas et iniustitia, per quam omnia vitia convalescunt et augentur. Haec animam ipsam pervertit, corrumpit naturam, subvertit hominem, ipsumque ignominiosissimis peccatis implicat,

likewise became a transgressor of the divine will. Therefore, he too was driven from this garden of delights into this valley of misery, made subject to ignorance and death, dying every hour, and becoming neglectful; and with the knowledge of God neglected, a wellspring of sins was opened up, crimes flowed forth, the companions of darkness fell away, and man, ignorant of God, was ignored by God.[48] Abandoning the knowledge of God, he was abandoned by God (as the Apostle Paul says) to his own desires, to degrading passions, and to a reprobate mind, and he became corrupt and abominable in all his pursuits.[49]

You see now how ignorance of God is the source of all evils, the origin of all sins, the root of wicked deeds, the tree of destruction, and the height of impiety and injustice, through which all vices gain strength and increase. This ignorance of God perverts the soul itself, corrupts nature, subverts man, and entangles him in the

---

[48] Genesis 3:9-24; Lazzarelli, *Crater Hermetis*, 14.2 (Hanegraaff and Bouthoorn, *Lodovico Lazzarelli*, p. 209): "For as long as the pure rays of wisdom shine into the soul, by which we perceive God and His powers, no messenger of lies will enter the understanding, but all such will be forced out towards the place of purgation. But when through the increasing distance from the essential One the dim light of our mind is made weaker, the companions of darkness seize the opportunity and couple with the effeminate and broken passions, that Moses calls the daughters of men."

[49] Romans 1:24-28.

corpus ipsum in omnem deformitatem naturaeque contumeliam demergit, in quibus et anima simul madens suffocatur, transformanturque homines in naturam ferarum, moresque beluarum, pejora quoque quam bruta saepe patiuntur. Unde praecipitantur in turpes sensuum illecebras, in lethiferas peccatorum sordes, corruunt in omne flagitium, et in naturae per[482]versionem, subiiciunturque cupiditatum imperio, ad quarum expletionem (ut inquit Hermes) ardenti quodam impetu perferuntur, rituque ferarum immoderato et irascuntur et cupiunt, quodque deterius est, nec finem imponunt libidini ullum, nec malorum inveniunt passionumque terminum, quae omnia Paulus in epistola ad Romanos clare edocet: hinc immundi spiritus, ultores scelerum, in tam nefariam labuntur animam, eamque flagellis verberant peccatorum, et violenta poena ad omnia peccatorum genera trahunt, raptant, compellunt ad neces, ad rapinas, ad libidines, et ad cuncta per quae delinquunt homines, vulnerantque eam insanabilibus vitiis, quae eisdem vitiata tanquam venenis infecta tumescit. Quod dolens Hermes

most shameful sins; it sinks the body into every deformity and affront to nature, in which the soul, drunk, is simultaneously suffocated, and men are transformed into the nature of wild animals and the manners of beasts, and often suffer worse than brutes. Hence they are driven to the vile allurements of the senses, fall into the deadly filth of sins, and plunge into all manner of disgrace and into the perversion of nature, becoming subject to the rule of their desires, towards the fulfillment of which (as Hermes says) they are carried with a certain burning impulse, and in the manner of wild beasts, they both rage and desire immoderately, and what is worse, they neither set any limit to their lust nor find any end to their evils and passions.[50] Paul clearly teaches all this in his Epistle to the Romans: hence unclean spirits, avengers of wicked deeds, slip into such a nefarious soul, scourging it with the whips of sins, and dragging it with violent punishment to all kinds of sins. They force, compel, and drive it to murder, rapine, lust, and all things by which men transgress. They wound it with incurable vices, by which, being corrupted, it swells as if infected by poisons. Lamenting this, Hermes

---

[50] *Asclepius* 7 (Copenhaver, *Hermetica*, p. 70): "Not all have gained true understanding, Asclepius. They are deceived, pursuing, on rash impulse and without due consideration of reason, an image that begets malice in their minds and transforms the best of living things into a beastly nature with brutal habits."

exclamat: Fit deorum ab hominibus dolenda secessio. Soli nocentes remanent angeli, qui humanitati commixti, ad omnia audaciae mala miseros manu injecta compellunt, in bella, in rapinas, in fraudes, et in omnia quae sunt animarum naturae contraria. Et alibi inquit: Permittitur daemonis ultoris arbitrio, qui, ignis acumen incutiens, sensus affligit magisque ad patranda scelera armat, ut turpioris culpae reus, acriori supplicio sit obnoxius, eumque sine ulla intermissione ad insanabiles concupiscentias inflammat. Vides modo quod qui Deum ignorant, a Deo ignorantur, et qui Dei notitiam relinquunt, a Deo relinquuntur.

exclaims: "a lamentable departure of the gods from men ensues. Only harmful angels remain, who, having mingled with humanity, take possession of the wretches and impel them to all ills of recklessness – into war, into plunder, into deceit, and into all things that are contrary to the nature of souls."[51] Elsewhere he says: "it is permitted to the avenging demon to act at will, who, inflicting the sharpness of fire, torments the senses and more fully arms them to commit crimes, so that being guilty of baser faults, they are subject to harsher punishments, inflaming them without any respite to incurable desires."[52] You see now how those who are ignorant of God are ignored by God, and those who abandon the knowledge of God are abandoned by God.

---

[51] *Asclepius* 25 (Copenhaver, *Hermetica*, p. 82): "How mournful when the gods withdraw from mankind! Only the baleful angels remain to mingle with humans, seizing the wretches and driving them to every outrageous crime – war, looting, trickery and all that is contrary to the nature of souls."

[52] *Corpus Hermeticum* 1.23 (Copenhaver, *Hermetica*, p. 5): "But from these I remain distant – the thoughtless and evil and wicked and envious and greedy and violent and irreverent – giving way to the avenging demon who [wounds the evil person], assailing him sensibly with the piercing fire and thus arming him the better for lawless deeds so that greater vengeance may befall him. Such a person does not cease longing after insatiable appetites, struggling in the darkness without satisfaction. [This] tortures him and makes the fire grow upon him all the more."

CAPUT II

Omnium itaque rerum cognoscere et amare principium ipsum omnium creatorem Deum, haec summa pietas, haec summa justitia, haec summa sapientia, summaque hominis felicitas est. Clamat ad nos Deus de coelo, de monte sancto suo: Contemplamini creaturas, audite angelos, auscultate filium meum, ut pii et justi sitis. Ecce, hi sunt tres libri cognitionis Dei, quos misit Deus in hunc mundum hominibus.

Primum librum creaturarum praepositum gentibus, qui sub lege naturae vivebant, qui habuerunt philosophos doctos per sensibiles creaturas, cognoveruntque Deum per illas, quemadmodum inquit Paulus: Invisibilia Dei per ea quae facta sunt intellecta conspiciuntur.

Secundo misit Deus librum legis et eloquiorum, quem dedit Judaei, annuncians verbum suum Jacob, justitias et judicia sua populo Israël. Non fecit taliter omni nationi, et judicia sua non manifestavit eis: Ipsi enim supra philosophos habebant prophetas edoctos per spirituales et an[483]gelicas creaturas, et cognoverunt Deum per illas. Unde ait illis Stephanus protomartyr:

CHAPTER II

Therefore, to know and love God Himself, the beginning of all things, the Creator of all, this is the highest piety, this the highest justice, this the highest wisdom, and the highest happiness of man. God cries out to us from heaven, from His holy mountain: "contemplate creation, listen to the angels, heed my Son, so that you may be pious and just." Behold, these are the three books of the knowledge of God, which God has sent into this world for men.

The first book, the book of creation, was presented to the nations who lived under the law of nature, who had philosophers learned in sensible creatures, and knew God through them, just as Paul says: "The invisible things of God are understood and seen through the things that are made."[53]

Secondly, God sent the book of the law and decrees, which He gave to the Jews, announcing His word to Jacob, and His statutes and judgments to the people of Israel. He has not done so with any other nation, and His judgments He has not revealed to them; for they had the prophets, learned beyond philosophers, through spiritual and angelic creatures, and they knew God through them. Hence, Stephen the protomartyr said to them: "you

[53] Romans 1:20.

Qui accepistis legem in dispositione angelorum. Et Dionysius ait: propheticam divinamque visionem gloriosos Hebraeorum vates adeptos esse, per medias coelestes virtutes. Unde tradit universa cabalistarum schola potiorem legis intentionem solum versari circa angelicum chorum, sublimem vero et ineffabilem essentiae trinitatem, adusque Messiae adventum incognitam fore.

Ultimo igitur misit nobis Deus tertium librum scilicet librum Evangelii datum Christianis, qui cognovimus Deum per ipsum Dei filium, patri coaeternum, factum hominem, Dominum nostrum Jesum Christum. Unde inquit Paulus, novissime diebus istis locutus est nobis Deus in Filio suo, quem constituit haeredem universorum, per quem fecit omnia, habemusque doctores Apostolos, doctos a filio Dei Jesu Christo.

received the law as ordained by the angels."[54] And Dionysius said: "the glorious prophets of the Hebrews attained divine prophecy and vision by means of heavenly powers."[55] Hence, the entire school of the Cabalists teaches that the higher intention of the Law revolves solely around the angelic choir, but also that the sublime and ineffable trinity of essence was to remain unknown until the coming of the Messiah.[56]

Finally, therefore, God sent us the third book, namely, the book of the Gospel given to Christians, by which we know God through the Son of God Himself, coeternal with the Father, made man, our Lord Jesus Christ. Hence Paul says: "in these last days, God has spoken to us by His Son, whom He appointed heir of all things, through whom He made all things,"[57] and we have as teachers the Apostles, who were taught by the Son of God, Jesus Christ.

---

[54] Acts 7:53.

[55] Dionysius, *De Coelesti Hierarchia*, 4.3: "But our illustrious fathers were initiated into these divine visions, through the mediation of the heavenly powers."

[56] Riccio, *Isagoge*, 17r.

[57] Hebrews 1:2.

CAPUT III

Nunc ergo singula pertractemus, et primo videamus quomodo cognoscatur Deus per creaturas. Sed non intelligamus, hic ita nos Deum cognoscere posse, ut qualis ipse sit in extrema ac solitaria sui ipsius a rebus separatione, ac in seipsum retractatione, ac quae sit ejus substantia in profundissimo suae divinitatis recessu dignoscamus. Hoc enim impossibile est, et super omnem intellectum incomprehensibile. Ideo ait Apostolus, Deum habitare lucem inaccessibilem. Et Propheta inquit, Posuit tenebras latibulum suum. Et Joannes ait, Deum nemo vidit, nec videre potest. Et Dionysius dicit: Porro ipsa divina, cujusmodi in suo principio suaque sede sint, nullus sensus attingit, nulla substantia, nullaque scientia penetrat; denique sive supersubstantialie illud occultum, sive Deum aut vitam, sive

CHAPTER III

Now, therefore, let us examine each point in detail, and first let us consider how God is known through creation. But let us not understand this to mean that we can know God in such a way that we can discern what He is like in His ultimate and solitary separation from things, in His withdrawal into Himself, and what His substance is in the deepest recesses of His divinity. This indeed is impossible and incomprehensible beyond all understanding.[58] Therefore, the Apostle says that God dwells in unapproachable light.[59] And the Prophet [David] says: "He made darkness His hiding place."[60] And John says: "no one has seen God, nor can anyone." And Dionysius states: "moreover, the divine itself, in its own principle and its own seat, is beyond the reach of any sense, any substance, or any knowledge. Finally, whether we call it that supersubstantial hiddenness, or God, or life, or

---

[58] Lazzarelli, *Crater Hermetis*, 19.3 (Hanegraaff and Bouthoorn, *Lodovico Lazzarelli*, p. 224-225): "So I do not say here that we should be able to know God in His transcendent being, in His all-encompassing enclosure of Himself within Himself, or as He is in the extreme and solitary retractedness of the profoundest depth and darkness of His divine being [cf. Dionysius, *De Mystica Theologia*, 1.997A], or that we could know what is His essence: that is exceedingly difficult, indeed impossible, for the human intellect cannot reach that high."

[59] I Timothy 6:16.

[60] Psalm 18:11 (Vulg. 17:12).

substantiam, sive lucem seu Verbum appellemus, nihil intelligimus aliud quam ex eo emanantes in nos participationes atque virtutes, quibus assumamur in Deum et quae nobis vel substantiam vel vitam vel sapientiam largiuntur. Cognoscimus itaque Deum per participationes quasdam ab eo emanantes in ea quae creata sunt, quas non intelligentes per quandam, ut ita dicam, reflexionem Deum cognoscimus; vel ut inquit Hermes: Contingit nobis hominibus, ut quasi per caliginem ea quae in coelo sunt videamus, quantum possibile est per conditionem sensus humani. Haec autem intentio pervidendi tantis bonis [484] angustissima est, latissima vero cum viderit felicitate conscientiae.

Itaque in creaturis propter participationem quandam Dei, Deus ipse suspicari et perscrutari potest: Deus enim per singula creata ubique splendet. Et omnibus se libenter ostendit (ut inquit Mercurius) non ubi sit loco,

substance, or light, or word, we understand nothing other than the participations and qualities that emanate from it into us, which draw us towards God and grant us either substance, or life, or wisdom."[61] Thus, we know God through certain participations that emanate from Him into created things, which, though we do not fully comprehend them, we recognize God through a kind of reflection, so to speak. Or, as Hermes says: "it happens for us men that we see the things that are in heaven as though through a fog, to the extent that it is possible through the condition of human sense. Our focus for perceiving such good things, however, is quite limited, but once it has perceived them, it becomes boundless by the felicity of its knowledge."[62]

Thus, in creatures, God Himself can be apprehended and investigated, due to a certain participation in God: for God shines forth everywhere through each created thing.[63] And He willingly shows Himself to all (as Mercurius says), "not in terms of where He is located,

---

[61] Dionysius, *De Divinis Nominibus*, 2.8.645A.

[62] *Asclepius* 32 (Copenhaver, *Hermetica*, p. 87): "And thus it comes about that we humans see the things that are in heaven as if through a mist, to the extent that we can, given the condition of human consciousness. When it comes to seeing great things, our concentration is quite confined, but once it has seen, the happiness of our awareness is vast."

[63] *Corpus Hermeticum* 5.2 (Copenhaver, *Hermetica*, p. 18): "For the lord, who is ungrudging, is seen through the entire cosmos."

nec qualis sit qualitate, nec quantus quantitate, sed hominem sola intelligentia mentis illuminans. Et alibi inquit: Deus omnia ob eam causam fabricavit, ut eum per singula cerneres. Haec Dei bonitas, haec ejus virtus est, illum fulgere per omnia. Nihil est vel in incorporeis etiam invisibile. Mens ipsa intellectione videtur; Deus autem in oratione conspicitur. Unde alibi inquit Mercurius: Denique cum Deum videre volueris, suscipe Solem, fili, respice Lunae cursus, suscipe syderum motus reliquorum. Quis perpetuum horum servat ordinem? Quis mensuram singulis motionis assignat? Quis trahit mundi machinam? Quis hoc utitur instrumento? Quis mare suis finibus circumscripsit? Quis terrae pondus sisit ac librat in medio?

nor in terms of what kind He is in quality, nor how great He is in quantity, but by illuminating man through the intelligence of the mind alone."[64] And elsewhere he says: "God made all things for this reason, that you might see Him through every being. This is the goodness of God, this is His power, that He shines through all things. Nothing is unseen, even among incorporeal beings. Mind itself is seen in [the act of] understanding, but God is seen in [the act of] praying."[65] Hence Mercurius says elsewhere: "finally, when you wish to see God, look upon the Sun, my son, consider the course of the Moon, observe the movements of the other stars. Who maintains the perpetual order of these things? Who assigns to each its measure of movement? Who drives the machine of the world? Who uses this instrument? Who circumscribed the sea with its limits? Who set the weight of earth and balances it in the middle?

---

[64] *Asclepius* 29 (Copenhaver, *Hermetica*, p. 84): "For the father and master of all, who alone is all, shows himself freely to all – not *where* as in a place nor *how* as through some quality nor *how much* as in a quantity but by illuminating people with the understanding that comes only through mind."

[65] *Corpus Hermeticum* 11.22 (Copenhaver, *Hermetica*, p. 42): "This is the goodness of god, this is his excellence: that he is visible through all things. For nothing is unseen, not even among the incorporeals. Mind is seen in the act of understanding, god in the act of making." Note that Perrone Compagni, *Ermetismo e Cristianesimo*, p. 108 correctly has "*Deus autem in operatione conspicitur*" [God is seen in the act of making] not "*oratione*" [in the act of praying].

Certe est aliquis horum author et Dominus. Unde etiam Dionysius ait: Forte id veraciter dicemus, nos Deum non ex ipsius natura cognoscere, id quippe ignotum omnemque superat rationem ac sensum, sed ex creaturarum omnium ordinatissima dispositione, ab ipso producta, ut imagines quasdam ac similitudines divinorum ipsius exemplarium prae se ferente, ad id quod omnia transcendit via et ordine pro viribus scandimus.

Eo usque ascenderunt philosophi gentium ex sola apprehensione creaturarum, hoc est intelligentia sua cuncta complexi quae creata sunt in terra, in aquis, in elementis, in coelo, et quae praeter ea super coelum sunt.

Surely there is someone who is their author and Lord."[66] Hence, Dionysius also says: "perhaps we might truthfully say that we do not know God by His nature, for that is unknown and surpasses all reason and sense, but by the most orderly arrangement of all created things produced by Him, which, bearing the images and likenesses of His divine exemplars, we gradually ascend, according to our strengths, to that which transcends all."[67]

The philosophers of the nations have ascended thus far by the mere apprehension of creatures, that is, by their intelligence comprehending all things that are created on earth, in the waters, in the elements, in the heavens, and those things which are beyond the heavens.[68]

---

[66] *Corpus Hermeticum* 5.3-4 (Copenhaver, *Hermetica*, p. 18-19): "If you want to see god, consider the sun, consider the circuit of the moon, consider the order of the stars. Who keeps this order? [...] Who determined the direction and the size of the circuit for each of them? Who owns this instrument, this [guardian of the] bear, the one that turns around itself and carries the whole cosmos with it? Who set limits to the sea? Who settled the earth in place? There is someone, Tat, who is maker and master of all this."

[67] Dionysius, *De Divinis Nominibus*, 7.3.869C-872A. Note that this whole paragraph draws closely and extensively from Lodovico Lazzarelli, *Crater Hermetis*, 9.4 (Hanegraaff and Bouthoorn, *Lodovico Lazzarelli*, p. 193).

[68] *Corpus Hermeticum* 4.5 (Copenhaver, *Hermetica*, p. 16): "But those who participate in the gift that comes from god, O Tat, are immortal rather than mortal if one compares their deeds, for in a mind of their own they have comprehended all – things on earth, things in heaven and even what lies beyond heaven."

Tandem pervenerunt ad primum motorem, et rerum omnium principium, intellectuque viderunt Deum omnipotentem, unum, aeternum, Creatorem omnium, ac summum bonum, sempiternam quoque ejus virtutem, et divinitatem, bonitatem, sapientiam, veritatem, justitiam, pulchritudinem, etc., quae vocat Paulus invisibilia Dei. Viderunt enim Deum in coelo et in terra, in igne, in aqua, in Spiritu, in animalibus, in arboribus, in omni corpore, et in omnibus creaturis, quemadmodum canit Lucanus:

Iupiter est quodcunque vides, quodcunque movetur.

Virgilius quoque inter pecora cecinit:

Iovis omnia plena.

Hinc Hermes ait: Homo effectus est divinorum operum contemplator; quae profecto, dum admiraretur,

At last they came to the prime mover and the principle of all things, and with their intellect, they perceived God Almighty – the one, eternal, Creator of all, and the highest good – along with His eternal power and divinity, goodness, wisdom, truth, justice, beauty, etc., which Paul calls "the invisible things of God."[69] For they saw God in heaven and on earth, in fire, in water, in the Spirit, in animals, in trees, in every body, and in all creatures[70], just as Lucan sings:

Jupiter is whatever you see, whatever moves.[71]

Virgil also sang among the flocks:

All things are full of Jove.[72]

Hence, Hermes says: "Man was made a contemplator of divine works, which, so long as he gazed upon them with

---

[69] Romans 1:20.

[70] *Corpus Hermeticum* 13.11 (Copenhaver, *Hermetica*, p. 51): "Since god has made me tranquil, father, I no longer picture things with the sight of my eyes but with the mental energy that comes through the powers. I am in heaven, in earth, in water, in air; I am in animals and in plants; in the womb, before the womb, after the womb; everywhere."

[71] Note that Agrippa here has *quodcunque movetur* (lit. "whatever is moved"), but Lucan, *De bello civili*, 9.578 has *quodcunque moveris* ("wherever you move"). Cf. Pico della Mirandola, *Heptaplus*, 7.Proem where both these lines of Lucan and Virgil's poetry first appeared together.

[72] Virgil, *Eclogae*, 3.

autorem illorum [485] cognovit. Facile enim et complete (prout humana sustinet promptitudo) Deum noscit qui mente facile singula ejus opera cernit. Omnis itaque homo potest Deum cognoscere, si velit.

Propterea inexcusabilis est homo ignorans Deum, et omnis qui, animam suam in corpus demergens, Deum se posse cognoscere diffidit. Sed absit haec impietas, recurre in te ipsum, emergas ex corpore, nihil supponas in te impossibile, confidas et intelliges, velis et consequeris. Sic denique Deum cognosces, si non diffidas

wonder, he assuredly recognized their author."[73] For indeed, anyone who easily perceives each of His works with a ready mind knows God easily and completely (as far as human alacrity allows).[74] Therefore, every man can know God, if they will it.

Hence, the man who is ignorant of God is inexcusable, and anyone who, drowning their soul in the body, doubts that they can know God.[75] But let this impiety be far from us – return into yourself, emerge from the body, suppose nothing impossible within you, have confidence, and you will understand; will it and you will attain it.[76] Thus, you will know God if you do not doubt

---

[73] *Corpus Hermeticum* 4.2 (Copenhaver, *Hermetica*, p. 15): "The man became a spectator of god's work. He looked at it in astonishment and recognized its maker."

[74] Cf. Riccio, *Isagoge*, 5^r.

[75] Romans 1:20; *Corpus Hermeticum* 11.21 (Copenhaver, *Hermetica*, p. 42): "But if you shut your soul up in the body and abase it and say, 'I understand nothing, I can do nothing; I fear the sea, I cannot go up to heaven; I do not know what I was, I do not know what I will be,' then what have you to do with god? While you are evil and a lover of the body, you can understand none of the things that are beautiful and good."

[76] *Corpus Hermeticum* 13.7 (Copenhaver, *Hermetica*, p. 50): "May it not be so, my child. Draw it to you, and it will come. Wish it, and it happens." *Corpus Hermeticum* 11.20 (Copenhaver, *Hermetica*, p. 41): "Make yourself grow to immeasurable immensity, outleap all body, outstrip all time, become eternity and you will understand god. Having conceived that nothing is impossible to you, consider yourself immortal and able to understand everything, all art, all learning, the temper of every living thing. Go higher than every height

de te ipso. Humanus enim animus (ut ait Hermes) omnia capit, omnia penetrat, elementis velocitate miscetur, acumine mentis in maris profunditatem descendit, omnia illi lucent, non coelum videtur altissimum, quasi enim ex proximo sagacitate omni intuetur. Intentionem animi ejus nulla aeris caligo confundit; non densitas terrae operam ejus impedit; non aquae altitudo profunda despectum ejus obtundit. Et alibi: Praecipito (inquit) animae tuae, quae citius quam praecipies, evolabit. Jubeto ut transeat in oceanum, illa priusquam jusseris, ibi erit, inde ubi nunc est, nequaquam discedens. Jubeto iterum ut in coelum volet, nullis pennis egebit, nihil ejus obstabit

---

and lower than every depth. Collect in yourself all the sensations of what has been made, of fire and water, dry and wet; be everywhere at once, on land, in the sea, in heaven; be not yet born, be in the womb, be young, old, dead, beyond death. And when you have understood all these at once – times, places, things, qualities, quantities – then you can understand god."

yourself.[77] For the human mind, as Hermes says, comprehends all things, penetrates all things, "mingles with the elements by its swiftness, plumbs the depths of the sea with its sharpness of mind; all things are illuminated[78] for it, heaven does not seem exceedingly high, for with all sagacity it perceives everything as if it were near. No fog of air clouds the focus of [man's] mind; no density of earth impedes its work; no profound depth of water dulls its gaze."[79] And elsewhere he says: "command your soul, which will take flight more quickly than you can command it. Order it to cross the ocean, and before you give the order, it will be there, never departing from where it is now. Command it again to fly to the heavens, and it will not lack wings; nothing will obstruct its

---

[77] *Corpus Hermeticum* 11.21 (Copenhaver, *Hermetica*, p. 42): "To be ignorant of the divine is the ultimate vice, but to be able to know, to will and to hope is the [straight and] easy way leading to the good." Cf. Lazzarelli, *Crater Hermetis*, 21.4 (Hanegraaff and Bouthoorn, *Lodovico Lazzarelli*, p. 231).

[78] Note that the correct Latin for *Asclepius* 6 according to Matteo Stefani's 2019 critical edition is *omnia illi licent* ("To him [i.e., man] all things are permitted") rather than Agrippa's *omnia illi lucent* ("All things are illuminated for it") which can be found in some manuscripts.

[79] *Asclepius* 6 (Copenhaver, *Hermetica*, 70): "He cultivates the earth; he swiftly mixes into the elements; he plumbs the depths of the sea in the keenness of his mind. Everything is permitted him: heaven itself seems not too high, for he measures it in his clever thinking as if it were nearby. No misty air dims the concentration of his thought; no thick earth obstructs his work; no abysmal deep of water blocks his lofty view. He is everything, and he is everywhere."

cursui, non Solis incendium, non aetheris amplitudo, non vertigo coelorum, non syderum reliquorum corpora, quin omnia penetrans ad supremum usque corpus transcendat. Quin etiam si volueris globos omnes transcendere coelorum, quodque superius est investigare, id quoque tibi licebit. Adverte modo quanta sit animae potestas, quanta virtus, quanta celeritas.

Propterea inexcusabilis est homo ignorans Deum. Magis autem ille qui cognoscens Deum quoquo modo, eundem non colit neque veneratur. Haec enim odiosissima est et inexcusabilis impietas, quam Paulus improperans gentibus ait ita: ut sint inexcusabiles; quia cum cognovissent Deum, non sicut Deum glorificaverunt, aut gratias egerunt. Philosophi namque gentium, cognoscentes

course, neither the burning of the Sun, nor the vastness of the aether, nor the whirling of the heavens, nor of the bodies of the other stars, but penetrating all things, it will transcend even the highest body. But if you wish to transcend all the spheres of the heavens and investigate what is above them, this too will be permitted to you."[80] Consider now how great the soul's power is, how great its virtue, how great its swiftness.

Therefore, the man who is ignorant of God is inexcusable. But more so is the one who, in any way knowing God, does not worship or venerate Him.[81] For this is the most hateful and inexcusable impiety, which Paul, reproaching the nations, expresses thus: "so that they are without excuse; because, when they knew God, they did not glorify Him as God, nor were they thankful."[82] For the philosophers of the nations, knowledgeable in

---

[80] *Corpus Hermeticum* 11.19 (Copenhaver, *Hermetica*, p. 41): "Command your soul to travel to India, and it will be there faster than your command. Command it to cross over to the ocean, and again it will quickly be there, not as having passed from place to place but simply as being there. Command it even to fly up to heaven, and it will not lack wings. Nothing will hinder it, not the fire of the sun, nor the aether, nor the swirl nor the bodies of the other stars. Cutting through them all, it will fly to the utmost body. But if you wish to break through the universe itself and look upon the things outside (if, indeed, there is anything outside the cosmos), it is within your power."

[81] Cf. Ficino, *De Christiana religione*, 4 (Attrell, Bartlett, and Porreca, *Marsilio Ficino: On the Christian Religion*, p. 53-54).

[82] Romans 1:20-21.

varias disciplinas, arithmeticam, musicam, geometriam, astronomiam, physicam, metaphysicam, dialecticam, et caeteras, cognoveruntque scientia sua unum solum ac verum Deum. Sed impii et ingrati de tanto beneficio, a pura sanctaque cognitione aversi, falsam quandam ejus imaginem temeraria cognitione, nulla vera ratione inspecta, sequentes ipsum non ut unum solum ac verum Deum coluerunt, nec gratias illi, quod illos divinitatis suae agnoscendae illustravit lumine, reddiderunt. Quare omnes illi impietatis injustitiaeque et ingratitudinis condemnabuntur, juxta verba Pauli dicentis: Revelatur [486] enim ira Dei de coelo super omnem impietatem et injustitiam hominum.

Impietas namque peccatum est erga Deum, injustitia erga homines: extrema autem impietas est non cognoscere Deum. Ex impietate intemperantia, et haec injustitiae fundamentum. Intemperantiam vero dicimus depravationem voluntatis ex sopore rationis ortam, affectu sensuali nimium dominante, ubi

various disciplines – arithmetic, music, geometry, astronomy, physics, metaphysics, dialectic, etc. – came to know, with their science, the one sole and true God.[83] Yet, being impious and ungrateful for such a great benefit, they turned away from pure and holy knowledge.[84] Following a false image of Him with reckless understanding, having examined no true reason, they did not worship Him as the one sole and true God, nor did they give thanks to Him for having enlightened them with the light of recognizing His divinity. Therefore, all those philosophers will be condemned for their impiety, injustice, and ingratitude, according to the words of Paul, who says: "for the wrath of God is revealed from heaven against all impiety and injustice of men."[85]

For impiety is a sin against God, and injustice is a sin against men; but the greatest impiety is not knowing God. From impiety comes intemperance, and this is the foundation of injustice. Indeed, we say intemperance is the corruption of the will arising from the sleep of reason, with excessive sensual desire dominating, where,

---

[83] *Asclepius* 12-13 (Copenhaver, *Hermetica*, p. 74): "What is it that the many do to make philosophy incomprehensible? How do they obscure it in the multiplicity of their reasoning?" "In this way, Asclepius: by combining it through ingenious argument with various branches of study that are not comprehensible – *arithmētikē* and music and geometry."

[84] *Asclepius* 14 (Copenhaver, *Hermetica*, p. 74): "the people who will come after us, deceived by the ingenuity of sophists, will be estranged from the true, pure and holy philosophy."

[85] Romans 1:18.

videlicet sopita ratione, ad imperium sensuum omnia aguntur. Unde haec sterilis anima dicitur, nullum fructum bonum producens in tempore suo, et haec est animae summa impietas, sterilem esse, de qua ait Mercurius: Impietas accidit illi, qui absque filiis e vita discedit, qua de causa daemonibus post obitum dat poenas. Sed frustra cognoscimus Deum, nisi illum rite colamus, et legitime cum hominibus vivamus. Unde inquit Hermes: Certamen religiosae pietatis est recognoscere Deum, injuriam inferre nemini: quod etiam praecipit Christus, dicens:

with reason being put to sleep, everything is done under the command of the senses.[86] Hence, this soul is called barren, bearing no good fruit in its time, and this is the greatest impiety of the soul: to be barren.[87] Concerning this, Mercurius says: "Impiety befalls the one who departs from life without children, for which reason he suffers punishment from demons after death."[88] But it is in vain to know God unless we worship Him properly and live with men justly. Therefore, Hermes says: "The struggle of religious piety is to know God and harm no one,"[89] which Christ also commands, saying:

---

[86] Ficino, *Theologia Platonica*, 18.10.6 (Allen and Hankins, *Platonic Theology*, p. 186-189): "The intemperate man is the one in whom the reason has been lulled to sleep or depraved by the dominance of excessive passions, and where all things are given over to the sway of the phantasy, and where the reason does not oppose desire."

[87] Cf. Matthew 7:16-20, Mark 11:12-14, and Luke 13:6-9.

[88] *Corpus Hermeticum* 2.17 (Copenhaver, *Hermetica*, p. 12): "Prudent people… regard the making of children as a duty in life to be taken most seriously and greatly revered, and should any human being pass away childless, they see it as the worst misfortune and irreverence. After death such a person suffers retribution from demons. This is his punishment: the soul of the childless one is sentenced to a body that has neither a man's nature nor a woman's – a thing accursed under the sun. Most assuredly then, Asclepius, you should never congratulate a childless person. On the contrary, show pity for his calamity, knowing what punishment awaits him."

[89] *Corpus Hermeticum* 2.18 (Copenhaver, *Hermetica*, p. 34): "Knowing the divine and doing wrong to no person is the fight of reverence."

Dilige Dominum Deum tuum, proximum tuum sicut te ipsum. Haec duo praecepta ad salutem necessaria sunt, suntque fons omnis boni: horum primum pietatis, alterum justitiae est. E contrario impietas et injustitia omnium malorum radix sunt, super quae revelatur ira Dei de coelo super illos, qui veritatem Dei in illis polluunt, violantque, et hi sunt qui Deum in cognitione non amant, et in scientia sua non frutificant, qui in sapientia sua non religiosi sunt, et in prudentia sua non prosunt hominibus.

Sed nunc consequentur de secundaria cognitione Dei, quae est per librum legis, dicamus.

"love the Lord your God, and your neighbor as yourself."[90] These two commandments are necessary for salvation and are the source of all good: of these the first is piety, the second, justice. Conversely, impiety and injustice are the root of all evils, upon which the wrath of God is revealed from heaven against those who pollute and violate the truth of God within themselves.[91] These are the ones who do not love God in their minds and do not bear fruit in their knowledge, who are not religious in their wisdom, and who do not benefit mankind in their prudence.

But now, let us speak about the second kind of knowledge of God, which is through the book of the law.

---

[90] Luke 10:27; cf. Deuteronomy 6:5 and 10:12; Matthew 19:19; Romans 13:9.

[91] Romans 1:18.

CAPUT IV

Secundus liber datus est Judaeis, liber legis, palam positus, et liber eloquiorum solis sapientibus traditus. Ipsi enim primi fuerunt, quibus cum multifariam Deus per angelos suos locutus est, et quibus data fuerunt oracula et arcana Dei, sicut ait Psalmista: Non fecit taliter omni nationi, et judicia sua non manifestavit illis. Constat autem ex sententiis Hebraeorum magistrorum, etiam et Christianorum doctorum, Moysen ipsum, magnum Hebraeorum legislatorem, praeter legem illam quam Deus dedit illi in monte Syna, quam ille quinque libris scriptam contentamque reliquit, revelatam quoque fuisse eidem Moysi ab ipso Deo veram legis expositionem, cum manifestatione omnium mysteriorum et secretorum, quae sub cortice et rudi facie verborum legis continentur. Unde legitur [487] Deus dixisse ad Esdram: Revelans revelatus sum super rubum et locutus sum Moysi, quando populus meus serviebat in Aegypto, et misi eum, et adduxi eum super montem Syna, et detinebam eum apud me diebus multis, et narravi illi mirabilia multa, et ostendi ei temporum secreta et finem, et praecepi ei dicens: Haec in palam facies verba, et haec abscondes.

CHAPTER IV

The second book was given to the Jews, the book of the law, openly presented, and the book of the oracles, entrusted only to the wise. For they were the first to whom God spoke in many ways through His angels, and to whom the oracles and secrets of God were given, as the Psalmist says: "He has not dealt so with any nation, and His judgments He has not made known to them."[92] It is well established by the teachings of Hebrew masters, as well as by Christian doctors, that Moses, the great lawgiver of the Hebrews, besides that law which God gave him on Mount Sinai and which he left written and contained in five books, was also revealed by God the true interpretation of the law, with the manifestation of all the mysteries and secrets that are contained beneath the outer shell and rough surface of the law's words. Hence, it is read that God said to Ezra: "I revealed myself in the bush and spoke to Moses when my people were serving in Egypt, and I sent him and brought him to Mount Sinai, and I kept him with me for many days, and I told him many wondrous things, and I showed him the secrets of times and their end, and I commanded him, saying: 'These words you shall make public, and these you shall hide.'"[93]

---

[92] Psalm 147:20 (Vulg. 147:9).

[93] IV Ezra 14:3-6. This and the following paragraph draw extensively from Giovanni Pico della Mirandola, *Apologia*, 26^{v}-27^{r}, a work which the young Prince of Concord had written in 1487

Constat itaque Moysen in monte duplicem legem, videlicet, literalem et spiritualem accepisse, et juxta praeceptum Dei utramque populo Judaico communicasse, illam videlicet scriptam vulgo palam statuisse, alteram vero solum septuaginta sapientibus communicasse, nec scriptis, nec ut ipsi scriberent, sed viva voce, et ut quisque eorum ordine perpetuo suis successoribus viva voce revelarent. Propter quam vivae vocis successivam traditionem dicta est scientia eloquiorum, quam Hebraei vocant Cabalam, propter receptionem tanquam haereditario jure unius ab altero. Cui sententiae correspondet etiam illud Hilarii in expositione Psalmi Quare fremuerunt gentes, ubi dicit Hilarius fuisse a Moyse institutum, in omni synagoga septuaginta esse seniores, quibus Moyses, praeter legem quam literis condidisset, secretiora mysteria intimavit. Et juxta hunc sensum exponit splendidissimus theologus Origenes illud dictum Pauli: Quia credita sunt illis eloquia Dei, scilicet praeter literalem legem Judaeis datam, etiam aliam fuisse spiritualem, quam Paulus vocat eloquia Dei: recentiores Hebraei Cabalam dicunt, quae omnium divinarum humanarumque rerum cognitionem in allegorico sensu legis Mosaicae comprehendit. Quod etiam Paulus confirmat, ubi dicit: Judaeos habere

---

to defend the orthodoxy of his *900 Conclusiones* in the face of condemnations led by the Thomist Dominican Bishop Pedro Garcia. In his *Apologia*, Pico relied on this passage in IV Ezra to legitimize his interest in Cabala in the eyes of the Catholic Church. See also Copenhaver, *Oration*, p. 133-135.

It is therefore established that Moses received a twofold law on the mountain, namely, the literal and the spiritual, and according to the command of God, he communicated both to the Jewish people. He set forth the literal law openly in writing to the common people, but the other, he communicated only to seventy wise men, neither in writing nor so that they might write it down, but orally, and so that each of them would reveal it to their successors orally in perpetual succession. Because of this successive oral tradition, this knowledge is called the science of the oracles, which the Hebrews call Cabala, on account of the reception, as if by hereditary right, from one to another. This view is supported by Hilary in his commentary on the Psalm "why do the nations rage?"[94] where Hilary says that it was instituted by Moses that in every synagogue there should be seventy elders, to whom Moses, besides the law that he had established in writing, revealed more secret mysteries. The illustrious theologian Origen, following this understanding, explains Paul's statement that "the oracles of God were entrusted to them,"[95] meaning that besides the literal law given to the Jews, there was also another spiritual one, which Paul calls "the oracles of God." The more recent Hebrews call it Cabala, which comprehends the knowledge of all divine and human things in the allegorical sense of the Mosaic law. Paul also confirms this when he says that the Jews have

---

[94] Psalm 2:1.

[95] Romans 3:2.

formam scientiae et veritatis in lege. Et Rabbi Moyses in secundo tractatu Morae inquit, totam legis sollicitudinem in hoc consistere, ut veridicas sententias de Deo angelicisque choris doceat, quibus edocti homines etiam ipsum mundum in suo ordine cognoscant.

Principalis itaque eruditio Cabalae prophetica est et illorum cognoscibilium, quae de Deo angelisque intelligi possunt. Hinc multiformia tam Dei quam angelorum sacra nomina invocanda edocet, variosque corporeos actus enumerat, quibus homines, tanquam similes facti diis conformando se divinis per quosdam gradus, ad aeterna patris lumina transcendunt, quibus repleti Dei cognitionem ultra naturae morem assequuntur, magis enim operantur invocata sacra nomina in mentem nostram illis rite expositam, quam corpus quodvis accedens ad aliud corpus operatur in illud, ceu ignis in stuppam. Habet praeterea lex Hebraica etiam hoc divinitatis, ut praeter [488]

"the form of knowledge and of truth in the law."[96] And Rabbi Moses, in the second tractate of the *Guide for the Perplexed*, says that the whole concern of the law consists in this: that it teaches true doctrines about God and the angelic choirs, by which men, having been instructed, may also come to know the world itself in its order.

Therefore, the principal teaching of the Cabala is prophetic and concerns those knowable things that can be understood about God and the angels. Hence, it teaches the invocation of the multiform sacred names of both God and the angels and enumerates the different corporeal actions by which men, becoming like gods and conforming themselves to divine things through certain steps, transcend to the eternal lights of the Father. Being filled with these lights, they attain knowledge of God beyond the normal order of nature. For the sacred names, when invoked correctly, influence our minds more powerfully than any physical body acting upon another body, like fire upon flax.[97] Furthermore, the Hebrew law also possesses this divine quality, that besides

---

[96] Romans 2:20.

[97] This paragraph draws extensively from the converso Paolo Riccio, *Isagoge*, 5^r-5^v, 12^v, 13^r, 17^v. According to Charles Nauert, *Agrippa and the Crisis of Renaissance Thought*, p. 41: "[Paola Zambelli] suggests that Agrippa must have known Paolo Ricci [1480-1541], the converted Jew who was an important religious controversialist and translator of the cabalistic *Sha'are Orah* and of a part of the Talmudic literature. But although Agrippa certainly did know some of this Ricci's translations, it is not so

Dei angelicaque nomina multiformia ibi latitantia, etiam ne elementum ullum transeat sine prophetico aliquo mysterio, quorum revolutione juxta regulas Cabalistarum saepe stupenda panduntur oracula. Unde ait Rabi Moyses secundo Morae divina nomina propheticaeque verba, transposito literarum ordine aliisque insolitis signaculis, saepe grandia sapientiae divinae oracula decernere. Quod etiam alter Moyses Gerundinus in exordio Geneseos, et tota Cabalistarum Schola confirmat, majores siquidem et propinquiores virtutes Dei sunt in divinis nominibus propheticisque characteribus quam in quovis corpore mundi. Ideo Dionysius nos illorum veneratione et contemplatione facilius ad Deum Patrem ascendere, suique splendoris plus quam ex rerum naturalium et creaturarum intuitu participes effici. Et nos de hac materia late et profunde scripsimus in libro de occulta philosophia, eo loco ubi de mysteriis et caeremoniis occultarum operationum tractatur.

---

certain that he knew the man himself. Ricci, a native of Germany, had left Pavia by 1514 to settle in Augsburg; and by 1516 he was serving as a physician to the Emperor Maximilian."

the many hidden names of God and the angels that lie within it, not even a single element passes without some prophetic mystery, of which by revolution according to the rules of the Cabalists, astounding oracles are often revealed.[98] Hence Rabbi Moses says in the second book of the *Guide for the Perplexed* that divine names and prophetic words, when the order of letters is transposed or other unusual signs are used, often produce great oracles of divine wisdom. This is also confirmed by the other Moses [Nachmanides] of Girona at the beginning of his Genesis commentary, as well as by the entire school of the Cabalists, who assert that the powers of God are greater and more at hand in divine names and prophetic characters than in any worldly body. Therefore, Dionysius says that through the veneration and contemplation of these, we ascend more easily to God the Father and participate more fully in His splendor than we do through the contemplation of natural things and creatures. We ourselves have written extensively and deeply on this subject in our book *On Occult Philosophy*, in the section where we discuss the mysteries and ceremonies of occult

---

[98] Cf. Pico della Mirandola, *Conclusiones*, 28.33 (in Farmer, *Syncretism and the West*, p. 358-359): "There are no letters in the whole Law which in their forms, conjunctions, separations, crookedness, straightness, defect, excess, smallness, largeness, crowning, closure, openness, and order, do not reveal the secrets of the ten numerations" [i.e. *sephirot*]. For the attribution of this passage to Menahem Recanati see Wirszubski, *Pico della Mirandola's Encounter with Jewish Mysticism*, p. 45.

Sed satis est hic nobis scire Judaeorum cognitionem de Deo multo fuisse sublimiorem et perfectiorem per legem, quam gentium per creaturas. Non tamen potuerunt nisi umbratilem quandam de Deo cognitionem habere. Veram autem et perfectam Dei cognitionem (ut tota Cabalistarum schola testatur) reservatam fuisse ad adventum Messiae, qui tandem venit, Dominus noster Jesus Christus, in quo perfecta sunt et perficiuntur omnia.

Sed redeamus ad Cabalam, quae est lex spiritualis, latens sub verbis legis literalis, quae sola viva voce tradebatur ab uno ad alterum. Haec lex spiritualis, post restitutionem Judaeorum a Babylonica captivitate per Cyrum regem Persarum, et instaurato templo sub Zorobabel per Esdram (qui tunc Judaicae ecclesiae praefectus erat) in synodo convocatis sapientibus ut afferret unusquisque in medium quae de legis mysteriis memoriter teneret, adhibitis notariis, primum scriptis mandata est, et in septuaginta volumina (tot enim in synodo illo erant sapientes) redacta est.

operations.[99] But it is enough here for us to know that the knowledge of God among the Jews was much higher and more perfect through the law than among the pagans through creation. Nevertheless, they could only have a shadowy knowledge of God.[100] The true and perfect knowledge of God (as the entire school of the Cabalists testifies) was reserved for the coming of the Messiah, who came at last – our Lord Jesus Christ – in whom all things are perfected and brought to completion.

But let us return to the Cabala, which is the spiritual law hiding beneath the words of the literal law, and was transmitted orally from one to another. This spiritual law, after the restoration of the Jews from the Babylonian captivity by Cyrus, king of the Persians, and the rebuilding of the temple under Zerubbabel[101] by Ezra (who was then the head of the Jewish assembly), was first committed to writing by wise men who were called together at a synod to bring forth what each had memorized concerning the mysteries of the law. Then, after the scribes were summoned, it was compiled into seventy volumes (for there were seventy wise men at that

[99] In Book III of the *Three Books of Occult Philosophy*, composed in 1510 though not published until 1533. Agrippa would greatly expand this book, especially as his knowledge of Cabala grew greatly in the Italian period.

[100] Hebrews 10:1.

[101] I.e. the Jewish governor of Judah for the Persian Empire who began to rebuild the Temple of Solomon in the 6th century.

De quibus ita loquitur Esdras: Exactis quadraginta diebus, loquutus est altissimus dicens: Priora quae scripsisti in palam pone, legant digni et indigni; novissimos autem septuaginta libros conservabis, ut tradas eos sapientibus de populo, quorum corda scis posse capere et servare secreta haec: in his enim est vena intellectus, sapientiae fons, et scientiae flumen. Continet enim lex ipsa ineffabilem de supersubstantiali deitate theologiam, de intelligibilibus angelicisque formis exactam metaphysicam, de mundo corporeo rebusque naturalibus firmissimam philosophiam. Atque hinc venit in usum, ut apud [489] recentiores Hebraeos etiam quaeque occultior et abditior, vel quae circa mirabilium effectuum secretas operationes versatur scientia, Cabala nuncupetur. Unde factum est ut etiam illi, qui secreto quodam foedere, pacto, et conventione cum daemonibus inita, stupenda facta jactitabant, quo improbitatem sui execrandi artificii superstitionisque tegerent, honestiori nomine Cabalistas sese vocitarunt. Hinc tandem Cabalae sanctum nomen in suspicionem venit, quemadmodum et sacrum magiae nomen, utrumque suspectum est, utrumque prophanatum est, juxta vetus proverbium, quo dicitur: sacra

synod).[102] Concerning these, Ezra speaks thus: "after forty days were completed, the Most High spoke, saying: 'publish openly the first things that you wrote down, so that the worthy and the unworthy may read them; but these last seventy books you shall keep and deliver only to the wise among the people, whose hearts you know are capable of comprehending and preserving these secrets: for in these books is the vein of understanding, the fountain of wisdom, and the river of knowledge."[103] Indeed, the Law itself contains an ineffable theology concerning the supersubstantial deity, the precise metaphysics concerning intelligible and angelic forms, and the most solid philosophy concerning the corporeal world and natural things. And hence it has come into use, that among the later Hebrews, even the more occult and hidden knowledge, or that which deals with the secret operations of miraculous effects, is called Cabala. Hence it has come about that even those who boasted of astonishing deeds through a certain secret covenant, pact, and agreement made with demons began to call themselves Cabalists under a more respectable name in order to conceal the wickedness of their execrable art and superstition. Thus, the holy name of Cabala came into suspicion, just as also happened to the sacred name of magic, both of which have become suspect, both of which have been profaned, according to the old proverb: "sacred

---

[102] This whole paragraph draws closely from Pico della Mirandola's *Oratio* (Copenhaver, *Oration*, p. 133-135).
[103] IV Ezra 12:38.

prophanantur quoniam a prophanis usurpantur.

Habebant itaque Judaei legem scriptam ad vulgus publicatam; habebant etiam eloquia Dei, scilicet altissimae divinitatis arcana mysteria, sub cortice verborum scriptae legis latitantia, solis sapientibus tradita, quae non licuit in vulgus prodere. Mysteria enim tanta divinitate plenissima stultae plebi communicare quid aliud esset, quam sanctum dare canibus, quod etiam Christus ipse in Evangelio suo vetuit.

Qui promissus per legem et desideratus in lege, tandem opportuno tempore venit adimpletor et perfector legis, quemadmodum ipse inquit: non enim veni solvere legem, sed adimplere. Erat enim tota lex in tres partes divisa: vel erant umbratiles figurae futurae lucis, vel sermones prophetici futurae veritatis, vel praecepta vivendi futurae perfectionis. Quod si solum literalem sensum legis apprehendas,

things are profaned when appropriated by the profane."[104]

The Jews, therefore, had a written law made public to the common people; they also had the utterances of God, namely, the mysteries of the highest divinity, hidden beneath the outer shell of the words of the written law, which were entrusted only to the wise and were not permitted to be revealed to the common people.[105] For to communicate to the foolish masses such mysteries filled to the brim with divinity would be nothing other than to give what is holy to dogs, which even Christ Himself forbade in His Gospel.[106]

He who was promised by the law and desired in the law, finally came at the appointed time as the fulfiller and perfecter of the law, as He Himself said: "I have not come to abolish the law, but to fulfill it."[107] For the entire law was divided into three parts: either they were shadowy figures of the future light, or prophetic words of future truth, or commandments of living for future perfection. But if you grasp only the literal sense of the law,

---

[104] Cf. Matthew 7:6.

[105] Pico della Mirandola, *Oratio* (Copenhaver, *Oration*, p. 131).

[106] Matthew 7:6-7; *Asclepius* 1: *Tractatum autem tota numinis maiestate plenissimum irreligiose mentis est multorum conscientie publicare* ("For it is the sign of an irreligious mind to divulge to the knowledge of the masses a discussion filled to the brim with the whole majesty of the divine presence"; cf. Copenhaver, *Hermetica*, p. 67).

[107] Matthew 5:18.

absque spiritu futurae lucis, veritatis, et perfectionis, nihil erit lege magis ridiculum, et anilis fabulae, milesiique sermonis magis simillimum. Porro venit Christus sol justitiae, vera lux, clarissima veritas, vera vitae perfectio omnibus hominibus, qui credunt in nomine ejus. Ipse adimplevit legem, ut ammodo non sit opus lege, nec ammodo cognoscimus Deum in caligine creaturarum, neque in umbra legis Judaicae, sed in lumine fidei Jesu Christi, qui est vera cognitio, sapientia Patris, intellectus hominis, in quo, ut inquit Paulus, recapitulantur omnia, et quae in coelis, et quae in terris sunt.

Ideo nunc consequenter dicamus de ultima et perfecta Dei cognitione, quae est per Evangelium Christi Jesu Domini nostri.

without the spirit of the future light, truth, and perfection, nothing will be more ridiculous than the law, and more like an old wives' tale or Milesian fable.[108] However, Christ came as the sun of justice, the true light, the clearest truth, the true perfection of life for all men who believe in His name.[109] He fulfilled the law so that from now on there is no longer a need for the law, nor do we now know God in the gloom of creatures, nor in the shadow of the Jewish law, but in the light of faith in Jesus Christ, who is true knowledge, the wisdom of the Father, and the understanding of man, in whom, as Paul says, all things are recapitulated, both those in heaven and those on earth.[110]

Therefore, let us now speak consequently of the ultimate and perfect knowledge of God, which is through the Gospel of our Lord Jesus Christ.

---

[108] Pico della Mirandola, *Heptaplus*, 7.Proem (Wallis, Miller, Carmichael, *On the Dignity of Man; On Being and the One; Heptaplus*, p. 147); Apuleius, *Metamorphoses*, 1.1.

[109] John 1:13.

[110] Ephesians 1:10.

CAPUT V

Omne studium amorque sapientiae ex Spiritu sancto est per Dominum nostrum Jesum Christum. Ipsa vera sapientia Dei cognitio est, illustratio mentis, voluntatis correctio, appetitioque rectae rationis, quaedam vitae certa lex, sanctificans [490] animam hominis, Deo disponens viam, quid agendum, quid omittendum demonstrans; quam nos sapientiam alio vocabulo theologiam vocamus. Haec sapientia veraque Dei cognitio, imo contactus quidam Dei essentialis melior quam cognitio, traditur divinitus in Evangelio. Neque enim Deus ipse sine Evangelio vere cognoscitur, neque Evangelium absque divina gratia vere intelligitur. Manifestum enim est, ea quae ex Deo tradita sunt non nisi ex Deo intelligi posse, sicut ait Propheta: In lumine tuo videbimus lumen: quam lucem Trismegistus Mercurius mentem vocat divinae essentiae, lucem ipsam exorientem Deo.

Intellectus tamen noster, nisi per mentem illuminetur divinam, ab errore non est immunis et frustra laborat in

CHAPTER V

All study and love of wisdom come from the Holy Spirit through our Lord Jesus Christ. True wisdom is knowledge of God, the enlightenment of the mind, the correction of the will, and the desire for right reason. It is a certain law of life, sanctifying the soul of man, directing the way to God, showing what should and what should not be done. This wisdom, which we also call by another name, theology, is true knowledge of God, or rather, a sort of essential contact with God that is better than knowledge. This wisdom is divinely imparted in the Gospel. Indeed, God cannot truly be known without the Gospel, nor can the Gospel be truly understood without divine grace. For it is evident that the teachings of God can only be understood through God, as the Prophet says: "in your light, we see light."[111] Hermes Trismegistus calls this light 'the mind of the divine essence,' the very light that arises from God.[112]

However, our intellect, unless it is illuminated by the divine mind, is not immune from error and labors in vain concerning

---

[111] Psalm 36:9 (Vulg. 35:10)

[112] *Corpus Hermeticum* 1.6 (Copenhaver, *Hermetica*, p. 2): "'I am the light you saw, mind, your god,' [Poimandres] said, who existed before the watery nature that appeared out of darkness. The lightgiving word who comes from mind is the son of god'"). Cf. Lazzarelli, *Crater Hermetis*, 5.2 (Hanegraaff and Bouthoorn, *Lodovico Lazzarelli*, p. 175-177).

divinis. Unde Paulus ait: Non sumus sufficientes aliquid cogitare ex nobis, sed sufficientia nostra ex Deo est, quem invocandum, ad quem orandum in omni rerum principio, maxime tamen in theologia, id fore agendum sacer praecipit Dionysius. Dixit etiam ipsa veritas Christus: Petite et dabitur vobis, pulsate et aperietur vobis, quaerite et invenietis, videlicet quaerendo in fide, firmiter credendo: credere enim (ut ait Hermes) ipsum intelligere est. Petendo denique in spe cum firma et indubia expectatione, laudando et adorando Jesum Christum, a quo tam divinissima cognitio in animam nostram descendit, ut nos spiritus sui illustret lumine. Pulsantes autem operatione charitatis cum vigiliis et jejuniis, et ardenti desiderio in omni vita cum imitatione Jesu Christi, quemadmodum inquit Joannes: qui dicit se manere in Christo debet,

divine matters.[113] Hence Paul says: "we are not sufficient to think anything of ourselves, but our sufficiency is from God,"[114] whom we must invoke and pray to at the beginning of all things, but especially in theology, as the holy Dionysius commands.[115] Christ Himself, who is the Truth, also said: "ask, and it will be given to you; knock, and it will be opened to you; seek, and you will find,"[116] that is, by seeking in faith and firmly believing – "for to believe," as Hermes says, "is to understand"[117] – and finally, by asking with hope, with firm and unwavering expectation, praising and adoring Jesus Christ, from whom such divine knowledge descends into our soul, that He might illuminate us with the light of His spirit. We knock, however, by the work of charity with vigils and fasts, and by a burning desire throughout life, in imitation of Jesus Christ. As John says: "he who says he abides in Christ ought himself also

---

[113] Reuchlin, *De verbo mirifico*, 1: *Intellectus nisi per mentem illuminetur, ab errore non est immunis.* ["The intellect, unless it is illuminated by mind, is not free from error."]

[114] II Corinthians 3:5.

[115] Lazzarelli, *Crater Hermetis*, 5.2 (Hanegraaff and Bouthoorn, *Lodovico Lazzarelli*, p. 175-177); Dionysius, *De Divinis Nominibus*, 3.1.680D.

[116] Matthew 7:7 and Luke 11:9.

[117] *Corpus Hermeticum* 9.10 (Copenhaver, *Hermetica*, p. 29): "To understand is to believe, and not to believe is not to understand."

sicut ille ambulavit, et ipse ambulare. Quam Paulus vocat fidem, quae per dilectionem operatur.

Idcirco frustra currunt, quicunque litigiosis quibusque disputationibus divina prosequuntur et sophismatum muniti ambagibus ac dialecticis praestigiis sacrarum litterarum fores se diffringere posse putant. Semper quaerunt magna disputantes, nihil tamen inveniunt, quia semet ipsos amittunt (ut ait Paulus) semper discentes et nunquam ad scientiam veritatis pervenientes. Hinc idem Paulus praecipit Corinthiis, ut obediant et firmiter perstent in fide, et caveant ne decipiantur per dialecticam et philosophiam, quae sunt inanes fallaciae, et inventa hominum, et secundum elementa hujus mundi corruptibilis: cujus cognitio omnis est a sensibus, ex quibus ratio omnem suam capit cognitionis materiam discurrendo, componendo, dividendo et colligendo universales propositiones ex experimentis. Deus autem et Jesus Christus

to walk just as He walked."[118] Paul calls this "the faith that works through love."[119]

And so they run around in vain, those who pursue the divine through contentious disputes and think they can force open the doors of sacred scripture, armed with the intricacies of sophisms and the tricks of dialectics.[120] They are always seeking, disputing over great matters, but find nothing, for they lose themselves, as Paul says, "always learning and never able to come to the knowledge of the truth."[121] Hence, Paul likewise orders the Corinthians to obey and firmly stand in faith, and to beware lest they be deceived by dialectic and philosophy, which are empty deceits, inventions of men, and in accord with the elements of this corruptible world.[122] All knowledge of this world comes from the senses, from which reason derives all its material for knowledge by reasoning, combining, dividing, and drawing universal propositions from experiences. But God and Jesus Christ

---

[118] I John 2:6.

[119] Galatians 5:6.

[120] Cf. Lazzarelli, *Crater Hermetis*, 11.4 (Hanegraaff and Bouthoorn, *Lodovico Lazzarelli*, p. 199): "So she who is said to be calling out in front of her house wants to be reputed wise even though she knows nothing at all, because she is striving after the wisdom of the flesh. Therefore she cries out in public and holds disputations in the squares, armed with tricky sophisms; but he who speaks as a sophist is hateful, and will be thwarted in all things. He does not receive God's grace, for he is bereaved of all wisdom, as we read in Ecclesiasticus."

[121] II Timothy 3:7.

[122] I Corinthians 16:13; Colossians 2:8.

supra mundum est, et creator mundi super omnes [491] naturas, qualitates, figuras, numeros, ordines, actiones, atque (ut ait Dionysius) supra omnem sermonem, positionem, ablationem, super omnem affirmationem et negationem, supra etiam illos supramundanos angelos et pennas ventorum, qui ascendit super Cherubim, et posuit nubem latibulum suum, qui est Rex regum, et Dominus dominantium, tum eorum quae sunt, tum eorum quae non sunt, qui inclinavit coelos, et descendit sicut pluvia in vellus, et in se assumpsit naturam humanam, et in ea inter homines factus est mirificus et admirabilis in omnibus operibus suis potentia sua supernaturali et divina.

Ad illum igitur vere cognoscendum dialectica et philosophia nequeunt ascendere, impeditae ratione, quae est inimica sanctae fidei. Unde ait Gregorius Nazianzenus libro secundo de

are above the world and are the Creator of the world, "above all natures, qualities, figures, numbers, orders, actions," and, as Dionysius says, "above all speech, position, negation, and affirmation,"[123] even above those supermundane angels and the "wings of the winds,"[124] who "rises above the Cherubim" and "has made the cloud His hiding place,"[125] who is the "King of kings and Lord of lords,"[126] both of what exists and what does not exist, who "bowed the heavens"[127] and "came down like rain upon the fleece,"[128] and took upon Himself human nature and, in it, was made wondrous and admirable in all His works among men by His supernatural and divine power.

Therefore, dialectic and philosophy are not able to ascend to the true knowledge of God because they are hindered by reason, which is an enemy of holy faith. Hence, Gregory Nazianzus says in his second book *On*

---

[123] Lazzarelli, *Crater Hermetis*, 20.1 (Hanegraaff and Bouthoorn, *Lodovico Lazzarelli*, p. 227): "As God is an incomprehensible intellect that is beyond anything, as Dionysius says in his *Mystical Theology* [*De Mystica Theologia*, 2.1000B and 5.1048B], inexpressible beyond any speech, beyond any determination or exclusion, affirmation or negation, we should firmly believe and simply profess that God is One in His Trinity and Three in His Unity, Father, Son, and Holy Spirit."

[124] Psalm 104:3 (Vulg. 103:3).

[125] Psalm 18:11-12 (Vulg. 17:11-12).

[126] I Timothy 6:15.

[127] Psalm 18:9 (Vulg. 17:10).

[128] Psalm 72:6 (Vulg. 71:6).

theologia: Quid enim tum suspicaberis divinum esse, si omnino logicis credis speculationibus? Aut ad quid te ratio inducet violenta sive examinata, tu qui gloriaris circa immensa? Fides ergo, omni cognitione praestantior, quatenus non inanibus commentationibus, sed divinae revelationi tota innititur, a primo lumine immediate descendens, sola potest ea quae supra mundum sunt apprehendere. Ipsa enim mundi exordium intelligit (ut ait Paulus: Fide intelligimus aptata esse secula verbo Dei) et supra statutae naturae limites ascendit, spaciaturque in illo latissimo campo, in ipso autore naturae. In hac fide Paulus dicit se accepisse apostolatum et praedicare Deum. Et scribens ad Corinthios ait: Praedicatio mea non est in persuasionibus humanae sapientiae, sed in ostensionibus spiritus et veritatis fidei Jesu Christi. Sola enim fides instrumentum est medium, qua sola possumus Deum cognoscere, et ut ajunt Platonici, qua sola ad Deum accedimus, divinamque nanciscimur protectionem ac virtutem.

Theology: "what, then, will you suppose to be divine if you entirely trust logical speculations? Or to what will impetuous or cautious reasoning lead you – you who boast in immeasurable things?"[129] Faith, therefore, is superior to all knowledge, insofar as it relies not on vain speculations but entirely on divine revelation, descending immediately from the first light, and it alone is able to grasp the things that are above the world.[130] For faith alone comprehends the origin of the world (as Paul says: "by faith, we understand that the ages were framed by the word of God"[131]) and ascends beyond the limits established by nature, wandering in that vast expanse, in the author of nature Himself. In this faith, Paul says he received his apostleship and preached God.[132] And writing to the Corinthians, he says: "my preaching is not in the persuasive arguments of human wisdom, but in the demonstration of the spirit and truth" of the faith of Jesus Christ.[133] For faith alone is the intermediate instrument by which we can know God, and, as the Platonists say, by which alone we approach God and obtain His divine protection and power.[134]

---

[129] Gregory of Nazianzus, *Oratio*, 28.32C.

[130] Here we see the kind of mystical skepticism Agrippa put on full display in *De incertitudine et vanitate scientiarum et artium* already taking shape.

[131] Hebrews 11:3.

[132] Romans 1:5.

[133] I Corinthians 2:4.

[134] Ficino, *De Christiana religione*, 37 (Attrell, Bartlett, and Porreca, *Marsilio Ficino: On the Christian Religion*, p. 219): "Faith, as Aristotle posits, is the foundation of knowledge, and by faith alone, as the Platonists prove, we draw nearer to God."

Sed videamus quae anima, quando et quomodo potest libere uti hoc instrumento. Certe nulla, nisi illa quae quando tota rationis intentione ascendendo in mentem, caput suum supremam ejus portionem, tota in eam convertitur: sicut quandoque ob inferiorum et sensibilium rerum amorem tota vertitur in phantasiam. Scimus utique humanam mentem superni vultus imaginem nobisque inscriptum lumen existere, quae de veritatis fonte migrans, sola veritatem capit et amplectitur: sed phantasmatum turbines eam (non quidem in se, sed in nobis) adeo obumbrant, distrahunt, dissipant, dispergunt, quo vix veritatis angustissimam portam intrare valeat. Anima itaque nostra, carne inclusa corruptibili nimioque ejus demersa commercio, nisi viam carnis superaverit fueritque pristinam naturam sortita evaserit[492]que mens pura, quasi par angelo, frustra laborat in divinis.

But let us see which soul, when and how it is able to use this instrument freely. Certainly none, except that which, when ascending with complete focus of reason into the mind, turns its head – its highest part – completely toward it: just as, at other times, due to the love of lower and sensible things, it turns entirely towards the phantasy.[135] We know, in any case, that the human mind is the image of a higher countenance and a light inscribed within us; it alone, flowing from the source of truth, grasps and embraces the truth. But the whirlwinds of phantasms obscure, divert, disorder, and disperse it – not in itself, but in us – such that it scarcely manages to enter the narrowest gate of truth.[136] Thus, our soul, enclosed in flesh subject to corruption and weighed down by excessive commerce with it, labors fruitlessly in divine matters unless it overcomes the way of the flesh, regains its original nature, and returns to being a pure mind, almost identical to an

---

[135] Ficino, *Theologia Platonica*, 13.4 (Allen and Hankins, *Platonic Theology*, p. 200-201): "To what is all this leading? That we might understand that it is possible for man's soul to be turned at times towards mind, its head, by the total concentration of its reason, just as it is turned at other times towards the phantasy, as we have already said, and towards the reason."

[136] Riccio, *Isagoge*, 15[v]-16[r]: "I surely know that human reason has within it the light of a higher countenance inscribed within us, which, flowing from the source of truth, grasps and embraces the truth. But the whirlwind of phantasms does not obscure this in itself, but rather in us, distracting and scattering it so greatly that it scarcely manages to enter the narrow gate of truth."

Sed quae anima haec est, nisi quae indubia spe et superni numinis desiderio phantasiam silere jubet, et quae veram fidem firmiter amplexa, assuetis rationis naturalis discursibus ammodo non confidit, et quae ardenti amore adhaerens Deo, sola vivit mente, evasit angelus, capit toto pectore Deum? Unde illud Hieremiae: In hoc glorietur, qui gloriatur, scire me.

angel.[137] But what soul can this be except one that, hoping without doubt and desiring the divine presence, commands the phantasy to keep silent, firmly embraces true faith, no longer trusts in the customary discursive process of natural reason, but, adhering to God with a burning love, lives by mind alone, becomes an angel, and grasps God with its whole heart?[138] Hence the words of Jeremiah: "let him who boasts, boast in this, that he knows me."[139]

---

[137] Cf. *Asclepius* 7 (Cf. Copenhaver, *Hermetica*, p. 70): "For man is the only twofold animal: one part of him is simple, which is, as the Greeks say, *ousiōdēs*, which we call 'a form of divine similitude'; the other part, however, is fourfold, which the Greeks call *hylicos* and we call 'worldly', and from it the body is made and by it is covered that which in man we have already said is divine, in which the divinity of a pure mind, concealed alone with its kindred (that is, the senses of a pure mind), rests with itself, as though enclosed within the wall of the body"; Plato, *Phaedrus*, 62b: "Now the doctrine that is taught in secret about this matter, that we men are in a kind of prison and must not set ourselves free or run away, seems to me to be weighty and not easy to understand"; Plato, *Cratylus*, 400c: "they think [the soul] has the body as an enclosure to keep it safe, like a prison, and this is, as the name itself denotes, the safe for the soul, until the penalty is paid".

[138] Ficino, *Theologia Platonica*, 13.4 (Allen and Hankins, *Platonic Theology*, p. 200-201): "Which soul does this? It is the one which orders the phantasy to be silent and which, burning with desire too for supernal divinity, does not trust itself to the customary discursiveness of the reason natural to it, but lives in the mind alone, issues as an angel, and takes God into its whole heart."

[139] Jeremiah 9:23.

Hinc Zoroastes vetustissimus philosophus: anima (inquit) hominis Deum quodammodo contrahit in se ipsam, quando nihil retinens mortale, tota divinis haustibus inebriatur; et tunc quoque talis anima saepe exultat in corporis harmoniam, quando scilicet post contemplationem rediens ad corporalia officia, producit in his fructus fidei, cibum justitiae. Ideo hujusmodi animam Joannes ait nasci iterum ex Deo, siquidem Dei summi lumen – quemadmodum radius Solis, corpus attenuans sursumque trahens et in igneam convertens naturam – per mentes angelicas usque ad animam nostram defluens, instigat quotidie animam carni immersam, ut denudata ab omni carnalitate deponat omnes potentias operationesque animales et rationales, ac sola mente vivens, spe decora, fide directa, amore flagrans, tota ad Deum conversa, et in Deo foecundata, Deo regenerante, fiat Dei filius pariatque novum Immanuel.

Hence Zoroaster, the most ancient philosopher, says: "the soul of man, in a certain way, contains God within itself when, retaining nothing mortal, it is entirely intoxicated with divine draughts"; and "then also" such a soul often "exults in the harmony of the body," when, having returned from contemplation to bodily duties, it produces in them the fruits of faith, the food of justice.[140] For this reason, John says that such a soul "is born again of God,"[141] because the supreme light of God – just as a ray of the sun, attenuating a body, draws it upward and transforms it into a fiery nature – flows down through the angelic minds to our soul, unceasingly urges the soul immersed in flesh to strip away all carnality, to lay aside all animal and rational powers and operations, and, living by mind alone, adorned with hope, directed by faith, inflamed by love, turned wholly toward God and made fruitful in God, with God regenerating it, to become a child of God and to bring forth a new Immanuel.[142]

---

[140] Ficino, *Theologia Platonica*, 13.4 (Allen and Hankins, *Platonic Theology*, p. 200-201): "Zoroaster signifies this when he says: 'In a way the human soul contracts God into itself when, retaining nothing mortal, it becomes utterly inebriated on the draughts divine. Then it exults too in the body's harmony.'"

[141] John 3:3-5.

[142] Ficino, *Theologia Platonica*, 13.4 (Allen and Hankins, *Platonic Theology*, p. 200-201): "The theology of the divine John says that such a soul is born again from God. For the influence of God on high, flowing down through the angelic minds to man's soul, daily moves the soul, immersed as it is in the body, to cast off its fleshly clothing, to lay aside its own soul-powers and activities, and instead of a soul to become an angel.

Et talis anima, quoties dimissis actionibus in se ipsam regreditur et ad aeternum Deum contemplandum se flectit, tunc nullo amplius terrenorum impetu torpens, sed Patre luminum fulta, ad sublimem divinae cognitionis ascendit apicem, ubi propheticis oraculis continuo impletur, saepe etiam ad miracula perpetranda Dei instrumentum elegitur. Cujus orationes etiam circa publicas mundi ipsius mutationes non fiunt irritae, quemadmodum Jacobus nos admonet, dicens: Helias homo erat similis nobis, et passibilis, et orans oravit ut non plueret super terram, et non pluit annos tres, menses sex; et rursum oravit, et coelum dedit pluviam, et terra dedit fructum suum.

Similarly, the sun's ray disperses the mists and draws them upwards and converts them into the fiery nature. He who commits himself entirely to this inspiration ceases to be a soul and becomes, being reborn from God, a son of God, an angel. Thus Plato in the *Timaeus* calls theologians the sons of God"; Riccio, *Isagoge*, 4^{v}: "For if you adorn with such a conception the chaste and undefiled maiden who is with you, you will indeed have in the womb and will give birth to a son, Immanuel." Cf. Isaiah 7:14 and Matthew 1:23.

And such a soul, whenever it returns into itself, having withdrawn from its actions, and turns itself to the contemplation of the eternal God, no longer numbed by the desire of earthly things but supported by the Father of lights, ascends to the lofty peak of divine knowledge, where it is continuously filled with prophetic oracles and frequently chosen for the performance of miracles as an instrument of God.[143] The prayers of such a soul are not in vain, even when they concern the public vicissitudes of the world itself, just as James reminds us, saying: "Elijah was a man like us, and subject to the same passions, and he prayed earnestly that it might not rain on the earth, and it did not rain for three years and six months; and again he prayed, and heaven gave rain, and the earth brought forth her fruit."[144]

---

[143] Ficino, *Theologia Platonica*, 13.5 (Allen and Hankins, *Platonic Theology*, p. 216-217): "But God has foreseen that such a soul is going to exist and exist as such not only because of supernal aid but also because of its own will, a will which acts freely precisely when, having set actions aside, it turns to contemplating and loving itself and its origin"; Riccio, *Isagoge*, 16^{r}; for the "Father of lights" see James 1:17.

[144] Ficino, *Theologia Platonica*, 13.5 (Allen and Hankins, *Platonic Theology*, p. 216-217): "God also selects such a soul to perform miracles. Even when the prayers of this soul concern the public vicissitudes of the world, they are not in vain it is asserted by Avicenna in his *Metaphysics* and by Proclus and Iamblichus"; James 5:17-18.

O magnum miraculum homo, praecipue autem homo Christianus, qui in mundo constitutus, ea quae supra mundum sunt ipsiusque mundi autorem cognoscit, tum in eo ipso inferiora quaeque cernit et intelligit: non solum ea quae sunt et quae fuerunt, sed et illa quae non sunt et quae ventura sunt. Magnum certe miraculum est homo Christianus, qui in mundo constitutus, supra mundum dominatur operationesque similes effecit ipsi Creatori mundi; quae opera vulgo miracula appellantur, quorum omnium radix et fundamentum fides est in Jesum Christum.

O a great miracle is man[145] – especially the Christian man – who, being placed in the world, knows the things that are above the world, and the author of the world itself, and in the same world perceives and understands lower things: not only those that are and those that have been, but also those that are not and those that will come.[146] Indeed, a great miracle is the Christian man who, having been placed in the world, rules over the world and performs works similar to those of the world's Creator. These works are commonly called miracles, the root and foundation of which is faith in Jesus Christ.[147] Through

---

[145] *Asclepius* 6 (Copenhaver, *Hermetica*, p. 69): "Because of this, Asclepius, a human being is a great wonder, a living thing to be worshipped and honored: for he changes his nature into a god's, as if he were a god; he knows the demonic kind inasmuch as he recognizes that he originated among them; he despises the part of him that is human nature, having put his trust in the divinity of his other part"; cf. Pico della Mirandola, *Oratio* (Copenhaver, *Oration*, p. 81).

[146] Reuchlin, *De verbo mirifico*, 2.c2r: "But come, Capnion: teach us about the wonder-working word… by which we are placed in nature above nature, as you were saying, so that we might be able to perform miracles: whether this is done by foreseeing (as in prophecies), or by directly accomplishing things whose natural cause is commonly unknown, and which even the most experienced men regard as worthy of wonder."

[147] Cf. Ficino, *Theologia Platonica*, 13.4 (Allen and Hankins, *Platonic Theology*, p. 182-183): "Not only in forming and shaping matter through the rational principle of art, as we said, does the human mind appropriate for itself the divine right; it does so too through [its] sovereignty in transmuting the species of things. The resulting work is called a miracle, not because it

Per hanc solam efficitur homo idem aliquid [493] cum Deo eademque potestate fruitur, quemadmodum Christus pollicitus est, dicens: Amen dico vobis, qui credit in me, opera quae ego facio, ipse faciet et majora horum faciet, quia ego vado ad Patrem. Et quicquid rogaverit Patrem in nomine meo, ego faciam: et quicquid rogaverit me, ego faciam, ut glorificetur Pater in Filio. Et alibi ait: Si habueritis fidem sicut granum sinapis, et dixeritis huic monti, jacta te ultra mare, fiet. Propterea dico vobis, quicquid petentes oraveritis, credite quia accipietis, et fiet vobis. Hinc est quod homines vere Christiani, ac Deo devoti, loquuntur linguis, praedicant futura, imperant elementis, pellunt nebulas, citant pluvias, praecipiunt ventis, avertunt tempestates, sanant aegrotos, illuminant caecos, curant claudos, mundant leprosos, ejiciunt daemonia, saepe suscitant mortuos, et hujusmodi. Sic prophetae, sic apostoli, sic multi sancti pontifices, sacerdotes, doctores, ceterique viri Dei maximis claruere clarentque potentiis.

---

is the supernatural work of our soul when it becomes God's instrument, but because it induces wonder, being a mighty event and one that happens rarely."

this faith alone, man becomes a thing identical with God and enjoys the same power, as Christ promised, saying: "Amen, I say to you, whoever believes in me will also do the works that I do; and greater works than these will he do, because I go to the Father. And whatever he asks the Father in my name, I will do it; and whatever he asks me, I will do it, that the Father may be glorified in the Son."[148] And elsewhere He says: "if you have faith as a grain of mustard seed, you will say to this mountain, 'cast yourself into the sea,' and it will move. Therefore I say to you, whatever you ask in prayer, believe that you will receive it, and it will be yours."[149] Hence it is that Christian men, especially those devoted to God, truly speak in tongues, foretell the future, command the elements, dispel the clouds, summon the rain, command the winds, avert storms, heal the sick, give sight to the blind, cure the lame, cleanse lepers, cast out demons, raise the dead often, and do things of this sort.[150] Thus have the prophets, the apostles, and many holy pontiffs, priests, doctors, and other men of God shone and continue to shine with the greatest powers.[151]

---

[148] John 14:12-14.

[149] Matthew 17:19 and 21:21; Mark 11:23-24.

[150] Ficino, *Theologia Platonica*, 13.4 (Allen and Hankins, *Platonic Theology*, p. 182-183): "Hence we are in awe when souls of men dedicated to God command the elements, rouse winds, compel clouds to rain, dispel mists, cure the diseases of human bodies, and so on."

[151] Lazzarelli, *Crater Hermetis*, 20.5 (Hanegraaff and Bouthoorn, *Lodovico Lazzarelli*, p. 229): "Thus Moses, thus

Maxime ergo concedens est illa potestas illos qui perfectiores in fide, quibus Paulus solum se dicit narrare sapientiam et segregatim praedicare Evangelium. Habet enim etiam Evangelium, quemadmodum Lex Mosaica, aliud in cortice propositum imbecillioribus, aliud in medulla, quod segregatim revelatum est perfectis, sicut de illis loquitur Paulus ad Hebraeos, vocans haec lac infantium, et elementa exordii sermonum Dei, illa autem nuncupat solidum cibum, sermonem justitiae, et perfectam Christi doctrinam, inquiens: Si ferri vultis ad perfectam Christi doctrinam, omittendus est sermo inchoationis, in quo videlicet tractatur de principiis et fundamentis divinae sapientiae quae sunt de poenitentia ab operibus mortuis, de baptismate, de sacramentis, de impositione manuum et de autoritate absolvendi, de resurrectione mortuorum, et judicio aeterno, et ejusmodi, quae omnia habentur in cortice Evangelii et in scholis tractantur a scholasticis theologis, et in problemata disputanda et discutienda deducuntur. Illa autem pertinentia ad meliorem sapientiam et perfectam doctrinam, videlicet quod sit donum coeleste, et manna absconditum, quod nemo scit nisi qui accipit, et quod sit bonum Dei verbum, melius illo quod foris vulgo traditur in parabolis,

---

Joshua, thus Elijah, thus the other prophets and holy men of God shone with the greatest powers."

Therefore, that power is especially fitting for those who are more perfect in faith; to them alone Paul claims to reveal wisdom and to preach the Gospel separately.[152] For the Gospel also, just like the Mosaic Law, has one meaning that is superficial, intended for the weaker, and another meaning that is internal, revealed separately to the perfect – just as Paul explains to the Hebrews, where he calls the former "milk for infants" and "the rudiments of the words of God," while he labels the latter "solid food," "the word of righteousness," and "the perfect doctrine of Christ." He says: "if you wish to be led to the perfection of Christ's doctrine, you must leave behind the elementary teaching, in which are discussed the principles and foundations of divine wisdom which concern repentance from dead works, baptism, the sacraments, the laying on of hands and the authority of absolution, the resurrection of the dead, and eternal judgment," and the like, all of which are contained in the outer shell of the Gospel and are handled in the schools by scholastic theologians, and are reduced to problems for disputing and discussing. However, that knowledge which pertains to a higher wisdom and perfect doctrine – namely, what the "heavenly gift"[153] is, and the "hidden manna,"[154] which no one knows except the one who receives it, and what "the goodness of the word of God is,"[155] better than that which is openly transmitted to the common people in parables,

[152] I Corinthians 2:6-7.

[153] Hebrews 6:4.

[154] Revelation 2:17.

[155] Hebrews 6:5.

quodque mysterium regni Dei datum nosse solis secretioribus discipulis, et quae virtutes seculi futuri, quae origo et finis animae, et ministeria angelicorum spirituum, quae conditio et qualitas illius immensae gloriae et felicitatis, quam expectamus, quam nec oculus vidit, nec auris audivit, nec in cor hominis ascendit: haec omnia continentur [494] in medulla et nucleo Evangelii et non nisi perfectioribus cognita sunt, quibus data est scientia potestatum et virtutum, miraculorum et prophetiae, et caetera, quae homines propriis viribus indagare non possunt, nisi qui subjecti fuerint virtuti Spiritus Sancti.

Qui ob hoc ad principatum in Ecclesia gerendum eliguntur et deputantur, ut ipsi, illuminati in fide, cognoscentes voluntatem Dei, instructi per Evangelium, juxta verba Pauli, sint duces caecorum, lumen eorum qui in tenebris sunt, eruditores insipientium, magistri infantium, habentes formam scientiae et veritatis in Evangelio, cujusmodi sunt in Ecclesia pontifices, episcopi, praelati, doctores, et quibus cura animarum et aedificatio Ecclesiae commissa est, ad quos Paulus scribens ait: Qui loquitur linguis, non

and what "the mystery of the Kingdom of God"[156] is, given to be known only to the more secret disciples, and what the virtues of the future age are, what the origin and end of the soul are, and the ministries of angelic spirits, and what the condition and quality of that immense glory and happiness is, which we await, which "no eye has seen, nor ear heard, nor has entered into the heart of man"[157] – all these are contained within the marrow and kernel of the Gospel and are known only to the more perfect, to whom the knowledge of powers and virtues, of miracles and prophecy, and other such things, has been given: things which men cannot investigate by their own strength, unless they have been subjected to the power of the Holy Spirit.[158]

Those who are chosen and appointed to hold authority in the Church are chosen for this reason: that they, being enlightened in the faith, knowing the will of God, and instructed by the Gospel, might be – according to the words of Paul – "guides to the blind, a light to those who are in darkness, instructors of the foolish, teachers of infants, having the form of knowledge and truth"[159] in the Gospel. In the Church, such are the pontiffs, bishops, prelates, doctors, and those to whom the care of souls and the edification of the Church has been entrusted, to whom Paul writes, saying: "he who speaks in tongues does not

---

[156] Luke 8:10; Matthew 13:11.

[157] I Corinthians 2:9.

[158] Hebrews 6:1-4; this paragraph draws closely and extensively from Francesco Giorgi, *De harmonia mundi*, 2.5.9.

[159] Romans 2:19-20.

hominibus loquitur, sed Deo, nemo enim audit; spiritus autem loquitur mysteria. Nam qui prophetat hominibus loquitur ad aedificationem et exhortationem et consolationem. Qui loquitur lingua semet ipsum aedificat, qui autem prophetat, Ecclesiam Dei aedificat. Et sequitur ibidem: Linguae in signum sunt, non fidelibus, sed infidelibus; prophetiae autem non infidelibus, sed fidelibus. Si ergo conveniat universa Ecclesia in unum, et omnes linguis loquantur, intret autem idiota infidelis, nonne dicet, quid insanitis? Si autem omnes prophetent, intret autem quis infidelis vel idiota, convincitur ab omnibus, dijudicatur ab omnibus: occulta enim cordis ejus manifesta sunt; et ita cadens in faciem, adorabit Deum, pronuncians quia vere Deus in vobis sit. Et tandem concludit: si quis videtur propheta esse aut spiritualis, cognoscet quae scribo vobis, quia Domini sunt mandata: si quis autem ignorat, ignorabitur. Ecce, Apostolus haec non ut consilium, sed divinum mandatum ac praeceptum proponit. Quare si pontifices, praelati, et doctores nostri divinae sapientiae propheticum spiritum non habuerint et admirandam eorum in Ecclesia professionem alicujus divinae potestatis effectu non comprobaverint, certe illorum spiritus mentis lumine hebet et fide in Christum debilis est, et languet carne supra spiritum nimium dominante. Quamobrem omnes

speak to men but to God, for no one hears him; but by the spirit he speaks mysteries. But he who prophesies speaks to men for their edification, exhortation, and consolation. He who speaks in tongues edifies himself, but he who prophesies edifies the Church of God."[160] And there it follows: "tongues are a sign not for believers but for unbelievers; prophecy, however, is not for unbelievers but for believers. If therefore the whole Church comes together in one place, and all speak in tongues, and an unlearned man or unbeliever enters, will they not say that you are mad? But if all prophesy, and an unbeliever or unlearned man enters, he is convinced by all, judged by all: for the secrets of his heart are revealed; and so, falling on his face, he will worship God, declaring that God is truly among you."[161] And finally he concludes: "if anyone considers himself to be a prophet or spiritual, let him acknowledge that the things I write to you are the commandments of the Lord. But if anyone is ignorant, let him be ignorant."[162] Behold, the Apostle proposes these things not as advice, but as a divine mandate and commandment. Therefore, if our pontiffs, prelates, and doctors do not possess the prophetic spirit of divine wisdom and fail to demonstrate their noble office in the Church by manifesting some divine power, then surely their spirit is weak in the light of mind and in their faith in Christ, and they languish under an excessive dominance of the flesh over the spirit. For this reason, all

---

[160] I Corinthians 14:2-4.

[161] I Corinthians 14:22-25.

[162] I Corinthians 14:37-38.

illi, tanquam steriles animae, impietatis et injustitiae a Deo judicabuntur atque condemnabuntur.

En habes modo qualem esse oporteat, qui Dei cognitionem assequi cupit et qui vere dici mereatur theologus, qui cum Deo loqui desiderat, et in lege ejus meditari die ac nocte. Sic namque Johannes Evangelista a Dionysio Theologus cognominatus est, a divina scilicet locutione.

Sed sunt quidam alii, qui linguis loquuntur, humanis scientiis inflati, [495] imo qui vita et linga de Deo mentiri non erubescunt, qui suo spiritu omnem Scripturam ad sua mendacia impudentissime torquent ac mysteria divina ad humanae rationis methodum exigunt; inventisque capitibus suis glossis sacrilegis adulterato verbo Dei, sua portenta stabiliunt ac sanctum theologiae nomen furto et rapina sibi temere usurpant solisque operam dant contentionibus et rixosis disputationibus, de quibus Paulus scribit ad Philippenses, dicens: Quidam propter invidiam et contentionem, quidam autem propter bonam voluntatem Christum praedicant. Et hi contentiosi sunt argumentatores isti, qui Dei notitiam argumentis et quaestionibus insequuntur, de quibus ait Psalmista: Corrupti sunt et abominabiles facti sunt in

these, as barren souls, will be judged and condemned by God as guilty of impiety and injustice.

Now you know how one ought to be who longs to attain the knowledge of God, and who truly deserves to be called a theologian – one who wishes to speak with God and to meditate on His law day and night.[163] For thus it is that John the Evangelist was given the name 'the Theologian' by Dionysius, namely, on account of his divine discourse.[164]

But there are certain others who, inflated by human sciences, speak in tongues, indeed who do not blush to lie about God both in their lives and in their speech. They shamelessly twist all Scripture to fit their lies according to their own spirit, and they force divine mysteries according to the method of human reason. With sacrilegious glosses devised by their own minds, they adulterate the word of God and establish their own monstrosities. They rashly usurp the holy name of theology by theft and plunder, dedicating themselves solely to disputes and contentious arguments, about which Paul writes to the Philippians, saying: "some indeed preach Christ out of envy and rivalry, but others out of good will."[165] And these contentious ones are those argumentative people who pursue the knowledge of God with arguments and questions, of whom the Psalmist says: "they are corrupt and have become abominable in their

[163] Psalm 1:2.

[164] Dionysius, *Epistle*, 10.1117A.

[165] Philippians 1:15.

studiis suis. Et Judas apostolus ait: Hi autem quaecunque quidem ignorant, blasphemant; quacumque autem naturaliter tanquam muta animalia norunt, in his corrumpuntur. Quos iterum alloquitur Esaias dicens: Sapientia tua et scientia tua ex ea ipsa decepit te; defecisti in multitudine consiliorum tuorum.

Carnalis enim est et mundana omnis doctrina ipsorum, gens ambitiosa, arrogans, confidens suis ingeniis, arbitrans se suis viribus Deum posse cognoscere et in omni re veritatem posse invenire, nec posse aliquid in sermonem venire, de quo non in utramque partem disertissime possint disputare, et probabilem sententiam proferre; populi astuti, abundantes alienis literis, ac simul artificiosa quadam dialectica freti, insolentes: cum nihil omnino sciant, cupiunt docti videri; ideo disputant palam in gymnasiis, sophismatum roborati diverticulis, dicentes et arbitrantes se esse sapientes. Sed his deliramentis ac versatilis ingenii versutiis miserabiliter decepti, quod putant sibi esse subsidio est illis impedimento, et evanescunt in cogitationibus suis, et traduntur a Deo in reprobum sensum; quo putant se maxime videre, et

ways."[166] And the apostle Jude says: "these people blaspheme whatever they do not know; and whatever they understand naturally, like dumb animals, in these they are corrupted."[167] To these Isaiah speaks again, saying: "your wisdom and your knowledge, they have deceived you; you have been worn out in the multitude of your counsels."[168]

Indeed, their doctrine is entirely carnal and worldly – an ambitious, arrogant race, confident in their own ingenuity, convinced that they can know God by their own strengths and can find truth in everything; convinced that there is no argument that can arise in a discussion about which they cannot argue most eloquently on both sides and offer a plausible opinion. They are a cunning people, rich in the learning of others, and at the same time, insolent, relying on a certain artificial dialectic: though they know absolutely nothing, they yearn to appear learned. Therefore, they debate publicly in schools, emboldened by the snares of sophistry, declaring and believing themselves to be wise. But miserably deceived by these delirious fantasies and the tricks of their shifting ingenuity, what they consider to be their support is actually their hindrance: they become vain in their thoughts, and are given over by God to a reprobate mind.[169] Where they think they see most clearly and

---

[166] Psalm 14:1 (Vulg. 13:1).

[167] Jude 1:10.

[168] Isaiah 47:10-13.

[169] Romans 1:21, 28.

veritatem posse invenire, eo maxime obscuratum est insipiens cor ipsorum; quo valent apud homines, apud Deum impotentes sunt, et dicentes se esse sapientes, stulti facti sunt. Qui enim sophistice loquitur, odibilis est, ait Ecclesiasticus; non illi data est a Domino gratia: omni enim sapientia defraudatus est. Maximum enim stultitiae argumentum est se ipsum putare sapientem, de qua sapientia dicit Apostolus: Prudentia carnis stultitia est apud Deum. Et Salomon vocat eam mulierem stultam et clamosam, plenam illecebris, nihil omnino scientem, cujus convivae sunt in inferno, et qui applicabitur illi descendet ad inferos. Ideo dicit Dominus: Perdam sapientiam sapientum,

believe they can find the truth, there their foolish heart is most darkened.[170] Where they prevail among men, they are powerless before God, and claiming to be wise, they became fools.[171] For he who speaks sophistically is detestable, says Ecclesiastes; to him grace has not been given by the Lord, for he has been deprived of all wisdom.[172] Indeed, the greatest proof of folly is to consider oneself wise, about which the Apostle says: "the wisdom of the flesh is foolishness with God."[173] Solomon too calls it "a foolish and clamorous woman, full of allurements, who knows nothing at all,"[174] whose "companions are in hell," and whoever associates with her will sink into the depths.[175] Thus says the Lord: "I will destroy the wisdom of the wise

---

[170] Romans 1:21.

[171] Romans 1:22.

[172] Ecclesiastes 37:23-24; Lazzarelli, *Crater Hermetis*, 11.4 (Hanegraaff and Bouthoorn, *Lodovico Lazzarelli*, p. 199): "But he who speaks as a sophist is hateful, and will be thwarted in all things. He does not receive God's grace, for he is bereaved of all wisdom, as we read in Ecclesiasticus."

[173] I Corinthians 3:19.

[174] Proverbs 9:13; Lodovico Lazzarelli, *Crater Hermetis*, 10.6 (Hanegraaff and Bouthoorn, *Lodovico Lazzarelli*, p. 197): "The wisdom of the flesh, an adulterous and foreign whore, of whom the Apostle has said: 'the knowledge of the flesh is foolishness with God' … He who turns towards her will go down to the depths of hell."

[175] Proverbs 9:18; Lodovico Lazzarelli, *Crater Hermetis*, 10.5 (Hanegraaff and Bouthoorn, *Lodovico Lazzarelli*, p. 195): "So Solomon calls divine wisdom the tree of life and the wife of our youth; the wisdom of the flesh and the contemplation of material things he calls a foolish and clamorous woman, full of

et prudentiam prudentum reprobabo. [496]

Vera enim sapientia non in clamosis disputationibus consistit, sed occulitur in silentio et religione per fidem in Dominum nostrum Jesum Christum, cujus fructus est vita aeterna: quam Paulus vocat scientiam quae secundum pietatem est, cujus ipse apostolatum accepit secundum fidem electorum Dei. Aliam vero esse scientiam contentionis, de qua Titum discipulum suum certiorem facit, sic monendo: Stultas autem quaestiones et genealogias, et contentiones, et pugnas legis devita, sunt enim inutiles et vanae. Super quo scribens, Hieronymus ita ait: Dialectici et Aristoteles (qui horum princeps est) solent argumentationum retia tendere et vagam theologiae libertatem in syllogismorum spineta concludere. Hi ergo, qui in eos totos dies et noctes terunt ut vel interrogent, vel respondeant, vel dent propositionem, vel accipiant, assumant, confirment atque concludant, eos quidem contentiosos vocant, qui ut libet non ratione, sed stomacho putant litigandum. Si igitur illi hoc faciunt, quorum proprie ars contentio est,

---

illicit lures, who knows nothing at all, a foreign and adulterous whore."

and the prudence of the prudent I will reject."[176]

Indeed, true wisdom does not consist in clamorous disputes, but is "hidden in silence"[177] and worship through the faith in our Lord Jesus Christ, whose fruit is eternal life. Paul calls this "the knowledge that accords with godliness," through which he himself received apostleship "according to the faith of God's elect."[178] There is, however, another kind of knowledge, that of contention, about which he informs his disciple Titus, admonishing him thus: "avoid foolish questions, genealogies, controversies, and polemics about the law, for they are useless and vain."[179] Writing on this, Jerome says the following: "the logicians and Aristotle (who is their leader) are accustomed to set the snares of argumentation and to confine the free spirit of theology within thickets of syllogisms. These, therefore – who spend their whole days and nights on this, whether asking questions or answering them, whether putting forward propositions or listening to them, assuming, confirming, and drawing conclusions – are called contentious, who think that one should argue not with reason but with the stomach. If, therefore, those whose art is contention do this,

---

[176] I Corinthians 1:19 and Isaiah 29:14.

[177] *Corpus Hermeticum* 13 (Copenhaver, *Hermetica*, p. 52-53): "It cannot be taught; it is a secret kept in silence."

[178] Titus 1:1.

[179] Titus 3:9.

quid debet facere Christianus, nisi omnino fugere contentiones? Haec ille.

Itaque et nobis, si volumus vere cognoscere Deum, postponenda est omnis turbida ratiocinatio, omnis sophistica argumentatio, omnis dialectica inquisitio. Ratio enim et inquisitio nonnullam subolent desperationem et diffidentiam. Fides autem fixa et tranquilla esse debet. Ideo dicit Ambrosius in libro De trinitate: Aufer argumenta ubi fides quaeritur, in ipsis gymnasiis suis jam dialectica taceat, piscatoribus creditur non dialecticis. Idem ad Gratianum de fide. Et Urbanus Papa scribens ad Carolum ait: Non in dialectica placuit Deo salvare populum suum: Regnum enim Dei in simplicitate fidei est, non in contentione sermonis. Nulla enim major pestis animae quam ratiocinatio, quam altercatio, quam disputatio de divinis, quae evertit rationem, pervertit intellectum, dejicit fidem. Ideo Paulus illam maxime vitandam jubet, et Jacobus appellat eam sapientiam terrenam, animalem, et diabolicam: hinc errores, hinc dubia, hinc mendacia, hinc haereses, hinc primum in humano genere peccatum ortum est.

what should a Christian do but flee from contentions altogether?"[180] So says Jerome.

Therefore, we too, if we truly wish to know God, must set aside all confused reasoning, all sophistical argumentation, and all dialectical inquiry. For reasoning and inquiry often carry about them a certain air of desperation and distrust. Faith, however, ought to be stable and serene. Thus, Ambrose says in his book *On the Trinity*: "remove arguments where faith is sought. In their own schools, let dialectic now be silent. It is believed by fishermen, not dialecticians."[181] He says the same in *On the Faith to Gratian*. And Pope Urban writing to Charles says: "it did not please God to save His people through dialectic; for 'the kingdom of God is in the simplicity of faith, not in the contention of words.'"[182] For there is no greater pestilence for the soul than reasoning, than altercation, than disputation about divine matters, which destroys knowledge, perverts understanding, and casts down faith. Paul, therefore, commands that it be avoided as much as possible, and James calls it "earthly, animal, and diabolical wisdom."[183] From this spring errors, doubts, lies, heresies; from this the first sin arose in mankind.

---

[180] Jerome, *On Titus*, 3.9.

[181] Ambrose, *De fide ad Gratianum*, 1.13.

[182] Gianfrancesco Pico della Mirandola, *De studio humanae et divinae philosophiae*, 1.3 in *Opera omnia*, vol. 2 (Basel: Henricpetrina, 1573), p. 11.

[183] II Timothy 2:14-16, 23; James 3:15.

Inventor autem hujus tam pestiferae facultatis diabolus, primus ille callidus et perniciosus sophista, quaestiunculas proposuit, disputationes invenit, et quasi scholam aliquam instituit. Non contentus quod se ipsum perdiderat, invenit artificium quo et alios perderet malumque suum augeret et propagaret. Idcirco non permittens hominem stare in simplici fide, voluit de praeceptis Dei quaestionem proponere, commodissimam hanc homines evertendi machinam arbitratus. Hinc [497] sophistae instar, Evam primo aggreditur, et illam exquistione et ratione in certamen provocat quaerens: Cur praecepit vobis Deus, ut non comedatis ex omni ligno paradisi? Cum quo si Eva non disputasset, decepta non fuisset. Quia vero cum diabolo in altercationem descendit, unica falsa et sophistica ratione decepta est, nec solum a fide jam decidit, sed et rationem simul amisit. Hinc coepit primo verba Dei falso interpretari, unde et mendacium commisit, simul ac de eloquiis Dei dubitare diffidereque praesumpsit. Ita enim respondit: de fructibus lignorum, quae sunt in Paradiso, vescimur; de fructu vero ligni, quod est in medio Paradisi, praecepit nobis Deus

The inventor of this most pestilential art, however, is the devil.[184] That cunning and pernicious sophist was the first to propose trifling *quaestiones*, to invent disputations, and to establish a kind of school, so to speak. Not content with destroying himself, he devised a craft by which he could also destroy others and augment and propagate his own evil. Therefore, not allowing man to remain in simple faith, he wished to propose a *quaestio* concerning God's commandments, considering this the most effective tool for overthrowing men. Thus, in the manner of a sophist, he first approached Eve and provoked her to a contest of inquiry and reasoning by asking: "why did God command you not to eat from any tree of paradise?"[185] If Eve had not disputed with him, she would not have been deceived; but because she stooped down into an argument with the devil, she was deceived by a single false and sophistical reasoning, and not only did she fall from faith, but she also lost reason at the same time. Hence she began to falsely interpret the words of God, and consequently, she committed a lie as soon as she dared to doubt and distrust what God had said. For thus she replied: "of the fruits of the trees that are in paradise we do eat; but of the fruit of the tree which is in the midst of paradise, God has commanded

---

[184] By such a statement, Agrippa is declaring open warfare against the proponents of Scholastic philosophy and what he believed were its insufficient means of knowledge production, i.e., the *disputatio*.

[185] Genesis 3:1.

ne comederemus et ne tangeremus illud, ne forte moriamur. Ecce quam falso interpretata est praeceptum Dei, dicendo nobis in plurali, quod Deus soli Adae in singulari praecepit, antequam Eva crearetur: insuper ne tangeremus, quo utrobique mentita est. Deinde etiam dubitavit, ubi subdit, ne forte. Vides quomodo callida illa et diabolica ex quaestionibus proposita disceptatio decepit rationem, ratio autem dejecit fidem.

Hic fructus, haec utilitas, hic finis disputationum sophisticarum, quae hoc tempore a recentioribus aliquot theosophistis, ac philopompis exercentur ad omnem vanitatem. Qui cum Aristotelem male conversum, et quaedam insuper commentaria, tum Petrum Lombardum, quem magistrum scientiarum vocant, ac neglecto Christi Evangelio apostolicisque dogmatibus, tanquam totius theologiae archetypum colunt, et nescio quae alia

us not to eat and not to touch, lest perhaps we die."[186] Behold how falsely God's precept was interpreted when she said "to us" in the plural, whereas God had commanded it only to Adam, in the singular, before Eve was created; moreover, she added "not to touch," thus lying in both respects. She then also expressed doubt when she added, "lest perhaps." You see how that cunning and diabolical dispute based on proposed *quaestiones* deceived reason, and reason, in turn, overthrew faith.[187]

This is the fruit, this is the benefit, this is the purpose of sophistical disputations, which are employed in our time by some of the more recent theosophists[188] and lovers of boastfulness, all in vain.[189] They, having neglected the Gospel of Christ and the apostolic doctrines, and having poorly understood Aristotle and certain commentaries besides, then Peter Lombard whom they call the master of sciences[190], worship him as the archetype of all theology, and who knows what other things of

---

[186] Genesis 3:2-3.

[187] This paragraph draws closely and extensively from Johannes Reuchlin, *De verbo mirifico*, 2.d3^{r}.

[188] Note that when Agrippa uses the word 'theosophists,' it is being used in the pejorative sense of 'sophists of god,' not in the positive sense used by 19th-21st century occultists.

[189] Marsilio Ficino, *Epistolarum libri XII*, vol. 1, p. 665: "There are many in our age who are not lovers of wisdom (*philosophi*), but lovers of boastfulness (*philopompi*), who arrogantly and excessively profess to hold the Aristotelian view."

[190] Perrone Compagni, *De triplici ratione cognoscendi Deum*, 164 correctly has *sententiarum* rather than *scientiarum* based on the *Magister Sententiarum* Peter Lombard's authorship of the

illius generis viderunt. Tunc freti sophistica sua insolentia, omnia se posse attentare, aggredi, dissolvere, et interpretari putant. Tunc irruentes suis ineptiis, inquinamentis et blateramentis, rixosisque disputationibus, ad quod artificium jam linguas armatas habent, omnia quae in fide et religione simplicia, sincera, et pura sunt, multiplicia, caliginosa, et sordida reddiderunt, omnemque theologiam suis absurdis altercationibus, ac futili verbositate confuderunt, conturbarunt, polluerunt, inveneruntque non divinam nec humanam quidem, sed nescio quam suam, non dico theologiam, sed squalidam, odiosam, cavillatoriam et diabolicam vanitatem, humanarum opinionum, philosophicarumque nugarum rhapsodiam.

Veram autem illam et vetustam theologiam, quae a primis sanctis et veris Christianis emanavit, in primis a Christo, et ab apostolis, quos sequuti ex Graecis Dionysius, cujus divinissima scripta, sed non omnia extant; item Divus Origenes, consumatissimus theologus, ex cujus innumeris fere scriptis ob ae[498]mulorum depravationem, paucissima extant: item Basilius, cognomento Magnus; Athanasius, Alexandrinus episcopus, qui contra Arrianos tanta constantia disputavit; Cyrillus ejusdem basilicae episcopus, qui praefuit concilio Ephesino, cujus egregia commentaria in Joannem extant;

Libri Quattuor Sententiarum (*Four Books of Sentences*) circa 1150.

that kind they have seen. Then, supported by their insolence in sophistry, they think they can attempt, undertake, resolve, and interpret everything. Then rushing in with their absurdities, pollutions, babblings, and contentious disputations, to which art they have now armed their tongues, they have rendered everything that is simple, sincere, and pure in faith and religion, complex, obscure, and sordid. They have confounded, muddied, and polluted all theology with their absurd altercations and pointless verbosity, and have invented, not a divine or even human theology, but a thing of their own, I know not what – I do not call it 'theology' – but a filthy, hateful, quibbling, and diabolical vanity, a patchwork of human opinions and philosophical trifles.

But that true and ancient theology which emanated from the first saints and true Christians – first from Christ and the apostles, who were followed by Dionysius from among the Greeks, whose most divine writings, though not all, are extant; and the divine Origen, the most perfect theologian, of whose nigh countless writings very few remain due to the corruption of his rivals; and Basil, surnamed the Great; and Athanasius, the Alexandrian bishop, who disputed with such constancy against the Arians; and Cyril, bishop of the same basilica, who presided over the Council of Ephesus, whose excellent *Commentaries on John* are extant;

Didimus, cognomento Caecus, qui scripsit de processu Spiritus sancti, quod opus Hieronymus in latinum sermonem transtulit; Eusebius Caesariensis, qui praeparationem in Evangelicam veritatem scripsit; multum quoque nobis in historia profuit Joannes, cognomine Chrysostomus ob eloquentiam; item Gregorius Nazianzenus, et plures alii; ex latinis praeterea Cyprianus, Lactantius, Tertullianus, Ambrosius, Ruffinus, Hieronymus, Augustinus, Leo, Gregorius, Beda, Anselmus, Bernardus, Cassaneus, et quos illa priora tempora genuere. Hos tam sanctos doctores, hanc inquam theologiam penitus posthabent, repudiant, et irrident, sine quibus tamen nil recte vel in suis queunt cognoscere.

Inventor hujus tam perniciosi magisterii fuit serpens ille, antiquus sophista, qui decepit Evam. Hunc imitantes recentiores quidam theosophistae, hoc seculo tanti flagitii principes, authores et propagatores extiterunt, quos innumerabiles alii ejusdem generis homines quotidie misere sequuntur. Hinc exorta est illa horrida et implicata sylva, caliginosusque lucus disputationum, in quo cum misero labore et damnabili studio, exiguo fructu assidue laborant, non fide, non spe, non charitate Christum imitantes, neque orationibus, jejuniis, vigiliis, petentes, quaerentes, pulsantes, ut aperiatur illis divinae cognitionis armarium, sed tanquam titani contra Deum belligerantes, daedalicis sophismatum machinis sacrarum literarum ostium se posse disrumpere arbitrantur.

and Didymus, surnamed the Blind, who wrote *On the Procession of the Holy Spirit*, a work which Jerome translated into the Latin tongue; and Eusebius of Caesarea, who wrote the *Preparation for the truth of the Gospel*; and much also has John, surnamed Chrysostom because of his eloquence, profited us in history; and Gregory of Nazianzus, and many others; and, moreover, from the Latins: Cyprian, Lactantius, Tertullian, Ambrose, Rufinus, Jerome, Augustine, Leo, Gregory, Bede, Anselm, Bernard, Cassian, and those whom those earlier times produced – these most holy doctors and this theology, I say, they utterly disregard, reject, and mock, but without which they are unable to rightly understand anything even in their own studies.

The inventor of this most pernicious discipline was that serpent, the ancient sophist, who deceived Eve. Following his example, some more recent theosophists, who in this age have become the leaders, authors, and propagators of such a great abomination, have emerged. Countless others of the same kind miserably follow them every day. Hence arose that horrid and tangled forest, and that dark grove of disputes, in which they labor incessantly in miserable toil and damnable study, with little fruit, imitating not Christ in faith, hope, or love, nor seeking, asking, and knocking with prayers, fasts, and vigils that the treasury of divine knowledge might be opened to them, but rather, like the Titans waging war against God, they think that they can batter down the door of the Holy Scriptures with the Daedalian machines of their sophistry.

Hinc quicquid a philosopho seu theologo aliquo dictum in manus eorum inciderit, id non resolvunt ad justa principia, sed deducunt longius, non ad primos fontes unde manavit, sed suis ineptiis ac ineptis distinctionibus dilacerant, dissipant, conterunt, quasi mortario in pulverem, ut viribus omnibus prae nimia tenuitate amissis, ante lucem et auram positum vel lenissimo vento evanescat. Hinc illud apud eos usurpatum proverbium, quo dicunt: unico flatu argumentum tuum dissolvam. Recte sane, vere ac sapienter dictum; nam nihil apud eos argumentatores est quam flatus, flauti obvians illumque discutiens. Hinc cum paulum a gymnasiis suis abierint, sedent muti et cogitabundi, tanquam stolidi et trunci inanimati, et tanquam ficulnea arida, non habent quod loquantur, quod [499] fructificent, quia non sunt cum suis condisputatoribus. Hinc natum illud apud vulgus proverbium: Maximos quosque scholasticos maxime stultos esse solere.

Accedit ad haec alia insolentia, qua recentiores isti theologi et canonistae, homines suae ignorantiae conscii, authoritati suae diffidentes, timentes quia illis non credatur,

Thus, whatever has been said by a philosopher or some theologian that falls into their hands, they do not explain according to sound principles, but deduce from it something very different, not according to the original sources from which it flowed; rather, with their absurdities and foolish distinctions, they chop it up, break it apart, and grind it down into powder, like in a mortar, so that, having lost all its strength from its excessive fineness, it vanishes in the slightest breeze when exposed to light and air. Hence that proverb used among them, in which they say, "I will dissolve your argument with a single breath." How well, truly, and wisely said! For among these arguers there is nothing but wind blowing against wind and dispersing it. Hence when they have left their schools for a short while, they sit silent and thoughtful, like stupid and lifeless logs, and like a dried-up fig tree, have nothing to say, no fruit to bear, because they are not with their fellow disputants. Hence that proverb was born among the common people: "the greatest schoolmen are usually the greatest fools."[191]

Added to this is another form of arrogance by which these recent theologians and canonists – men conscious of their own ignorance, unsure of their own authority, and fearful that they will not be believed – cite

[191] Note here the *paronomasia*, or the use of words similar in sound to achieve a humorous effect, between *scholasticos* ('schoolmen' or 'scholastics') and *stultos* ('fools') which is impossible to render in English translation.

tam capitulatim tamque articulatim testimonia citant, in singulis verbis et interpunctionibus occupati, neque hoc raro, neque ex remotiore antiquitate, sed etiam ex novissimis, et suis fere contemporaneis, suique similibus quibusque scriptoribus, et hoc tam continue et tam assidue, jactantes se congerie illorum testimoniorum, non ut doceant alios, sed ut ipsi memoriae laudem aucupentur et multa legisse videantur, non considerantes, quod si ex dictis vel scriptis suis unicuique quod suum est distribuerint, nihil quod eorum sit remansurum. Sed illo errore et proprii ingenii inopia vagantes, quasi rustica quaedam secta, cum ipsi nihil sciant, nec ex se aliquid edere possint, omnia studia sua in excerpendo et compilando consumunt. Quibus contenti, cum nihil omnino sciant, quam aliorum laboribus et exemplis uti, sapientiae nomen temere sibi arrogant; atque hoc consilio mirum quam sibi placeant, quam egregie doctos se putent. Non sic fecerunt prisci illi theologi, viri sapientia graves, authoritate venerabiles, vita sancti, quales illi quos supra memoravimus, fuerunt. In quorum scriptis tam simplex, tam rara invenitur scripturarum citatio, ubicunque aliquid memorandum est, et illa quidem ex Veteri Testamento, ex Evangeliis, ex apostolis, ex remotiore antiquitate, nihil se jactantes, homines sane in divina gratia solum confidentes, suae sapientiae conscii, et doctores optimi,

testimonies chapter-by-chapter or article-by-article while being concerned with individual words and punctuation marks, and not infrequently. Nor do they cite from writers of a more distant antiquity, but from the most recent, their nigh contemporaries, very much like themselves. And this they do so continuously and so incessantly, boasting of their heap of testimonies, not to teach others, but to seek praise for their own memory and to appear well-read, not considering that if they were to distribute to each person what belongs to him from their sayings or writings, nothing of their own would remain. But wandering in that error and poverty of their own genius, given that they know nothing themselves and can produce nothing themselves, they consume all their time studying in making excerpts and compilations, like some band of brigands. Content with these, since they know nothing at all, other than how to use the labors and examples of others, they rashly arrogate to themselves the name of wisdom; and with this counsel, it is amazing how pleased they are with themselves, how excellently learned they think themselves to be. Those ancient theologians – men grave in wisdom, venerable in authority, holy in life, like those whom we mentioned above – did not behave in this way. In their writings, the most simple and infrequent quotations of texts are found wherever something worth remembering is mentioned, and indeed these are from the Old Testament, from the Gospels, from the apostles, and from more remote antiquity, never boasting, men truly confiding solely in divine grace, conscious of their wisdom, and the best of

doctores optimi, nullorum judiciorum timentes, veraces, non respicientes in faciem hominum. Qui ex suis thesauris nobis largiti sunt munera, imitantes Christum, qui tamquam bonus paterfamilias de thesauris suis protulit nova et vetera, in omnibus verbo et opere fructificantes in hominibus fructum verae religionis et fidei ad salutem aeternam.

Sed redeamus unde digressi sumus. Quantum namque in divina cognitione peccant, qui exili rationis discursu Deum se cognoscere posse praesumunt, innumera fere in eorum traditionibus discrimina ostendunt. Nulla enim eis quaestio, quantumcunque levis, proponitur, quam non litigiosis ratiunculis daedalicisque labyrinthis involvant; ac sese invicem canum more, rabidis latratibus, morsibusque condemnant, quod eorum scripta et volumina abunde satis ostendunt. [500] Quod si juxta Aristotelis sententiam veritatis conditio est, ut undique sibi consonet, estque consonantia opinionum veritatis vestigium, necessario sequitur ex opposito, id quod ubique sibi dissonat verum esse non posse. Ideo apud istos argumentatores, et recentiores theosophistas, nec veritas quidem ulla esse potest, nec ullum quidem veritatis vestigium, necesseque est hanc inconditam atque portentosam nec nisi humanarum de divinis opinionum coacervationem aliquando mole sua ruituram.

teachers, fearing no judgments, truthful, paying no regard to the appearance of men.[192] They have bestowed gifts upon us from their treasures, imitating Christ, who, "like a good head of house, brought forth from his treasures things new and old,"[193] in all things bearing fruit in word and deed among men, the fruit of true religion and faith unto eternal salvation.

But let us return to where we digressed. Therefore, by the nigh innumerable distinctions in their traditions, they generally reveal how greatly they sin in divine knowledge who presume they can know God by the feeble discourse of reason. For no question, however trivial, is proposed to them which they do not entangle in litigious arguments and Daedalian labyrinths. Like dogs, they condemn each other with rabid barking and biting, as their writings and volumes clearly reveal. And if, according to Aristotle, the nature of truth is that it is always consistent with itself, and if the consistency of opinions is a sign of truth, it necessarily follows that what is everywhere discordant with itself cannot be true.[194] Therefore, among these arguers and recent theosophists, there can be no truth at all, nor even any trace of truth, and it is inevitable that this disordered and monstrous heap of merely human opinions about divine matters will eventually collapse under its own weight.

---

[192] Matthew 22:16.

[193] Matthew 13:52.

[194] Riccio, *Isagoge*, 15^{v}.

Sed heu miseri, ignorantia adhuc late patet in orbe; nemo mente pius Dei cognitionem requirit; omnes fere sumus ignorantiam professi. Theologia nova, novi doctores, doctrina nova, nihil antiquum, nihil sanctum, nihil vere religiosum, et quod deterius est, si qui sunt qui huic pristinae theologiae ac religioni se dedicant, insani, ignari, irreligiosi, interdum etiam haeretici vocantur, atque (ut inquit Hermes) odio habentur, etiam periculum capitale in eos constituitur, contumeliis afficiuntur, saepe vita privantur.

Attamen redire ad primos fontes et puram aquam haurire, ubi est immaculata forma pietatis et justitiae, licebit semper et disputare et docere, et facere, favente nobis

But alas, wretched ones, ignorance still spreads widely in the world; no one with a pious mind seeks the knowledge of God; almost all of us profess ignorance. New theology, new doctors, new doctrine – nothing ancient, nothing holy, nothing truly religious.[195] And what is worse, if there are any who dedicate themselves to this ancient theology and religion, they are called madmen, ignorant, irreligious, and sometimes even heretics, and (as Hermes says) are hated; even the threat of death is made against them, they are subjected to insults, and are often deprived of life.[196]

Nevertheless, it will always be possible to return to the first sources and draw up the pure water where the immaculate form of piety and justice flows, and to dispute, to teach, and to act with the help of our

---

[195] This is an allusion to the famous lament of Hermes in *Asclepius* 25 (Copenhaver, *Hermetica*, p. 82): "They will establish new laws, new justice. Nothing holy, nothing reverent nor worthy of heaven or heavenly beings will be heard of or believed in the mind."

[196] *Asclepius* 25 (Copenhaver, *Hermetica*, p. 82): "But – believe me – whoever dedicates himself to reverence of mind will find himself facing a capital penalty"; *Corpus Hermeticum* 9 (Copenhaver, *Hermetica*, p. 28): "One who has come to know god, filled with all good things, has thoughts that are divine and not like those of the multitude. This is why those who are in knowledge do not please the multitude, nor does the multitude please them. They appear to be mad, and they bring ridicule on themselves. They are hated and scorned, and perhaps they may even be murdered."

Domino Deo nostro Jesu Christo Nazareno crucifixo, qui magni consilii Angelus, vero mentes lumine illustrat, quem verum Deum et verum hominem profitemur, ac futuri Patrem saeculi, judicemque expectamus.

crucified Lord God Jesus Christ of Nazareth, who, as the Angel of Great Counsel, enlightens minds with true light. Him we profess as true God and true man, and await as Father of the world to come and judge.[197]

[197] Isaiah 9:6; Lazzarelli, *Crater Hermetis*, 1.1 (Hanegraaff and Bouthoorn, *Lodovico Lazzarelli*, p. 167).

CAPUT VI

Quoniam igitur nunc gentes ab ipsa creaturarum conditione, Deum primam causam omnium productricem cognoscunt, et ipsa conditio ostendit, qui condidit eam et ipsa factura monstrat qui fecit eam, et mundus manifestum facit qui se disposuit; Judaei quoque in primis a protoplasti traditione: deinceps a Moyse et prophetis eundem Deum fabricatorem coeli et terrae acceperunt, et per legis ministerium cognoverunt; nos autem in Evangelio ab apostolis: Qui est idem Deus super omnes Deos, et nomen ejus super omne nomen, et hujus Verbum, naturaliter invisibile, caro factum, in visibilem et palpabilem hominem, et usque ad mortem humilians se, mortem autem Crucis, et eos qui in eum credunt, similes sibi, incorruptibiles, et impassibiles futuros, et percepturos regnum coelorum, accipimus perfectam agnitionem. Propterea inexcusabilis est homo, qui ignorat Deum, maledictus autem, qui illum agnoscens non veneratur, impossibile [501] enim est (ut ait Apostolus)

CHAPTER VI

Since, therefore, the nations now know God as the first cause of all things from the very foundation of creation, and this foundation reveals who created it, and the work itself shows who made it, and the world makes it obvious who arranged it, and the Jews too received the same God, Creator of heaven and earth, first of all from the tradition of the first man, then from Moses and the prophets, and came to know Him by means of the law, though we, through the Gospel from the apostles, have received perfect knowledge of Him who is the same God above all gods, and whose name is above every name, and whose Word, naturally invisible, was made flesh, became a visible and tangible man, humbling Himself even to death – death on the cross – and we know that those who believe in Him will become like Him, subject to neither corruption nor suffering, and will receive the kingdom of heaven, therefore, man is without excuse if he does not know God, and accursed is he who, knowing Him, does not worship Him.[198] "For it is impossible," as the Apostle says,

---

[198] Ficino, *De Christiana religione*, 4 (Attrell, Bartlett, and Porreca, *On the Christian Religion*, p. 53-54): "Nothing displeases God more than being despised; nothing pleases Him more than being worshipped. He punishes more mildly those who transgress His divine laws in part but strikes with thunder those who rebel against His authority out of ingratitude, malice, and arrogance. Therefore, divine providence does not at any time permit any region of the world to be utterly devoid of every

ut qui semel sunt illuminati, et gustaverunt donum coeleste, et participes facti sunt Spiritus sancti, gustaveruntque bonum Dei verbum virtutesque seculi venturi, et prolapsi sunt, rursum renovari ad poenitentiam.

Nos itaque dictamine creaturarum moniti, et annunciatione prophetarum edocti, ac praedicatione apostolorum informati, audemus dicere: quod unus solus est verus Deus increatus, immensus, aeternus, omnipotens, Pater, Filius, et Spiritus Sanctus, tres quidem personae sibi invicem coaeternae et coaequales, una tamen essentia et substantia naturaque simplex omnino, ut sic unum Deum in Trinitate et Trinitatem in Unitate fateamur, neque confundentes personas, neque substantiam separantes. Nam Pater ab aeterno genuit Filium, suamque illi dedit substantiam, ac nihilominus retinuit: Filius quoque nascendo Patris accepit substantiam, non tamen personam propriam Patris assumpsit, neque Pater illam in Filium transtulit, sunt enim ambo unius et ejusdem substantiae, sed diversarum

---

religion, though He does permit different rites of worship to be observed in different times and places… [God] prefers to be worshipped in whatever way, even incompetently, provided it is in keeping with human nature, than not to be worshipped at all out of pride. Indeed, for men who are intemperate but submissive to Him to a degree, He either corrects them like a father or at least punishes them less. As for the impious, the utterly ungrateful, and those rebelling out of their own free will, however, He casts them out and torments them as enemies."

"for those who have once been enlightened, who have tasted the heavenly gift, have become partakers of the Holy Spirit, have tasted the good Word of God and the powers of the world to come, and have then fallen away, to be renewed again to penance."[199]

Thus we – instructed by the testimony of creation, taught by the proclamation of the prophets, and informed by the preaching of the apostles – dare to say that there is one true God, uncreated, immeasurable, eternal, omnipotent, Father, Son, and Holy Spirit, three persons, coeternal and coequal with one another, yet one essence, substance, and entirely simple nature, so that we confess one God in Trinity and Trinity in Unity, neither confusing the persons nor dividing the substance. For the Father eternally begot the Son, and gave Him His substance, yet retained it nonetheless. The Son also, in being begotten, received the substance of the Father, but did not take the Father's own person, nor did the Father transfer it to the Son, for they are both of one and the same substance, but of different persons.

[199] Hebrews 6:4.

personarum. Filius quoque hic licet Patri coaeternus sit ex substantia Patris ante saecula genitus, tamen nihilominus ex substantia Virginis in seculo natus est, et vocatum est nomen ejus Jesus, qui est Christus, perfectus Deus, perfectus homo, ex anima rationali et humana carne subsistens, cui nihil humanum defuit praeter peccatum: una persona, duae naturae, ante saecula genitus Deus sine matre, in seculo natus homo sine patre de virgine ante et post partum incorrupta, passus in cruce mortuus est, sed in cruce vitam illustravit, et mortem morte resolvit. Sepultus est, et descendit ad inferos, sed animas Patrum reduxit ex inferis, et resurrexit tertia die per virtutem propriam, et ascendit in coelos, et misit Spiritum Sanctum Paracletum, et iterum venturus est judicare vivos et mortuos. Ad cujus adventum omnes homines resurrecturi sunt in carne sua propria, et reddituri sunt de factis propriis rationem.

Haec est perfecta Dei agnitio, in qua oportet nos salvos fieri: quam qui non agnoverit, aut agnoscentibus non crediderit, aut de ea dubitare praesumpserit, a spe vitae et salutis aeternae alienus est.

The Son, though coeternal with the Father and begotten from the substance of the Father before the ages, was nonetheless born in time from the substance of the Virgin, and His name was called Jesus, who is the Christ, perfect God, perfect man, subsisting in a rational soul and human flesh, lacking nothing human except sin: one person, of two natures, begotten as God before the ages without a mother, born as man in time without a father from a virgin who remained uncorrupted before and after childbirth. He suffered on the cross and died, but on the cross He illuminated life, and by His death, He destroyed death. He was buried and descended to the dead, but He brought back the souls of the Fathers from the dead, and He rose again on the third day by His own power, ascended into heaven, and sent the Holy Spirit, the Comforter, and He will come again to judge the living and the dead. At His coming, all men will rise in their own flesh, and will give an account of their own deeds.[200]

This is the perfect knowledge of God, through which we must be saved: whoever has not recognized it, or has not believed those who do, or has presumed to doubt it, is a stranger to the hope of life and to eternal salvation.

---

[200] Here Agrippa publicly affirms his orthodoxy using material drawn directly from the Athanasian creed and Reuchlin, *De verbo mirifico*, 3.f6^{v}-f7^{r}.

Epistolae

Venerabili Patri Sacrae Theologiae Magistro Aurelio ab Aquapendente Augustiniano

Henricus Cornelius Agrippa Salutem Dicit.

Ex literis quas ad me secundo huius mensis dedisti, perspexi erga me animi tui candorem P. R. et cognovi te virum cyclice doctum, eorumque quae adhuc in tenebris delitescunt curiosum exploratorem. Gavisus sum ilico, atque mihi gratulor, nactum me amicitiam talis viri, qui cum possem aliquando et genium et ingenium excolere: teque nunc (teste hoc chirographo) inter amicissmos recipio.

Sed heus tu qui sunt duces tui quos sequeris. Tu qui audes irremeabilem domum intrare Dedali, atque tremendi Minois, ire per excubias, et te committere Parcis? Qui sunt magistri tui, tu qui versaris circa immensa, ausus conari vagum stabilem, perfidum affidum, ac deorum omnium fugacissimum redere,

Epistles

To the Venerable Father Aurelius of Aquapendente, Master of Sacred Theology of the Augustinian Order (1527)

Heinrich Cornelius Agrippa sends greetings.

From the letters which you sent me on the second of this month, I have noticed the candor of your spirit towards me, most reverend Father, and I have recognized you as a man learned in letters, and a curious investigator of those things which still lie hidden in darkness. I rejoiced immediately, and I congratulated myself on having gained the friendship of such a man, who might, at some time, help to cultivate both my spirit and my talent. And now (as this letter bears witness), I count you among my closest friends.

But hey, who are the guides whom you follow? You, who dare to enter the inescapable house of Daedalus and to pass through the guards of fearsome Minos, committing yourself to the Fates? Who are those teachers of yours, you who are wrapped up in immense matters, who dares to attempt to make the wandering steadfast, the faithless trustworthy, and the most elusive of all the

vel ipsa Adrastia constatiorem? Cave ne decipiare ab his qui fuerunt decepti. Neque enim hic te dirigere poterit quantacumque librorum lectio, quum non nisi mera aenigmata sonent. O quanta leguntur scripta de inexpugnabili magicae artis potentia, de prodigiosis astrologorum imaginibus, de monstrifica alchymistarum metamorphosi, deque lapide illo benedicto, quo Midae instar contacta aera, mox omnia in aurum argentumve permutentur, quae omnia comperiuntur vana, ficta et falsa quoties ad literam practicantur. Atque tamen traduntur ista, scribunturque a magnis gravissimisque philosophis et sanctis viris, quorum traditiones quis audebit dicere falsas? Quin imo credere impium esset, illos data opera scripsisse mendacia.

Alius est ergo sensus quam literis traditur, isque variis obductus mysteriis, sed hactenus a nullo magistrorum palam explicatus, quem nescio siquis sine perito fidoque magistro sola librorum lectione possit adsequi, nisi fuerit divino numine illustratus quod datur paucissimis: ideoque in vacuum currunt multi qui haec secretissima naturae arcana prosequuntur, ad nudam lectionis seriem referentes animum. Nam inauspicato ingenio a vero intellectu prolapsi, in [348] falsas imaginationes, exteriorum spirituum vaframentis irretiti,

gods even more constant than Adrasteia[201] herself? Beware lest you be deceived by those who were themselves deceived. For no amount of book reading will be able to guide you here, since they speak nothing but pure riddles. O how many works do we read about the invincible power of the magical arts, about the ominous images of astrologers, about the monstrous metamorphoses of the alchemists, and about that blessed stone, with which, like Midas, bronze is quickly transformed into gold or silver when touched – all of these are found to be vain, fictitious, and false whenever they are practiced to the letter. And these things are handed down and written by great and serious philosophers and holy men. Who would dare to say their traditions are false? Nay, it would rather be impious to believe that they deliberately wrote those lies.

Therefore, there is another meaning than that which is conveyed by the words, and it is veiled in various mysteries, but so far not one of the masters has openly explained it. I do not know if anyone, without an experienced and trustworthy master, can attain this by the mere reading of books – unless he is illuminated by a divine presence, which is granted to so very few. Hence, the masses rush in vain towards these most secret mysteries of nature, directing their minds only to the bare reading of the text. For, having by ill-fated genius fallen from true understanding into false imaginations, ensnared by the deceits of external spirits – those over

---

[201] I.e., the Greek goddess of fate or necessity.

illorum quorum dominari datum est, periculosi servi effecti sunt, et ignorantes semetipsos, abeunt retro post vestigia gregum suorum, quaerentes extra se quod intus possident. Atque hoc est quod te nunc scire volo, quia in nobis ipsis est omnium mirabilium effectuum operator, qui quicquid portentosi mathematici, quicquid prodigiosi magi, quicquid invidentes naturae persecutores alchymistae, quicquid daemonibus deteriores malefici necromantes promittere audent, ipse novit discernere et efficere, idque sine omni crimine, sine dei offensa, sine religionis iniuria. In nobis inquam est ille mirandorum operator:

Nos habitat, non tartara, sed nec sydera coeli,
Spiritus in nobis qui viget, illa facit.

Verum de his nobis quam latissime tecum conferendum esset, sed coram: Non enim committuntur haec literis, nec scribuntur calamo, sed spiritu spiritui, paucis sacrisque verbis infunduntur. Idque si quando nos ad te venire contigerit.

Caeterum quos postulas libros, aliqui illorum aliquando fuerunt penes me, sed iam non sunt: qui vero penes vos circumferuntur libri adolescentiae meae, de Occulta philosophia intitulati, horum priores duo in multis deficiunt, tertius totus mancus, nec nisi scriptorum meorum epitome quoddam continet. Sed ego totum opus, favente Domino, integrum recognitumque aliquando

whom we were given charge to rule[202] – they have become dangerous slaves. Ignorant of themselves, they retreat, following the tracks of their own herds, seeking outside themselves what they possess within. And this is what I now want you to know: the operator of all wondrous effects lies within ourselves. It knows how to discern and accomplish whatever portentous astrologers, prodigious magi, alchemists – the envious persecutors of nature – and wicked necromancers worse than demons dare to promise, and all this without any crime, without offending God, without injury to religion. In us, I say, is that operator of wonders:

It dwells within us, not in Tartarus, nor in the stars of heaven;
All this is brought to pass by the spirit which lives in us.

But regarding these matters, we should talk about this as extensively as we can, but in person. For these things are not entrusted to letters, nor written with a pen, but are infused from spirit to spirit with few and sacred words. And this, if ever it should happen that we come to you.

As for the books which you request, some of them were once in my possession, but now they are not. However, those books from my youth which are circulated among you, entitled *On Occult Philosophy*, the first two of these are lacking in many respects, and the third is entirely incomplete, containing nothing but a synopsis of my writings. But I, with the Lord's favor, will someday

---

[202] For the authority of Christ's followers over demons, see Matthew 10:1, 10:8; Mark 3:14-15, 6:7, 6:13; Luke 9:1, 10:17-20; Acts 8:7.

in lucem dabo; clave tamen operis solis amicissimis reservata, quorum te unum esse non dubites.

Vale felicissime, e Lugduno. XXIIII. Septemb. Anno. M.D.XXVII.

Ad eundem

Ex humanissimis tuis literis (venerande pater) quasi ad speculum animum tuum introspexi totum, illumque amplector totus, voloque sic tibi persuasum habeas, te mihi supra quam literis demonstrari possit gratissimum fore, altissimeque insidere animo: me vero talem esse, qui ex abundantia cordis hoc scribam, quique eos qui se meae amicitiae commiserunt, nulla unquam tempestate soleam deserere. Quare ut tu vota consequaris tua, meis non minora, ego propediem ad te veniam. Ubi cum coram dabitur mutuas audire et reddere voces, scio amicitiam nostram indissolubilem fore perpetuoque duraturam.

Iam vero quod ad postulatam Philosophiam attinet, te scire volo, quod omnium rerum cognoscere opificem

bring forth the whole work into the light of day, complete and revised; however, the key of the work will be reserved only for my closest friends, among whom you should not doubt yourself to be one.

Farewell most happily, from Lyon, 24 September, in the year 1527.

To the Same Aurelius of Aquapendente (1527)

From your most courteous letters, venerable Father, I have, as if gazing into a looking-glass, fully observed your soul, and I embrace it entirely. I wish you to be assured that you are more dear to me than can be demonstrated by letters, and that you dwell most deeply in my heart. Indeed, I am someone who writes this from the abundance of my heart and who is never accustomed, in any storm whatsoever, to abandon those who have entrusted themselves to my friendship. Therefore, so that you may achieve your desires – no less than mine – I will come to you very soon. When we can hear and exchange words with each other in person, I know our friendship will be indissoluble and will perpetually endure.

But now, regarding the Philosophy you have requested, I wish you to know that to know the maker of

ipsum deum, et in illum tota similitudinis imagine (ceu essentiali quodam contactu sive vinculo) transire, quo ipse transformeris efficiareque deus quemadmodum de Mose ait dominus, inquiens: Ecce ego constitui te deum Pharaonis. Haec est illa vera et summa mirabilium operum occultissima philosophia: Clavis eius intellectus est: quanto enim altiora intelligimus, tanto sublimiores induimus virtutes, tantoque maiora et facilius et efficacius operamur. Verum intellectus noster carni inclusus corruptibili, nisi viam carnis superaverit, fueritque propriam naturam sortitus, divinis illis virtutibus non poterit uniri (non enim nisi sibi quamsimillibus congrediuntur) ac [348] pervidendis illis occultissimis dei et naturae secretis, omnino inefficax est, atque hoc opus, hic labor est, superas evadere ad auras.

Quomodo enim qui in cinere et mortali pulvere seipsum amisit, deum ipsum inveniet? Quomodo apprehendet spiritualia carni immersus et sanguinis? An videbit dominum homo et vivet? Quem fructum adferet granum frumenti si prius mortuum non fuerit? Mori enim oportet, mori inquam mundo et carni, ac sensibus omnibus, ac toto homini animali, qui velit ad haec secretorum penetralia ingredi, non quod corpus separetur ab anima, sed quod

all things, God himself, and to pass over into Him in the full image of His likeness (as if by some essential contact or bond), whereby you yourself are transformed and made God, just as the Lord said of Moses, saying: "behold, I have appointed thee the god of Pharaoh."[203] This is that true and highest most occult philosophy of wondrous works. Its key is intellect: for the higher we understand, the more sublime virtues we array ourselves with, and the greater things we accomplish, more easily and more effectively. But our intellect, enclosed in corruptible flesh, unless it overcomes the way of the flesh and attains its own proper nature, cannot be united with those divine virtues (for they associate only with those most similar to themselves) and is utterly ineffective in perceiving those most hidden secrets of God and nature. And this is the task, this is the labor: to escape to the higher airs.

For how will someone who has lost himself in ash and mortal dust find God Himself? How will one, immersed in flesh and blood, grasp spiritual things? Will a man see the Lord and live?[204] What fruit will a grain of wheat bring forth if it has not first died?[205] For it is fitting to die – to die, I say, to the world and to the flesh, and to all the senses, and to the entire animal man – whoever wishes to enter into these inner sanctuaries of secrets; not that the body is separated from the soul, but that the

---

[203] Exodus 7:1.

[204] Exodus 33:20.

[205] John 12:24.

anima relinquat corpus: de qua morte Paulus scribit Colossensibus: Mortui estis, et vita vestra abscondita est cum Christo. Et alibi clarius de seipso ait: Scio hominem in corpore vel extra corpus, nescio, deus scit, raptum usque ad tertium coelum, et quae reliqua sequuntur. Hac inquam pretiosa in conspectu domini morte, mori oportet, quod contingit paucissimis, et forte non semper: Nam pauci quos aequus amavit Iupiter, aut ardens evexit ad aethera virtus, diis geniti potuere. Primum qui non ex carne et sanguine, sed ex deo nati sunt: proxime, qui naturae beneficio ac

soul relinquishes the body. Of this death Paul writes to the Colossians: "you have died, and your life is hidden with Christ."[206] And elsewhere he speaks more clearly about himself, saying: "I know a man, whether in the body or outside the body, I do not know – God knows – who was caught up to the third heaven,"[207] and what follows. In this death, I say, precious in the sight of the Lord, it is fitting to die – a death which happens to so very few, and perhaps not always.[208] For few, whom fair Jupiter loved, or whom burning virtue carried to the heavens – those born of the gods – have been able to do so.[209] First, those who are born not of flesh and blood, but of God; next, those who, by the benefit of nature and

---

[206] Colossians 3:3.

[207] II Corinthians 12:2.

[208] Here Agrippa is referring to Psalm 116:15, "precious in the sight of the Lord is the death of his saints," and the *Binsica* or 'death of the kiss' (*mors osculi*) motif discussed by Pico della Mirandola in *900 Conclusiones* 11.11 (Farmer, *Syncretism and the West*, p. 524-525): "The way in which rational souls are sacrificed by the archangel to God, which is not explained by the Cabalists, only occurs through the separation of the soul from the body, not of the body from the soul except accidentally, as happens in the death of the kiss..." "*Modus quo rationales animae per archangelum deo sacrificantur, qui a Cabalistis non exprimitur, non est nisi per separationem animae a corpore, non corporis ab anima nisi per accidens, ut contigit in morte osculi...*" Cf. Maimonides, *Guide for the Perplexed*, 3.51 (Friedländer, p. 390-391).

[209] An allusion to classical mythology, where only select heroes and demigods like Hercules are granted ascent to the heavens due to their virtue or favor from the gods.

coelorum genethliaco dono, ad id dignificati sunt: caeteri meritis nituntur et arte, de quibus viva vox te certiorem reddet.

Verum hoc te admonitum volo, ne circa me decipiaris, ac si ego aliquando divinae passus, tibi ista praedicem aut tale quid mihi arrogare velim, vel concedi posse sperem, qui hactenus humano sanguine sacratus miles, semper fere aulicus, cum carnis vinculo charissimae uxori alligatus, omnibusque instabilis fortunae flatibus expositus, totusque a carne, a mundo, a domesticis curis transversum actus, tam sublimia immortalium deorum dona non sum adsecutus: Sed accepi me volo velut indicem, qui ipse semper prae foribus manens, aliis quod iter ingrediendum sit, ostendit. Caeterum de amore in te meo tu quidem minime falleris, beneficiis meis quid debeas, non video, quippe qui non contulerim in te quicquam, nisi quod paratus sum dum dabitur occasio, conferre omnia.

Tu nunc felicissime Vale, e Lugduno XIX. Novemb. Anno M.D.XXVII.

the natal gift of the heavens, have been dignified for that; the rest rely on merits and art, about whom word of mouth will inform you.

But I wish to warn you of this, lest you be deceived about me, as if I, having at any time experienced divine things, proclaim these to you, or wish to arrogate such a thing to myself, or hope that it can be granted to me – I who, up till now, consecrated as a soldier by human blood, almost always a courtier, bound by the bond of the flesh to a most dear wife, and exposed to all the unstable blasts of fortune, and wholly driven astray by the flesh, by the world, by domestic cares, have not attained such sublime gifts of the immortal gods. Nevertheless, I wish to be accepted as a guide, who himself remains ever before the doors and shows others which path must be entered upon. Moreover, concerning my love towards you, you are certainly not mistaken; as for what you owe for my benefits, I see nothing, since I have not bestowed anything upon you, except that I am prepared, when the opportunity arises, to bestow all things.

Now, farewell most happily, from Lyon, 19 November, in the year 1527.

Cuidam Amico Suo in Aula Regis

Henricus Cornelius Agrippa cuidam amico suo in aula Regis. Salutem dicit.

Solebant veteres aedito proverbio insignem stultitia notare Noctuas Athenas inferre: sed non minoris stultitiae est, impietatis autem maximae, daemones inferno addere. Scis quem dico infernum, illam inquam scelerum scholam, quam indignatus alibi suis coloribus egregie depinxi aulam. Sed nunquam antea tam iusta scribendi simul et indignandi occasio data est atque nunc, si per occupationes liceret rem pro dignitate tractare. Continere tamen nequeo calamum, quin [349] argumentum eius tibi exponam.

Audi nunc igitur rem stultam simul et impiam: Accersitus est e Germania non modicis sumptibus vir quidam daemoniorum, hoc est cacomagus, in quo potestas daemonum inhabitat, ut sicut Iannes et Mambres resisterunt Mosi, sic iste resistat Caesari. Persuasum est enim illis a patre mendaciorum,

To a Certain Friend at the King's Court (1528)

Heinrich Cornelius Agrippa sends greetings to a certain friend of his at the King's court.

The ancients used to denote outstanding foolishness with a well-known proverb: "to bring owls to Athens."[210] But no less foolish is it, and of the greatest impiety, to add demons to hell. You know what I call hell – that is, that school of crimes, which, indignant, I have elsewhere excellently depicted in its true colors: the court. But never before has such a just occasion for writing and at the same time for indignation been given as now, if my occupations allowed me to handle the matter as it deserves. Nevertheless, I cannot restrain my pen from laying out its subject to you.

Hear now, therefore, a matter both foolish and impious: A certain man of demons – that is, an evil sorcerer, in whom the power of demons dwells – has been summoned to Germany at no small expense, so that just as Jannes and Jambres resisted Moses, this man may resist Caesar.[211] For they have been persuaded by the father of lies[212] that he is

---

[210] I.e., γλαῦκ' εἰς Ἀθήνας. Just like "carrying coals to Newcastle," to bring owls to Athens is pointless, because the city already has its own, sacred to the goddess Athena.

[211] II Timothy 3:8.

[212] I.e., Beelzebub, see Matthew 12:22-30; Mark 3:22; and John 8:44.

illum futurorum omnium praescium, arcanorum quorumcunque consiliorum conscium, ac deliberatarum cogitationum interpretem: tanta praeterea praeditum tu potestate, ut possit regios pueros reducere per aëra, quemadmodum legitur Abacuc cum suo pulmento traductus ad lacum leonum: possetque sicut Helisaeus obsessus in Dothaim, ostendere montes plenos equorum et curruum igneorum, exercitumque plurimum: insuper et revelare et transferre thesauros terrae, quasque volet coget nuptias amoresque aut dirimere: deploratos quosque curabit morbos, stygio pharmaco, puta radicatam ethicam, confirmatam hydropem, inossatam elephantiam, et quam

Solvere nodosam nescit medicina podagram,
Multaque praeterea quae fama obscura recondit.

Vides ubi fides eorum locata est, ubi spes reposita, qui elementa, coelum, fata, naturam, providentiam, Deum, omnia unius magi imperio subiicere conantur, et regni quaerunt salutem, a publicae salutis hostibus daemonibus, dicentes in corde suo cum Ochozia: Non est deus in Israël, eamus ad consulendum Belsebub,

the knower of all futures, the confidant of every arcane counsel, and the interpreter of deliberate thoughts. Moreover, endowed with such great power that he can carry royal youths through the air, just as it is read that Habakkuk, with his stew, was transported to the lions' den.[213] And that he could, like Elisha besieged in Dothan, show mountains full of horses and fiery chariots, and a vast army.[214] What is more, he can reveal and relocate the treasures of the earth, and compel whatever marriages and loves he wishes or dissolve them. He will cure every deplorable disease with Stygian drugs, diagnose deeply-rooted consumption, advanced dropsy, ingrained swelling, and

the knotty gout for which medicine has no cure;
and many other things which obscure rumor conceals.[215]

You see where their faith has been placed, where their hope has been set, those who try to subject the elements, the heavens, fate, nature, providence, and God – all things – to the command of one magician, and who seek salvation for the kingdom from demons, the enemies of public well-being, saying in their hearts with Ahaziah: "there is no God in Israel; let us go to consult Beelzebub,

---

[213] In apocryphal additions to the Book of Daniel (i.e., the tale of 'Bel and the Dragon' in Daniel 14), the prophet Habakkuk is miraculously transported by an angel to bring food to Daniel after he was cast into the lions' den.

[214] II Kings 6:15-17.

[215] Ovid, *Ex Ponto*, 1.3.23 (Wheeler, *Ex Ponto*, p. 282): "tollere nodosam nescit medicina podagram."

deum Acharon. Et sicut Saul locutus ad Pythonem, ait: Philistiim pugnant adversum me, et Dominus recessit a me, et exaudire noluit, vocavi ergo te. Adeo ne et penes istos desperatum est de Deo, ut requirenda censuerint auxilia daemonum? Nonne hoc est iuxta verbum Iudae et Petri, dominum nostrum Iesum Christum salvatorem, et qui nos redemit, deum abnegare, et superinducere sibi celerem perditionem? Nonne thesaurizant sibi iram indignationis domini, mittentem in eos immissiones per angelos malos? Nonne traditi sunt in reprobum sensum, qui veritatem arcanique consilii petunt a patre mendaciorum diabolo, et victoriam postulant aliunde qui a domino exercituum?

Atque tamen huic tam nefario idololatriae et sacrilegiorum artifici, audaciam praestat, quae istis tam impense favet orthodoxa illa mater, et Christianissimi filii accommodatur autoritas, et sacris pecuniis largiuntur munera, conviventibus etiam atque tam nephariam operam conducentibus columnis ecclesiae, episcopis et cardinalibus, et impietatis ministro impii applaudunt proceres, quemadmodum operibus lupi congratulantur corvi. Quod maius peccatum commiserunt Pharao, Balach, Saul, Achab cum sua Iezabel? Ochozias, Nabuchodonosor, Balthassar, Sennacherib, et caeteri cultores

the god of Ekron."[216] And just as Saul, speaking to the Pythoness, said: "the Philistines fight against me, and the Lord has departed from me, and does not answer; therefore, I have called upon you."[217] Has it come to this, that even among these people, hope in God is so lost that they think they must seek help from demons? Is this not, as Jude and Peter say, denying our Lord Jesus Christ, the Savior and God who redeemed us, and to bring upon themselves swift destruction? Do they not store up for themselves the wrath of the Lord's indignation, sending upon them judgements through evil angels? Have they not been given over to a reprobate mind, those who seek the truth and secret counsel from the father of lies, the devil, and ask for victory from elsewhere than from the Lord of Hosts?

And yet, such audacity is granted to this most nefarious craftsman of idolatry and sacrilege by that so-called orthodox mother who so fervently supports him, and by the authority conferred upon him by the most Christian sons, and gifts are lavishly bestowed upon him with sacred funds, while the pillars of the Church – bishops and cardinals – dine with him and support this most wicked work. The impious princes also applaud this minister of impiety, just as ravens congratulate the works of the wolf. What greater sins were committed by Pharaoh, Balak, Saul, Ahab with his Jezebel, Ahaziah, Nebuchadnezzar, Belshazzar, Sennacherib, and the other worshippers

---

[216] II Kings 1:16.

[217] I Samuel 28:15-25.

Baal? Vocavit Pharao contra Mosen magos suos, et illi victi in tertia plaga confessi sunt digitum dei: rex autem obstinatus per decem plagas periit in mari rubro. Vocavit Balach Moabites Balaam ariolum ut malediceret Israël, et deus ipse maledictionem convertit in benedictionem, Balach vero maledictus est. Quid Saulo Samuelis sui aut Pythonis profuere responsa? Nonne confossus est in monte Gelboë: Achab et Iezabel nefariis nuptiis coniuncti confidebant in prophetas [350] Baal, et iuxta verbum dei egressus est spiritus mendax in ore omnium prophetarum, Achab ascensuro in Ramod Balaad prospera promittentium, ceciditque Achab, et Iezabel praecipitata est, et canes comederunt eos. Corripitur Asa rex Iuda a propheta domini, quia in aegritudine sua non quaesivit dominum, sed in artem medicorum confisus est. Nonne maius peccatum habituri sunt, qui relinquentes deum salvatorem, et salubres naturae vires, salutem quaerunt a Satana?

Fecit ita quondam Ochozias, proptereaque audiuit a propheta domini, supra lectulum quem ascendisti non descendes, sed morte morieris. Percurratur caeterorum infidelium regum series, etiam gentilium historiae: Zoroastres,

of Baal? Pharaoh summoned his magicians against Moses, and when they were defeated in the third plague, they confessed it was the finger of God; yet the obstinate king perished after the ten plagues in the Red Sea.[218] Balak, king of Moab, summoned Balaam the diviner to curse Israel, but God Himself turned the curse into a blessing, and Balak was cursed. What did the responses from his Samuel or the Pythoness avail Saul? Was he not pierced through on Mount Gilboa? Ahab and Jezebel, joined in their nefarious marriage, placed their trust in the prophets of Baal, and according to the word of God, a lying spirit came forth in the mouth of all the prophets, promising Ahab prosperity as he was preparing to ascend to Ramoth-Gilead.[219] Ahab fell, Jezebel was cast down, and the dogs ate them. Asa, king of Judah, was rebuked by the prophet of the Lord because in his sickness, he did not seek the Lord but trusted in the art of physicians. Will not those be guilty of a greater sin who forsake God the Savior, and the healing powers of nature, and seek salvation from Satan?

Ahaziah once did this, and because of it, he heard from the prophet of the Lord: "You shall not come down from the bed upon which you have ascended, but you will surely die."[220] Let us consider the series of other unfaithful kings, even from the histories of the pagans: Zoroaster,

---

[218] Exodus 14:27; Psalm 136:15.

[219] I Kings 22:1-36.

[220] II Kings 1:16; the reference to Ahaziah emphasizes the king's reliance on false gods, leading to his death as prophesied by Elijah.

Diotharus, Croesus, Pompeius, Pyrrhus, Crassus, Nero, Iulianus, quid lucrati sunt in magis et divinatoribus suis, qui mentiti sunt illis felicia? Nonne omnes ad nihilum redacti sunt, et male perierunt in peccatis suis? Sic solent impiae illae nugae semper perniciem suis adferre cultoribus, quibus profecto qui maxime confidunt, maxime omnium redduntur infelicissimi. Non inficior, sunt naturales scientiae, sunt metaphysicae artes, sunt occulta ingenia, quibus citra dei offensionem, citra fidei et religionis iniuriam tueri possunt regna, explorari consilia, vinci hostes, eripi captivi, adaugeri divitiae, conciliari hominum benevolentia, depelli aegritudines, conservari sanitas, prolongari vita, restitui iuventutis robur. Sunt insuper sacrae religionis intercessiones, publicae supplicationes, privatae bonorum preces, quibus non solum iram dei flectere, sed et simul illum nobis beneficum impetrare possumus.

Quod si praeterea ars quaedam est praescientiae et mirandorum operum, quam Calo magiam sive Theurgiam veteres vocant, certe haec istis nugatoribus et daemoniorum mancipiis incognita est. Quippe explorare de futuris aut imminentibus aliisve occultis, et quae hominibus divinitus portenduntur veridicas sententias, atque operari opera virtutum communem naturae consuetudinem excedentia, non nisi profundae et perfectae doctrinae, integerrimaeque vitae ac fidei est, non hominum levissimorum ac indoctorum. Hominibus autem innocentibus et doctis in lege Domini,

Diotharus, Croesus, Pompey, Pyrrhus, Crassus, Nero, Julian – what did they gain from their magicians and diviners, who falsely promised them prosperity? Did they not all come to nothing and perish miserably in their sins? In this way, such impious trifles always bring ruin to their followers, and those who place the greatest trust in them become the most unfortunate of all. I do not deny that there are natural sciences, metaphysical arts, and hidden talents, which, without offending God or harming faith and religion, can be used to defend kingdoms, uncover counsels, defeat enemies, free captives, increase wealth, win human favor, drive away sickness, preserve health, prolong life, and restore the vigor of youth.[221] Moreover, there are intercessions of sacred religion, public supplications, and private prayers of the good, by which not only can we turn aside God's wrath, but also obtain His favor and blessings.

Moreover, if there is a certain art of foreknowledge and miraculous works, which the ancients called celestial magic or theurgy, surely this is unknown to those triflers and slaves of demons. Indeed, to explore the future or imminent matters, or other hidden things, and to provide truthful judgements about those things divinely foretold to men, and to perform works of power that exceed the common course of nature – this belongs only to profound and perfect knowledge, to those of the most upright life and faith, not to the most frivolous and unlearned men. But to innocent and learned men in the law of the Lord,

---

[221] Cf. Attrell and Porreca, *Picatrix*, p. 16-26.

pro voto fidei servit omnis creatura, et exaudiuntur ad quaecunque petierint. Sic Heliam corvus pavit, et ad preces eius terra fructus retinet, coelum negat pluviam, et in impios evomit ignes suos. Sic Helisaeo serviunt ursi, militant angeli, flumina siccis transeuntur pedibus. Danieli posita ferocitate neglectaque fama adblandiuntur leones: Et succensus in fornace ignis non urit pueros. Eiusmodi sunt non cacomagorum, non goeticorum, non daemoniorum, sed fidelium divinorumque hominum opera: non enim daemones, sed spiritus Dei ministrant illis.

Sunt fateor aliqui, etiam in hunc diem (et forte plures) viri sapientia graves, scientia insignes, virtutibus et potestatibus pollentes, vita et moribus integri, prudentia invicti, etiam aetate et robore dispositi, ut reipublicae consilio et opera plurimum possint prodesse: sed hos aulici vestri contemnunt, ut ab instituto eorum longe diversos, quibus pro sapientia malitia est, fraus et [351] dolus pro consilio, astus

all creation serves at the command of their faith, and they are heard in whatever they ask. Thus, a raven fed Elijah, and at his prayers the earth withheld its fruit, the heavens denied rain, and upon the wicked it spewed forth its fires.[222] Thus, bears serve Elisha, angels fight, and rivers are crossed with dry feet.[223] The lions, having set aside their ferocity and fame, fawned over Daniel; and the fire lit in the furnace does not burn the youths.[224] Such are neither the works of evil sorcerers, nor of goetic practitioners, nor of demons, but of faithful and divine men: for it is not demons, but the spirits of God who minister to them.[225]

I admit that even today (and perhaps more than before), there are men of great wisdom, notable for their knowledge, powerful in virtues and abilities, upright in life and morals, invincible in prudence, and even strong in age and constitution, who can greatly benefit the state with their counsel and deeds. But your courtiers despise these men, as being far removed from their way of thinking, for in their minds, malice stands in place of wisdom, fraud and deceit in place of counsel, craftiness

---

[222] See I Kings 17:4-6 for Elijah and the ravens; I Kings 17:1; James 5:17 for Elijah's prayer for a three-and-a-half-year drought; and 2 Kings 1:10-12 for fire from heaven.

[223] See II Kings 2:23-24 for the bears that maul a crowd of forty-two boys that mock Elisha for his baldness; II Kings 19:35 for the angel of the Lord who slays eighty-five thousand Assyrians; and Exodus 14:29 for the Hebrews crossing the Red Sea.

[224] Daniel 6:1-28 and 3:1-30.

[225] Cf. Matthew 4:11 and Hebrews 1:14.

et calliditas pro scientia, deceptio et perfidia pro prudentia est. Regionis locum possidet superstitio, et in afflictionibus blasphematur Deus: et quae (ut ait Apostolus) in infirmitate perficitur fides, contemnitur: sed recurritur ad invocamenta malorum daemonum. Bonus quisque apud eos irridetur, audax hypocritis provehitur, veritas pro crimine est, laus et praemia stultitiae et sceleribus reposita sunt.

O stulti et impii, qui his artibus stabilire vultis regnum, quibus olim potentissima imperia ceciderunt funditusque eversa sunt. De quibus vere dictum est per Hieremiam: Cecidit corona nostra, vae quia peccavimus. Quod utinam non tam vere quam excogitata ingeniosa forte in vos quadraret. Siquidem ille versiculus collectis invicem numerabilibus literis. M.C.V.I. annum exprimit M.D.XXIIII. quo iuxta vestrum calculum, rex vester apud Papiam captus est. Nonne haec vidistis et admirati estis, quae ante facta quam fuissent impossibilia iudicastis? Et adhuc superbistis et obdurati estis in infelicitatibus vestris. Contemnitis prophetas, et Dei comminationes vobis pro fabulis sunt. En prope est, et adhuc videbitis et sentietis magnalia Dei in orbe terrarum, et collapsi in fata contremiscetis, quia veniet super vos repente miseria

and cunning in place of knowledge, and deception and treachery in place of prudence. Superstition holds place in the land, and in hardships, God is blasphemed; and that faith which (as the Apostle says) is made perfect in weakness, is scorned: but recourse is made to the invocations of evil demons. Any good man is ridiculed by them; the reckless is promoted by hypocrites; truth is treated as a crime; and praise and rewards are reserved for folly and wickedness.

O foolish and wicked ones, who wish to stabilize your kingdom by means of these arts, by which long ago the most powerful empires have fallen and been utterly overthrown. Of which it was truly said by Jeremiah: "our crown has fallen, woe to us because we have sinned!"[226] Would that this did not apply to you as truly as it fits by ingenious design! Indeed, that verse, when the letters are calculated and added together, expresses the year 1524, in which, according to your calculation, your king was captured at Pavia. Did you not see these things and wonder at them – things you thought impossible before they happened? And even now you remain proud and hardened in your misfortunes.[227] You scorn the prophets, and God's warnings are like fables to you. Behold, it is nigh, and soon you will see and feel the great works of God around the whole world, and, collapsing into ruin, you will tremble at fate, for misery will come upon you suddenly,

---

[226] Lamentations 5:16.

[227] The language here echoes Exodus 7:13-8:19 with the hardening of Pharaoh's heart in the face of the catastrophes brought about by the ten plagues of Egypt.

quam nescitis: quo tunc fugietis? State cum incantatoribus vestris et cum multitudine maleficiorum vestrorum, si forte quid prosint vobis, aut possitis fieri fortiores. Nonne accersitus Germanicus cacomagus salvabit vos, et mendaces faciet prophetas, ac praevalebit contra iram domini, et liberabit vos a malo? Non sic impii non sic. Nisi dominus aedificaverit et custodierit civitates et regnum, in vanum laborant et vigilant omnes custodes eius. Solius Dei est, non daemonum, non magorum, suspendere aut mutare prophetarum sententiam: si vos toto corde conversi ad eius misericordiam, vestram mutaveritis malitiam atque perfidiam. Sic nanque Nabuchodonosor Danielis consilio peccata eleemosynis redimens, et iniquitates in misericordiis pauperum; imminentem Dei iram ad tempus effugit, donec in aula Babylonis voce elationis suae rursus illam in se revocavit. Achab impiissimus cum sua Iezabele, cui mortem per Heliam dominus nunciavit, quia conversus est ad Deum, sanctus est iterum sermo domini ad Heliam: Quia reveritus est Achab faciem meam, non inducam malum in diebus eius. Ninivitae quia ex edicto regis et principum egerunt poenitentiam ad praedicatione Ionae, ab imminenti protinus excidio liberati sunt. Intimavit Esaias Ezechiae sententiam, ut disponeret domui suae cito moriturus: Ille oravit et flevit, et sanatus est, adauctis ei annis vitae quindecim: Sic enim ad eum per eundem prophetam locutus est dominus:

and you will not know from where: where then will you flee? Stand with your enchanters and with the multitude of your sorceries, if perhaps they might help you, or you might be made stronger. Will your summoned German sorcerer not save you? Will he make the prophets liars? Will he prevail against the Lord's wrath, and deliver you from evil? Not so, wicked ones, not so. Unless the Lord builds and guards our cities and our kingdom, all its guardians labor and watch in vain.[228] It is God alone, not demons or magicians, who has the power to suspend or change the will of the prophets – if you with your whole heart turn to His mercy, and change your wickedness and treachery. Thus, by the counsel of Daniel, Nebuchadnezzar redeemed his sins with alms, and his iniquities with mercy toward the poor; he escaped the imminent wrath of God for a time, until in the court of Babylon, by the voice of his pride, he again called it upon himself. The most impious Ahab, with his Jezebel, to whom the Lord announced death through Elijah, when he turned to God, the word of the Lord came again to Elijah, saying: "because Ahab has humbled himself before me, I will not bring evil in his days."[229] The Ninevites, because they repented at the preaching of Jonah by the decree of the king and his nobles, were immediately delivered from impending destruction. Isaiah announced to Hezekiah the sentence that he should set his house in order, as he would soon die; but he prayed and wept, and was healed, with fifteen years added to his life. For thus did the Lord speak

[228] Psalm 127:1 (Vulg. 126:1).
[229] I Kings 21:29.

Vidi lachrymas tuas, et exaudivi orationem tuam: ecce ego adiiciam super dies tuos quindecim annos. Insuper et de manu regis Assyriorum eruam te, et civitatem istam, et protegam eam. Tantum potuit conversio et oratio pii regis, ut qui pro se solo oravit, tamen non pro se solo impetravit, sed etiam pro civitate et populo. Solus dominus est qui salvum fecit regem, [352] et qui sapientiam dat filio regis. Ad hunc magistrum confugere oportet, qui quaerunt salutem, non ad magos et ariolos.

Induimini iustitiam, et timete dominum, vos qui quaeritis felicia. Si regni firmitas quaeritur, scriptum est: Iusti haereditabunt terram. In memoria aeterna erit iustus, et in aeternum non commovebitur. Si securitas quaeritur: Qui timent dominum, ab auditione mala non timebunt, sed et omnes despicient inimicos. Si honor et opes quaeruntur: Gloria et divitiae in domo eius. Si laus et favor: Generatio rectorum benedicetur. Si potentia: Potens erit in terra ipse et semen eius:

to him through the same prophet: "I have seen your tears and have heard your prayer; behold, I will add fifteen years to your life. Moreover, I will deliver you from the hand of the king of the Assyrians, as well as this city, and I will protect it."[230] Such was the power of the conversion and prayer of the pious king, that although he prayed for himself alone, he nevertheless procured favor not only for himself but also for the city and the people. It is the Lord alone who saved the king, and who gives wisdom to the king's son. It is to this master that one seeking salvation ought to flee, not to magicians and soothsayers.

Clothe yourselves in righteousness and fear the Lord, you who seek happiness.[231] If the stability of the kingdom is sought, it is written: "the righteous will inherit the land."[232] "The righteous will be in everlasting remembrance, and he will not be moved forever."[233] If security is sought: "those who fear the Lord will not fear bad news, but will look down upon all their enemies."[234] If honor and wealth are sought: "glory and riches are in his house."[235] If praise and favor: "the generation of the upright will be blessed."[236] If power: "he and his seed will be mighty upon

---

[230] II Kings 20:6.

[231] Colossians 3:12; Proverbs 9:10.

[232] Psalm 37:29 (Vulg. 36:29).

[233] Psalm 112:6 (Vulg. 111:6).

[234] Psalm 112:8 (Vulg. 111:8).

[235] Psalm 112:3 (Vulg. 111:3).

[236] Psalm 112:2 (Vulg. 111:2).

fortitudo eius exaltabitur in gloria. Si nuptiae et coniugii prosperitas: Uxor eius sicut vitis habundans in lateribus domus, et filii eius sicut novellae olivarum. Si corporis sanitas et robur: Non dabit dominus sanctos suos videre corruptionem. In omnibus denique beatus est, qui timet dominum, qui immaculatus in via, qui non abiit in consilio impiorum, qui miseretur super egenum et pauperem: nam in die mala liberabit eum dominus, et non tradet eum in manu inimicorum eius: peccatores autem videbunt et irascentur, dentibus frement et tabescent, desiderium eorum peribit. Haec nunc admonuisse satis. Nolo enim curiosius hanc rem prosequi, ne forte malitia subiectae materiae calamum protrudat quo non expedit.

Vale ex Lutetia Parisiorum XIII. Februarii Anno. M. D. XXVIII. Romano calculo.

the earth; his strength will be exalted in glory."[237] If marriage and prosperity in wedlock: "his wife will be like a fruitful vine on the sides of the house, and his sons like olive shoots."[238] If health and strength of the body: "the Lord will not allow His holy ones to see corruption."[239] Finally, blessed in all things is the man who fears the Lord, who is blameless in his way, who has not walked in the counsel of the ungodly, who has mercy upon the needy and poor.[240] For in the day of trouble, the Lord will deliver him, and He will not give him over into the hand of his enemies. But the wicked will see and be enraged, they will gnash their teeth and waste away; their desire will perish.[241] I think I have now said enough on this matter, for I do not wish to pursue it further, lest perhaps the malice of the subject at hand might push the pen where it ought not to go.

Farewell from Paris, February 13, 1528, according to the Roman calendar.

---

[237] Psalm 112:2 (Vulg. 111:2).

[238] Psalm 128:3 (Vulg. 127:3).

[239] Psalm 16:10.

[240] Psalm 1:1, 41:1 (Vulg. 40:1), and 112:1 (Vulg. 111:1).

[241] Psalm 112:10 (Vulg. 111:10).

Censura sive retractatio de magia ex sua declamatione de Vanitate scientiarum et excellentia Verbi dei

DE MAGIA IN GENERE

Exigit etiam hic locus, ut de Magia dicamus, nam et ipsa cum astrologia sic coniuncta atque cognata est, ut qui magiam sine astrologia profiteatur, is nihil agat, sed tota aberret via. Suidas magiam a Magusaeis, et nomen, et originem traxisse putat. Communis opinio est nomen esse Persicum, cui astipulantur Porphyrius et Apuleius, et significare eorum lingua idem quod sacerdotem, sapientem sive philosophum. Magia itaque omnem philosophiam, physicam, et mathematicam complexa, etiam uires religionum illis adiungit. Hinc et goetiam et theurgiam in se quoque continet. Qua de causa magiam plerique bifariam dividunt in naturalem uidelicet et ceremonialem.

Critique or Retraction on Magic from His Declamation on the Vanity of the Sciences and the Excellence of the Word of God (1533)

ON MAGIC IN GENERAL

This topic also requires us to speak about magic, for it itself is also so closely connected and related to astrology that anyone who professes magic without astrology accomplishes nothing and strays completely from the path. Suidas believes that magic took both its name and origin from the Magi. The common opinion is that the name is Persian, which Porphyry and Apuleius support, and that in their language, it signifies the same as priest, wise man, or philosopher. Magic, therefore, having encompassed all philosophy, physics, and mathematics, also adds to them the powers of religions. Hence, it also contains within itself both goetia and theurgy. For this reason, many divide magic into two kinds, namely natural and ceremonial.[242]

---

[242] Giambattista della Porta, *Natural Magick*, p. 1-2 draws closely and extensively from this section of Agrippa's *De incertitudine* to introduce his own treatment of natural magic.

DE MAGIA NATURALI

Naturalem magiam, non aliud putant, quam naturalium scientiarum summam potestatem, quam idcirco summum philosophiae naturalis apicem, eiusque absolutissimam consummationem vocant, et quae sit activa portio philosophiae naturalis, quae naturalium [353] virtutum adminiculo, ex mutua earum et opportuna applicatione opera edit, supra omnem admirationis captum: qua magia Aethiopes maxime et Indi utebantur, ubi herbarum et lapidum, et caeterorumque ad id spectantium facultas suppetebat. Eius memimisse uolunt Hieronymum ad Paulinum, ubi ait Apollonium Tyaneum fuisse magum, seu philosophum, ut Pythagorici. Eius etiam generis fuisse magos, qui Christum natum muneribus invisentes adoraverunt, quos evangeliorum interpretes exponunt Chaldaeorum philosophos: quales fuere Hiarchas apud Bragmanas, Tespion apud Gymnosophistas, Budda apud Babylonios, Numa Pompilius apud Romanos,

ON NATURAL MAGIC

They consider natural magic to be nothing other than the highest power of the natural sciences, which they therefore call the supreme peak of natural philosophy and its most perfect consummation. It is the active part of natural philosophy, which, through the aid of natural virtues and the mutual and timely application of these virtues, performs works beyond all comprehension of admiration. This magic was particularly used by the Ethiopians and the Indians, where the knowledge of herbs, stones, and other related faculties was available for this purpose.[243] It is said that Jerome mentioned it in his letter to Paulinus, where he states that Apollonius of Tyana was a magician, or rather, a philosopher, like the Pythagoreans.[244] It is also said that the Magi, who visited the newborn Christ with gifts and adored Him, were of this kind.[245] These the interpreters of the Gospels explain as philosophers of the Chaldeans. Of such kind were Hiarchas among the Brahmins, Tespion among the Gymnosophists, Budda among the Babylonians, Numa Pompilius among the Romans,

---

[243] Cf. *Picatrix* 2.5.1 (Attrell and Porreca, *Picatrix*, p. 84).

[244] Jerome, *Letter* 53.1: "Apollonius too was a traveller – the one I mean who is called the sorcerer by ordinary people and the philosopher by such as follow Pythagoras. He entered Persia, traversed the Caucasus and made his way through the Albanians, the Scythians, the Massagetae, and the richest districts of India."

[245] Matthew 2:1-12.

Zalmoxides apud Thracas, Abbaris apud Hyperboreos, Hermes apud Aegyptios, Zoroastes Oromasi filius apud Persas. Nam Indi, et Aethiopes, et Chaldaei, et Persae hac maxime praecelluere magia: qua idcirco (ut narrat Plato in Alcibiade) imbuuntur Persarum regum filii, ut ad mundanae reipublicae imaginem suam et ipsi rempublicam administrare, distribuereque condiscant, et Cicero in Divinationum libris ait, neminem apud Persas regno potiri, qui prius magiam non didicerit.

Zalmoxis among the Thracians, Abaris among the Hyperboreans, Hermes among the Egyptians, and Zoroaster, the son of Oromasius, among the Persians. For the Indians, Ethiopians, Chaldeans, and Persians particularly excelled in this magic, which is why (as Plato narrates in the *Alcibiades*) the sons of the kings of the Persians are imbued with it so that they may learn to govern and manage their republic according to the image of the world's republic.[246] Cicero, in his books *On Divination*, says that no one among the Persians could attain the throne without first learning magic.[247]

---

[246] Plato, *Alcibiades I*, 121e-122a: "When the boys are seven years old, they are given horses and have riding lessons, and they begin to follow the chase. And when the boy reaches fourteen years he is taken over by the royal tutors, as they call them there: these are four men chosen as the most highly esteemed among the Persians of mature age, namely, the wisest one, the justest one, the most temperate one, and the bravest one. The first of these teaches him the magian lore of Zoroaster, son of Horomazes; and that is the worship of the gods: he teaches him also what pertains to a king. The justest teaches him to be truthful all his life long; the most temperate, not to be mastered by even a single pleasure, in order that he may be accustomed to be a free man and a veritable king, who is the master first of all that is in him, not the slave; while the bravest trains him to be fearless and undaunted, telling him that to be daunted is to be enslaved."

[247] Cicero, *De divinatione*, 1.90-91: "Among the Persians the augurs and diviners are the magi, who assemble regularly in a sacred place for practice and consultation, just as formerly you augurs used to do on the Nones. Indeed, no one can become

Magia itaque naturalis ea est, quae rerum omnium naturalium atque coelestium vires contemplata, earundemque sympathiam curiosa indagine scrutata, reconditas ac latentes in natura potestates ita in apertum producit: inferiora superiorum dotibus, tanquam quasdam illecebras, sic copulans, per eorum mutuam applicationem ad invicem, ut exinde stupenda saepe consurgant miracula, non tam arte quam natura, cui se ars ista ministram exhibet haec operanti. Nam magi, ut naturae accuratissimi exploratores, conducentes ea, quae a natura praeparata sunt, applicando activa passivis, saepissime ante tempus a natura ordinatum effectus producunt, quae vulgus putat miracula, cum tamen naturalia opera sint, interveniente sola temporis praeventione: ut si quis in mense Martio rosas producat, et maturas uvas, aut satas fabas, vel petroselinum intra paucas horas excrescere faciat in perfectam plantam, et iis maiora, ut nubes, pluvias, tonitrua, et diversorum generum animalia, et rerum transmutationes quam plurimas, cuiusmodi multas fecisse se iactat Rogerius Bachon pura et naturali magia.

---

king of the Persians until he has learned the theory and the practice of the magi."

Thus natural magic is that which, having contemplated the forces of all natural and celestial things, and having carefully investigated their sympathy through diligent inquiry, brings forth into the open the hidden and latent powers in nature: thus combining lower things with the qualities of higher ones, as though by certain allurements, through their mutual application to one another, such that astounding miracles often arise from them, not so much by art as by nature, to which this art presents itself as a servant to the one performing the work. For magicians, as the most meticulous explorers of nature, by using what has been prepared by nature, most frequently produce effects before their time ordained by nature by applying active things to passive ones, which the common people believe to be miracles, although they are natural works, with only the intervention of temporal acceleration, like if someone were to produce roses and mature grapes in the month of March, or cause sown beans or parsley to grow into a complete plant within a few hours, and even greater things, like clouds, rain, thunder, various kinds of animals, and numerous transmutations of things, of the kind which Roger Bacon boasts to have performed with pure and natural magic.

Scripserunt de illius operibus Zoroastes, Hermes, Euanthes rex Arabum, Zacharias Babylonius, Ioseph Hebraeus, Bocus, Aaron, Zenotenus, Kirannides[248], Almadal[249], Thetel[250], Alchindus[251], Abel, Ptolemaeus, Geber, Zahel, Nazabarub, Tebith, Berith, Solomon, Astaphon, Hipparchus, Alcmaeon, Apollonius, Triphon,

---

[248] A Hermetic text, the *Kyranides* (Greek: Κυρανίδες), rather than an individual. It is a compilation of magical and medical knowledge containing information on natural remedies, magical stones, and talismans, and was translated into Latin by Pascal the Roman during the reign of the 12th-century Byzantine Emperor, Manuel I Komnenos.

[249] Again, not an individual, but a reference to the *Ars Almandal Salomonis*, a magical text containing instructions on how to build a portable altar with four candles and a wax tablet used for summoning spirits in the smoke of suffumigation. See Regan, "The *De consecratione lapidum*: A Previously Unknown Thirteenth-Century Version of the Liber Almandal Salomonis," p. 277-333 and the digital edition of the *Ars Almadel* by Joseph Peterson (esotericarchives.com/solomon/almadel.htm) who writes:" in addition to the unique version published by Vajra Regan, two main versions are known, distinguished as *Almandal* and *Almadel*. The former is closer to the Arabic source, while the latter apparently represents a significant revision and Christianization of the text."

[250] Possibly Techel, author of the *Liber Sigillorum*. See Ockenström and Regan, "The Hermetic Origins of the Liber sigillorum of Techel," p. 173-266.

[251] I.e. the 9th century Arab philosopher Al-Kindi, though in this context, it is likely Agrippa is referring to the *De radiis stellarum* which is now believed to be only pseudepigraphically attributed to Al-Kindi; see Matton, "D'un rayonnement des grammairiens latins ou le *De radiis* n'est pas d'al-Kindi," p. 443-456.

Zoroaster, Hermes, Evanthes, king of the Arabs, Zacharias the Babylonian, Joseph the Hebrew, Bocus, Aaron, Zenotenus, Kyranides, Almadal, Thetel, Al-Kindi, Abel, Ptolemy[252], Geber[253], Zahel[254], Nazabarub, Tebith[255], Berith[256], Solomon, Astaphon, Hipparchus, Alcmaeon[257], Apollonius, Triphon, and many others wrote on works of

---

[252] I.e., Claudius Ptolemaeus (c. 100 - c. 170 AD) was an Alexandrian mathematician, astronomer, geographer, and astrologer, whose works became highly influential in both the medieval Islamic world and Europe. He is best known for his treatise on astronomy, the *Almagest*, which outlined the geocentric model of the universe, as well as his *Tetrabiblos*, in which he systematized the principles of Hellenistic astrology within a natural philosophical framework. Most relevant here is the *Centiloquium*, which is a collection of a hundred aphorisms of astrological wisdom and practical insight pseudepigraphically attributed to Ptolemy.

[253] I.e., Jabir ibn Hayyan, the most influential (and mysterious) of all the Arab alchemists.

[254] A.k.a. Zehel, i.e., Sahl ibn Bishr al-Israili, an 8-9th century astrologer and polymath whose work was translated into Latin by John of Seville in the 12th century and from there found its way into works such as the *Liber hermetis de sex principium rerum*. Possibly even the same author as 'Techel' mentioned earlier in the list.

[255] I.e., Thabit ibn Qurra, the Sabian mathematician, physician, and astronomer from Harrān who authored a work of astrological magic that circulated throughout Europe as the Latin *De Imaginibus*.

[256] Uncertain identity, but in some magical traditions, "Berith" is associated with a demon or a spirit in the *Goetia*. The god Baal Berith is also mentioned in Judges 8:33, 9:4, and 9:46.

[257] I.e., Alcmaeon of Croton, the Ancient Greek natural philosopher and alleged disciple of Pythagoras.

et plerique alii, quorum aliqua opera adhuc integra, et pleraque fragmenta adhuc extant, et ad manus meas aliquando pervenerunt. Ex recentioribus vero scripserunt in naturali magia pauci, et illi quidem pauca, ut Albertus[258], Arnoldus de Villanova[259], Raimundus Lullius, Bachon, et Apponus, et autor libri, ad Alfonsum, sub Picatricis nomine editus, qui tamen una cum naturali magia plurimum superstitionis admiscet, quod quidem fecerunt et alii.

---

[258] While this attribution is now doubted, Albertus Magnus was long thought to be responsible for composing the *Speculum Astronomiae* in defence of astrology as a science compatible with Christian doctrine. Aside from this attribution, Albertus wrote many works on natural philosophy like *De re metallica*, leading to his association with many spurious alchemical and magical texts.

[259] A medieval alchemist, physician, and apocalyptic thinker known to have made use of talismanic images in his medical practice. See *Picatrix* 2.12.44 (Attrell and Porreca, *Picatrix*, 59) for the golden image of Leo he used to treat Pope Boniface VIII's kidney stones. Arnald's failed astrological predictions also earned him some opprobrium from Giovanni Pico della Mirandola in his *Disputationes adversus astrologiam divinatricem* (*Opera omnia*, p. 551: "*Arnaldus Hispanus, nobilis quidem medicus, sed ad superstitiones Paulo nimis propensius ex astrologica vanitate, plerisque aliis adiectis, Antichristum nobis anno gratiae 1345 comminabatur.*" ["Arnaldus of Spain, indeed a noble physician, but somewhat too inclined to superstitions due to astrological vanity, along with several other things, was threatening us with the Antichrist in the year of grace 1345."]

this kind, some of whose whole works, and some fragmentary, are extant to this day, and have at times come into my possession. Among more recent authors, few have written on natural magic, and those few have written little, such as Albert, Arnald of Villanova, Raymond Llull[260], [Roger] Bacon[261], and [Pietro] d'Abano[262], and the author of the book addressed to [King] Alfonso, published under the name *Picatrix*, who nevertheless mixes in a great deal of superstition with natural magic, as indeed others have also done.[263]

---

[260] The so-called *doctor illuminatus*, Ramon Llull was a Majorcan polymath and Franciscan tertiary who wrote on a great variety of philosophical works, upon some of which Agrippa has left us commentaries. Nevertheless, Llull was also subject to numerous pseudepigraphically-attributed works on alchemy, magic, and Cabala (e.g., *De auditu kabbalistico; sive, ad omnes scientias introductorium*, first printed in Venice, 1518). See Blau, "Appendix B: Was Raymond Lull a Cabalist?" in *The Christian Interpretation of the Cabala*, p. 117-118.

[261] I.e., Roger Bacon, the 13th-century English philosopher and Franciscan friar who produced an edited and annotated manuscript of the Latin *Secretum secretorum* (or *Sirr al-Asrar*), a pseudo-Aristotelian 'mirror for princes' which deals in part with Hermetic and magical themes. See Roger Bacon, *Secretum Secretorum*, p. 1-175.

[262] An Italian philosopher and physician attributed with the authorship of such magical works as the *Heptameron*, a work with ritual instructions for the conjuration of angels.

[263] Authors left unglossed in this section are either unknown (e.g., Bocus, Nazabarub, Astaphon), or known well-enough not to merit an explanatory note (e.g., Zoroaster, Hermes, Solomon).

DE MAGIA MATHEMATICA

Sunt praeterea alii naturae sagacissimi aemulatores, inquisitoresque audacissimi, qui absque naturalibus virtutibus, ex solis mathematicis disciplin[354]is, adscitis coelorum influxibus, sese naturae operum similia producere posse pollicentur, ut corpora euntia vel loquentia, quae tamen non habeant virtutes animales: qualis fuit columba Architae lignea, quae uolabat, et statuae Mercurii, quae loquebantur: et caput aeneum ab Alberto Magno fabricatum, quod locutum perhibent. Excelluit in istis Boethius, vir maximus ingenii, et multiplicis eruditionis: ad quem de istiusmodi scribens Cassiodorus: Tibi (inquit) ardua cognoscere, et miracula monstrare propositum est: tuae artis ingenio metalla mugiunt, Diomedes in aere gravius buccinatur, aeneus anguis insibilat, aves simulatae sunt, et quae vocem propriam nesciunt habere, dulcedinem cantilenae probantur emittere, parva de illo referimus, cui coelum imitari phas est. De istis puto artificiis dictum est, quod apud Platonem legimus in undecimo *de Legibus*: Ars data est mortalibus, qua res posteriores quasdam generarent, non quidem veritatis et divinitatis participes, sed simulacra quaedam sibiipsis cognata deducerent: atque eo usque progressi sunt magi homines audacissimi omnia perpetrare, favente maxime antiquo illo et valido serpente

ON MATHEMATICAL MAGIC

There are, moreover, other very wise imitators and very bold investigators of nature, who, without relying on natural powers, promise that they can produce works similar to those of nature using only the mathematical disciplines and the influences of the heavens, such as moving or speaking bodies that still do not possess animal life, like the wooden dove of Archytas that could fly, the statues of Mercurius that could speak, and the brazen head made by Albertus Magnus, which is said to have spoken. Boethius, a man of great talent and diverse learning, excelled in these matters. Writing to him about such things, Cassiodorus said: "it is your purpose to know the difficult and to reveal marvels: through the ingenuity of your art, metals bellow; Diomedes in brass sounds his horn more powerfully; a brazen serpent hisses; birds are counterfeited; and those things that do not know how to produce their own voice are shown to emit the sweetness of song." Here we are merely talking about the little things done by a man for whom it is lawful to imitate the heavens. I believe these artifices are what we read about in the eleventh book of *The Laws* according to Plato: art was given to mortals that they might create some inferior things, not indeed participants in truth and divinity, but that they might bring forth certain images akin to themselves. And so the boldest of magi have advanced to the point where they attempt to accomplish everything, aided especially by that ancient and powerful serpent, the

scientiarum pollicitatore, ut similes illi tanquam simiae, deum et naturam aemulari conarentur.

promiser of sciences, so that they, like apes, would attempt to ape God and nature.

DE MAGIA VENEFICA

Est praeterea naturalis magiae species, quam veneficiam, sive pharmaciam vocant, quae poculis, phyltris, variisque veneficiorum medicamentis perficitur: cuiusmodi Democritus confecisse legitur, quo boni felices, fortunatique filii gignantur: et aliud, quo avium uoces rite intelligamus, sicut de Apollonio narrant Philosostratus atque Porphyrius. Vergilius etiam de quibusdam herbis Ponticis locutus dixit:

His ego saepe lupum fieri, et se condere sylvis
Moerim, saepe animas imis exire sepulchris,
Atque satas alio vidi traducere messis.

Et Plinius narrat, quendam Demarchum Parrhassium in sacrificio, quod Arcades Iovi Lycaeo humana hostia faciebant, immolati pueri exta degustasse, et in lupum se convertisse: propter quam hominem in lupos immutationem, putat Augustinus Pani Lycaeo, et Iovi Lycaeo nomen esse impositum. Narrat idem Augustinus, dum esset in Italia, quasdam

ON WITCHCRAFT

There is a type of natural magic, which they call witchcraft (*veneficium*) or *pharmakeia*, which is accomplished through potions, philters, and various poisonous drugs. Democritus is said to have prepared something of this kind, by which good, happy, and fortunate children are born; and another, by which we might rightly understand the calls of birds, just as Philostratus and Porphyry recount about Apollonius.[264] Virgil also spoke of certain Pontic herbs and said:

By these I've often seen Moeris become a wolf
and hide himself in the woods; often souls I've seen
rise from deep graves, and crops transplanted elsewhere.[265]

Pliny also recounts that a certain Damarchus of Parrhasia, during the sacrifice that the Arcadians made to Jupiter Lycaeus with a human victim, tasted the entrails of the sacrificed boy and turned into a wolf: Augustine thinks that the name Pan Lycaeus and Jupiter Lycaeus were given on account of this transformation of a man into a wolf.[266] Augustine also recounts how, while he was in Italy, certain

---

[264] Philostratus, *Life of Apollonius of Tyana*, 4.3.

[265] Here Virgil makes reference to a law in the Twelve Tables of Rome which forbade the use of magic for transferring crops from one farmer's field to another's. See Pliny, *Naturalis Historia*, 28.4.

[266] Augustine, *De civitate Dei*, 18.17: "In support of this story, Varro relates others no less incredible about that most famous

foeminas magas, Circes instar, dato viatoribus veneficio in caseo, eos in iumenta vertisse: cumque portassent quae placuissent onera, rursus in homines restituisse, idque patri cuidam Praestantio tunc accidisse. Sed et ne quis haec putet omnino deliramenta esse et impossibilia, is recodetur quomodo sacrae litterae narrant, Nabuchodonosor regem mutatum in bovem, et septem annis foeno vixisse, tandemque Dei misericordia in hominem rediisse: cuius corpus post mortem illius filius Euilmerodach in escam dedit vulturibus, ne quando resurgeret a mortuis, qui iam de bestia redierat in hominem, et eiusmodi plura de magis Pharaonis narrat Exodus. Verum de iis sive magis sive veneficis loquitur Sapiens,

---

sorceress Circe, who changed the companions of Ulysses into beasts, and about the Arcadians, who, by lot, swam across a certain pool, and were turned into wolves there, and lived in the deserts of that region with wild beasts like themselves. But if they never fed on human flesh for nine years, they were restored to the human form on swimming back again through the same pool. Finally, he expressly names one Demaenetus, who, on tasting a boy offered up in sacrifice by the Arcadians to their god Lycaeus according to their custom, was changed into a wolf, and, being restored to his proper form in the tenth year, trained himself as a pugilist, and was victorious at the Olympic games. And the same historian thinks that the epithet Lycaeus was applied in Arcadia to Pan and Jupiter for no other reason than this metamorphosis of men into wolves, because it was thought it could not be wrought except by a divine power. For a wolf is called in Greek λυκὸς, from which the name Lycaeus appears to be formed. He says also that the Roman Luperci were as it were sprung of the seed of these mysteries."

witch women, like Circe, gave poison in cheese to travelers, turning them into pack animals; and after they had carried what burdens they pleased, they turned them back into humans again, which happened to a certain Praestantius' father.[267] But so that no one thinks these are entirely delusions and impossible things, let him remember how the sacred scriptures recount that King Nebuchadnezzar was transformed into an ox, and for seven years lived on grass, and was finally turned back into a man by God's mercy: his son Evil-Merodach[268] fed his body to vultures after his death, so that he might never rise from the dead, having already returned from beast to man. The book of Exodus also recounts many such things about Pharaoh's magicians. Indeed, the Wise One speaks

---

[267] Augustine, *De civitate Dei*, 18.18: "For a certain man called Praestantius used to tell that it had happened to his father in his own house, that he took that poison in a piece of cheese, and lay in his bed as if sleeping, yet could by no means be aroused. But he said that after a few days he as it were woke up and related the things he had suffered as if they had been dreams, namely, that he had been made a sumpter horse, and, along with other beasts of burden, had carried provisions for the soldiers of what is called the Rhoetian Legion, because it was sent to Rhoetia. And all this was found to have taken place just as he told, yet it had seemed to him to be his own dream." Though this story sounds entirely fanciful, in more recent years, scopolamine and other tropane alkaloids derived from Datura and similar solanaceous plants have been used by prostitutes on unsuspecting johns to unwittingly clear out not only their bank accounts of funds, but even their apartments of furniture.

[268] I.e., Amel-Marduk, the third ruler of the Neo-Babylonian empire.

dum dicit: Exhorruisti illos deus, quia horribilia opera tibi faciebant per medicamina. Illud praeterea vos scire volo, non solum [355] naturalia scrutari hos magos, verum etiam ea quae naturam comitantur, ac quodammando exuunt, ut motus, numeros, figuras, sonos, uoces, concentus, lumina, et animi affectus atque verba. Sic Psylli et Marsi convocabant serpentes, alii aliis deprimentes fugabant: Sic Orpheus Argonautarum tempestatem hymno conpescuit: et Homerus narrat Ulyssi sanguinem uerbis restrictum: et lege duodecim tabularum iis qui messes excantassent, poena constituta est: ut non dubium sit, magos etiam solis verbis et affectibus, aliisque similibus, non in seipsos modo, sed etiam in res extraneas saepe mirum aliquem producere effectum: quae omnia non secus vim insitam in res alias profundere, illasque ad se trahere, vel abs se repellere, seu alio quovis modo afficere putant, quam magnes ferrum, et succinum paleas trahunt: sive adamas, et allium magnetem ligant: sicque per hanc rerum gradariam ac concatenatam sibi sympathiam, non solum dona naturalia et coelestia, sed etiam intellectualia et divina Iamblichus, Proclus, atque Synesius, ex magorum sententia, desuper suscipi posse confirmant, quod Proclus in libro de Sacrificio et Magia fatetur, scilicet per huiusmodi rerum consensum, magos etiam numina evocare solitos. Ad tantam enim quidam eorum devoluti sunt insaniam, ut ex diversis stellarum constellationibus, per temporum intervalla,

of these matters, whether of magicians or witches, when he says: "You abhorred them, O God, because they performed terrible deeds with drugs." Moreover, I want you to know that these magi not only investigate natural things but also those things that accompany nature, and, in a certain way, transcend it, such as motion, numbers, figures, sounds, voices, harmonies, lights, emotions, and words. Thus, the Psylli and Marsi summoned serpents, with some driving them away by suppressing others; thus Orpheus calmed the storm for the Argonauts with a hymn; Homer relates how Ulysses staunched blood with words; and by the law of the Twelve Tables, a penalty was established for those who enchanted crops. As such, there is no doubt that magicians can often produce some wondrous effect, not only from themselves but also from external things, through words, emotions, and other such means which they believe exert an inherent force on other things, drawing them to themselves or repelling them, or affecting them in some other way, just as a magnet attracts iron, or amber attracts chaff, or as diamond and garlic binds the magnet. And thus through this gradated and interconnected sympathy of things, Iamblichus, Proclus, and Synesius, according to the magicians' view, confirm that not only natural and celestial gifts but also intellectual and divine ones can be received from above, as Proclus admits in his book *On Sacrifice and Magic*, namely that through such agreement of things, magicians were accustomed to summon divine powers. Some of them, indeed, have fallen into such madness that they believe – from the various constellations of the stars, through intervals of

et quadam proportionum ratione rite observatis, constructam imaginem coelitum nutu vitae intellectusque spiritum accepturam putent, quo consulentibus illam respondeat, et occultae veritatis arcana revelet. Hinc patet haec naturalem magiam nonnunquam in goetiam et theurgiam renatam, saepissime malorum daemonum vaframentis, erroribusque, obretiri.

time, and by certain proportions duly observed – that an image they construct will receive a spirit of life and intellect by the will of the celestials, so that it might answer those who consult it and reveal the secrets of hidden truth. Hence it is evident that this natural magic sometimes transforms into goetia and theurgy, and most often becomes entangled with the tricks and errors of evil demons.

DE GOETIA ET NECROMANTIA

Ceremonialis autem magiae partes sunt goetia atque theurgia. Goetia, immundorum spirituum commerciis inauspicata, nefariae curiositatis ritibus, illicitis carminibus, et deprecamentis concinnata, omnium legum placitis est exterminata et execrata. Huius generis sunt, quos necromanticos et maleficos hodie nuncupamus.

Gens inuisa deis, maculandi callida coeli,
Quas genuit natura mali, qui sidera mundi,
Iuraque fixarum possunt peruertere rerum.
Nam nunc stare polos, et flumina mittere norunt,
Aethera sub terras adigunt, montesque revellunt.

Hi sunt ergo, qui defunctorum inclamant animas, et illi quos veteres dicebant epodos, qui excantant pueros, et in eloquium oraculi eliciunt, et qui daemones paredros circunferunt, quale quidam de Socrate legimus: et qui, ut dicitur, spiritus pascunt in vitro, per quos se prophetare mentiuntur. Et hi omnes bifariam procedunt. Nam alii daemones malos virtute quadam maxime divinorum nominum adiuratos, advocare et cogere student: quippe cum omnis creatura timet, et reveretur nomen illius, qui fecit eam, non mirum si goetici, et quique etiam infideles, pagani, Iudaei, Saraceni, et cuiuscunque prophani colle[356]gii sive sectae homines, divini nominis invocatione daemones adstringant. Alii autem nefandissimi, detestando et omnibus ignibus plectendo scelere, se

ON GOETIA AND NECROMANCY

The parts of ceremonial magic are goetia and theurgy. Goetia, inauspicious from its dealings with unclean spirits, is constructed through the rites of unlawful curiosity, illicit incantations, and supplications, and has been condemned and execrated by all the decrees of law. Those of this kind are what we today call necromancers and sorcerers.

A race hated by the gods, cunning in defiling the heavens,
whom the nature of evil has produced, who can overturn
The stars of the world and the laws of fixed things. For now they
know how to make the poles stand still, and to divert rivers,
They force the sky beneath the earth, and tear up mountains.

These are, therefore, those who call upon the souls of the dead, and those whom the ancients called *epodes*, who chant over boys and draw forth the utterance of an oracle, and who carry attendant demons around, such as we read of a certain Socrates: and who, as it is said, feed spirits in a glass, by which they falsely claim to prophesy. And all these proceed in two ways. For some strive to call up and compel evil demons by a certain power, especially by the adjurations of divine names: indeed, since all creation fears and reveres the name of the one who made it, it is no wonder if the goetic practitioners, along with the infidels, pagans, Jews, Saracens, and men of any profane group or sect, constrain demons by invoking the divine name. But others, most abominable, submitting themselves to

daemonibus submittentes, illis sacrificant et adorant, idololatrae et vilissimae deiectionis rei effecti sunt: quibus criminibus, etsi priores non sunt obnoxii, tamen manifestis periculis se exponunt. Nam etiam coacti daemones invigilant, semper quo errantes nos decipiant. Ex horum vero goeticorum anagyri, profluxerunt omnes isti tenebrarum libri, quos improbatae lectionis Ulpianus Iurisconsultus appellat, protinusque corrumpendos esse statuit.

Cuiusmodi primus excogitasse dicitur Zabulus quidam illicitis artibus deditus, deinde Barnabas quidam Cyprius: et hodie adhuc confictis titulis circumferuntur libri, sub nominibus Adae, Abelis, Enoch, Abrahae, Salomonis: item Pauli, Honorii, Cypriani, Alberti, Thomae, Hieronymi, et Eboracensis cuiusdam: quorum nugas stulte secuti sunt Alphonsus rex Castellae, Robertus Anglicus,

demons by committing a crime that is detestable and deserving of punishment by all fires, sacrifice to them and worship them, having become idolaters and guilty of the vilest defilement: even if they were not previously guilty of these crimes, they nevertheless expose themselves to manifest dangers. For even when compelled, demons are vigilant, always deceiving us as we go astray. Indeed, from the noxious fruits of these goetic practitioners have emerged all those books of shadows, which Ulpian the Jurist calls "disreputable reading," and decrees that they must be destroyed immediately.

The first to have invented such things is said to have been a certain Zabulus, devoted to illicit arts, and then a certain Barnabas of Cyprus; and even today, books with forged titles are circulated under the names of Adam, Abel, Enoch, Abraham, and Solomon; likewise, under the names of Paul, Honorius, Cyprian, Albert, Thomas, Jerome, and a certain man from York, whose nonsense Alphonso the King of Castile[269], Robert the Englishman[270],

---

[269] I.e., Alphonso X, "The Wise," patron of the translation of the Arabic astro-magical treatise, the *Ghāyat al-Hakīm*, into Castilian Spanish between 1256-1258, which was soon after translated into Latin; see *Picatrix* 1.1.1 (Attrell and Porreca, *Picatrix*, p. 37).

[270] This could refer to one of two different *Roberti Anglici*: either the 14th-century Dominican known for his *De Magia Caeremoniali*, *Correctorium Alchymiae*, and *De Mysteriis Secretorum* among other works, or alternatively the 13th-century astronomer known for his commentary on Sacrobosco's *De Sphera Mundi*, also credited (probably incorrectly) with

Bacon, et Apponus, et plerique alii deplorati ingenii homines. Praeterea non homines modo, et sanctos, et patriarchas, et angelos Dei tam execrabilium dogmatum fecerunt autores, sed et libros a Raziele et Raphaele, Adami et Tobiae, angelis traditos ostentant: qui libri tamen acutius inspicienti, suorum praeceptorum canonem, ritum, consuetudinem, verborum et charecterum genus, extructionis ordinem, insulsam phrasim, aperte sese produnt, non nisi meras nugas ac imposturas continere, ac posterioribus temporibus ab omnis antiquae magiae ignaris, perditissimis perditionum artificibus esse conflatatos, ex prophanis quibusdam observationibus nostrae religionis ceremoniis permixtis insitisque, ignotis multis nominibus, et signaculis, ut perterreant rudes et simplices, et stupori sint insensatis, et his qui nesciunt bonas literas.

Neque tamen propterea patet has artes fabulas esse: nam nisi re vera essent, atque per illas multa mira ac noxia fierent, non tam arcte de illis statuissent diuinae et humanae leges, eas exterminandas esse de terra. Cur autem goetici istis solis malis utantur daemonibus, ea ratio est, quia boni angeli difficilie comparent, quia Dei iussum expectant, nec nisi mundis corde et uita sanctis hominibus congrediuntur: mali autem faciles se exhibent ad

---

Alkindus de Judiciis ex Arabico Latinus factus per Robertum Anglicum anno Domini 1272.

Bacon, D'Abano, and many others of deplorable intellect foolishly followed. Moreover, not only have they made men, saints, patriarchs, and God's angels into authors of such execrable doctrines, but they also put out books supposedly handed down by Raziel and Raphael to Adam and Tobit. However, to one who looks more closely at these books – the rule of their teachings, the rite, the custom, the kind of words and characters, the order of construction, and the foolish phrasing – all these openly reveal themselves to contain nothing but pure nonsense and deceit. They were fabricated in more recent times by the most corrupt of all deceivers, who were entirely ignorant of ancient magic, and who mixed profane observations with the ceremonies of our religion, inserting many unknown names and seals to terrify the uneducated and simple, to astonish the senseless, and to deceive those who do not know good literature.

Yet it does not follow that these arts are mere fables: for if they were not real, and if through them many wondrous and harmful things were not accomplished, divine and human laws would not have so strictly decreed that they be eradicated from the earth. But the reason why goetic practitioners use only these evil demons is because good angels rarely appear, since they await the command of God, and they do not associate except with those who are pure in heart and holy in life: but the evil ones easily present themselves

invocandum, falso faventes, et divinitatem mentientes, semper praesto, ut astu suo decipiant, ut uenerentur, ut adorentur: et quia mulieres secretorum avidiores sunt, ac minus cautae, atque in superstitionem proclives, faciliusque illuduntur, ideo illis se praebent faciliores, faciuntque ingentia prodigia: cuiusmodi de Circe, de Medea, de aliis canunt poetae: testantur Cicero, Plinius, Seneca, Augustinus, et multi alii, tum philosophi, tum catholici doctores et historici, ipsae etiam sacrae literae. Nam in libris regum legimus Pythonissam mulierem, quae erat in Endor, evocasse animam Samuelis prophetae, licet plerique interpretentur non fuisse animam prophetae, sed malignum spiritum, qui illius sumpserit imaginem. Tamen Hebraeorum magistri dicunt, quod etiam Augustinus ad Simplicianum fieri potuisse non negat, quia fuerit verus spiritus Samuelis, qui ante completum annum a disces[357]su ex corpore facile euocari potuit, ut prout docent goetici. Quinetiam magi, necromantici, illud naturalibus quibusdam viribus ac uinculis fieri posse autumant, sicut nos in libris nostris de Occulta philosophia tractamus. Ideoque antiqui patres, rerum spiritualium periti, non sine causa ordinauerunt, ut corpora mortuorum sepelirentur in loco sacro, et luminibus socientur, aqua benedicta aspergantur, thure et incenso suffumigentur, et expientur orationibus quousque super terram extiterint.

when invoked, falsely appearing to give favor, and pretending divinity, always ready to deceive with their cunning, to be venerated, and to be worshiped.[271] And because women are more eager for secrets, less cautious, more inclined to superstition, and more easily deceived, they therefore make themselves more accessible to demons, and perform great wonders, of the sort that poets sing about Circe, Medea, and others, testified by Cicero, Pliny, Seneca, Augustine, and many others, both philosophers and Catholic doctors, and historians, and even by the Holy Scriptures themselves. For in the books of Kings we read that a woman, a Pythoness, who was in Endor, summoned the soul of the prophet Samuel, although many interpret that it was not the soul of the prophet, but an evil spirit who assumed his image. However, the Hebrew masters say, and even Augustine in his letter to Simplicianus does not deny that it could have happened, that it was indeed the true spirit of Samuel, who, before the completion of a year from his departure from the body, could easily be summoned, as the goetic practitioners teach. Moreover, magi and necromancers claim that this could be accomplished by certain natural forces and bonds, as we discuss in our books *On Occult Philosophy*. Therefore, the ancient fathers, skilled in spiritual matters, did not without reason ordain that the bodies of the dead be buried in a sacred place, and accompanied by lights, sprinkled with holy water, suffumigated with smoke and incense, and purified with prayers as long as they remain above the earth.

---

[271] Cf. Augustine, *De civitate Dei*, Chap. 9.

Nam ut aiunt magistri Hebraeorum, omne corpus nostrum, et carnale animal, et quicquid in nobis super materia carnis male disposita innititur, relinquitur in cibum serpenti, et ut ipsi vocant Azazeli, qui est dominus carnis et sanguinis, et princeps huius mundi, et vocatur in Levitico princeps desertorum, cui dictum est in Genesi: Terram comedes omnibus diebus uitae tuae. Et in Esaia: Pulvis panis tuus. Hoc est, corpus nostrum creatum ex pulvere terrae, quamdiu non fuerit sanctificatum, et transmutatum in melius, ut non amplius serpentis, sed dei sit effectum, videlicet ex carnali spirituale, iuxta verbum Pauli dicentis: Seminatur quod animale est, et resurget quod spirituale est. Et alibi: Omnes quidem resurgent, sed non omnes immutabuntur, quia multi remansuri sunt in perpetuum cibum serpentis. Hanc itaque turpem et horridam carnis materiam, ac serpentis cibum morte deponimus, illam aliquando in meliorem sortem, et spiritualem transmutatam reassumpturi, quod erit in resurrectione mortuorum. Et iam factum est in his, qui primitias resurrectionis degustarunt, et multi hoc ipsum virtute deifici spiritus in hac vita consecuti sunt, Enoch, et Helias, et Moses, quorum corpora transmutata in naturam spiritualem,

For as the Hebrew masters say, our entire body, the carnal animal, and whatever in us rests upon the poorly disposed matter of the flesh, is left as food for the serpent, and as they themselves call it, Azazel – who is the lord of flesh and blood, and the prince of this world, and is called the prince of the desert in Leviticus, to whom it was said in Genesis: "dust you shall eat all the days of your life;"[272] and in Isaiah: "dust shall be your food"[273] – this means that our body, created from the dust of the earth, as long as it is not sanctified and transformed for the better, so that it no longer belongs to the serpent but to God (namely, transformed from carnal to spiritual according to the word of Paul who says: "it is sown a natural body, it is raised a spiritual body;"[274] and elsewhere: "all will indeed rise, but not all will be changed,"[275] since many will remain forever as food for the serpent), therefore, in death we cast off this vile and horrid matter of the flesh, and food for the serpent, so that we may one day take it up again in a better state, transformed into a spiritual form, which will happen in the resurrection of the dead. And this has already happened to those who have tasted the first fruits of the resurrection, and many have attained this very thing by the power of the deifying spirit: Enoch, Elijah, and Moses, whose bodies, having been transformed into a spiritual

---

[272] Genesis 3:14.

[273] Isaiah 65:25: "The wolf and the lamb shall feed together; the lion and the ox shall eat straw; and dust shall be the serpent's food: they shall not hurt nor kill in all my holy mountain, saith the Lord."

[274] I Corinthians 15:44.

[275] I Corinthians 15:51.

non uiderunt corruptionem: nec sicut caetera cadavera potestati serpentis relicta sunt. Atque haec est illa disceptatio diaboli cum Michaele de corpore Moysi, cuius meminit in epistola sua Iudas, sed de Goetia et Necromantia haec satis.

DE THEURGIA

Theurgiam uero plerique putant haud illicitam, quasi haec bonis angelis, diuinoque numine regatur, cum saepissime tamen sub dei et angelorum nominibus malis daemonum fallaciis obstringatur: non solum siquidem naturalibus viribus, sed etiam certis ritibus et ceremoniis coelestes, et per illas divinas virtutes nobis conciliamus et attrahimus: de quibus multis regulis antiqui magi editis voluminibus pertractant. Omnium autem ceremoniarum pars maxima, in munditia servanda consistit, primum quidem animi, deinde etiam corporis, et eorum quae circa corpus sunt, ut in cute, in uestibus, in habitaculis, in vasis, in utensilibus, oblationibus, hostiis, sacrificiis, quorum munditia ad diuinorum consuetudinem, et contuitum disponit, et in sacris summopere efflagitatur, iuxta uerba Isaiae: Lavamini et mundi estote, et auferte malum cogitationum vestrarum. Immunditia vero quia aerem frequenter

nature, did not see corruption, nor were they left to the power of the serpent like other corpses. And this is that dispute between the Devil and Michael over the body of Moses, which Jude mentions in his epistle.[276] But this is enough about goetia and necromancy.

ON THEURGY

Many indeed believe that theurgy is not illicit, as though it were governed by good angels and a divine presence; nevertheless, it is most often tangled up with the deceptions of evil demons lurking beneath the names of God and his angels: for we bring about and attract celestial and divine virtues to ourselves not only through natural powers, but also through certain rites and ceremonies, concerning which many rules have been discussed thoroughly in the volumes written by ancient magi. However, the greatest part of all these ceremonies consists in maintaining purity, first of mind, then also of body, and of those things around the body, such as the skin, clothing, dwellings, vessels, utensils, offerings, victims, and sacrifices, whose purity disposes them towards divine custom and favor, and is greatly demanded in sacred matters, according to the words of Isaiah: "wash yourselves and be clean, and remove the evil of your thoughts."[277] Indeed impurity, because it frequently

[276] Jude 1:9.

[277] Isaiah 1:16.

et hominem inficit, mundissimum illum coelestium et divinorum influxum disturbat, et mundos dei spi[358]ritus fugat. Verum nonnunquam immundi spiritus, et deceptrices potestates, ut venerentur et adorentur pro diis, etiam hanc munditiam exquirunt: ideo hic maxima opus est cautela, de quibus late in libris nostris *de Occulta philosophia* disseruimus. Verum de hac theurgia, sive divinorum magia plura disputans Porphyrius, tandem concludit theurgicis consecrationibus posse quidem animam hominis idoneam reddi, ad susceptionem spirituum et angelorum, ad videndos deos: reditum vero ad deum hac arte praestari posse infitiatur omnino. Eius itaque scholae sunt, ars Almadel, ars notoria, ars Paulina, ars revelationum, et eiusmodi superstitionum plura, quae eo ipso sunt perniciosiora, quo apparent imperitis diviniora.

contaminates both the air and man, disturbs that most pure influence of celestial and divine powers, and drives away the pure spirits of God. Sometimes, however, unclean spirits and deceptive powers, in order to be venerated and worshipped as gods, also demand this purity: therefore, the utmost caution is needed here, about which we have extensively discussed in our books *On Occult Philosophy*. Indeed, Porphyry, discussing this theurgy or divine magic more thoroughly, concludes in the end that the soul of man can be made suitable by theurgic consecrations for the reception of spirits and angels and for seeing the gods: however, he completely denies that a return to God can be achieved by this art. There are schools, therefore, such as the *Ars Almadel*, the *Ars Notoria*, the *Ars Paulina*, the *Ars Revelationum*, and many more superstitions of this kind, which are all the more destructive, the more divine they appear to the inexperienced.

DE CABALA

Verum occurrunt hic mihi verba Plinii, qui, est et alia inquit magices factio, a Mose etiam num et Latopea Iudaeis pedens, quae verba me de cabala Iudaeorum commonefaciunt, quam in monte Sina a deo ipso Mosi datam penes Hebraeos constans opinio est, ac deinceps per successionum gradus citra literarum monumenta, usque in Ezrae tempora posterioribus sola viva voce tradita: quemadmodum Pythagorica dogmata olim ab Archippo et Lysiade, qui in Graecia Thebis scholas habuere tradebantur, in quibus discipuli memoriter doctorum praecepta tenentes, ingenio et memoria pro libris utebantur: sic et Iudaei quidam literas aspernati, in memoria et observatione, ac vocali traditione hanc collocarunt: unde cabala ab Hebraeis, quasi solo auditu unius ab altero receptio, nuncupata est. Ars (ut fertur) pervetusta, nomen autem non nisi recentibus temporibus apud Christianos cognitum.

Eius vero duplicem tradunt scientiam, unam de *Bresith*, quam et cosmologiam vocant, videlicet rerum creaturum naturalium et coelestium vires explicantem, et legis bibliaeque arcana philosophicis rationibus exponentem: quae profecto hac ratione nihil differt a magia naturali, in qua Salomonem regem praestitisse credimus. Legitur namque in sacris Hebraeorum historiis, illum disputare solitum a cedro Libani,

ON CABALA

But here the words of Pliny come to my mind: "there is," he says, "another faction of the magical art stemming from the Jews Moses and Latopea," which reminds me of the Cabala of the Jews, which, according to the consistent opinion among the Hebrews, was given to Moses by God Himself on Mount Sinai and was subsequently handed down orally through successive generations, without the aid of written records, until the time of Ezra. Just as the Pythagorean doctrines were once passed down by Archippus and Lysis, who had schools in Thebes, Greece, where the students, holding the precepts of their teachers in memory, used intellect and memory instead of books: so too did some Jews, disdaining written letters, place this knowledge in their memory, observation, and oral tradition: whence it was called 'Cabala' by the Hebrews as if it were a 'reception' from one to another by ear alone. The art (as it is said) is very ancient, but the name was not known among Christians until more recent times.

Nevertheless, they transmit its knowledge in two parts, one concerning *Bresith* – which they also call 'cosmology' – explaining the forces of natural and celestial created things, and expounding the mysteries of the law and the Bible with philosophical reasoning. In this respect it differs in no way from the natural magic in which we believe King Solomon excelled. For it is read in the sacred histories of the Hebrews that he was accustomed to speak about all manner of things from the cedar of Lebanon to

usque ad hyssopum, item de iumentis, volucribus, reptilibus, et piscibus, quae omnia magicas quasdam naturae vires prae se ferre possunt.[278] Ipse quoque inter posteriores Moyses Aegyptius, in expositionibus suis super Pentateuchum, et plures thalmudistae hanc insecuti sunt.

Alteram vero eius scientiam vocant de Mercava, quae est de sublimioribus divinarum, angelicarumque, virtutum, ac sacrorum nominum, et signaculorum contemplationibus, quaedam quasi symbolica theologia, in qua literae, numeri, figurae, res et nomina, et elementorum apices, ac lineae, puncta et accentus, omnia sunt profundissimarum rerum, et magnorum arcanorum

---

[278] Flavius Josephus, *Antiquities of the Jews*, 8.2.42: "Now the sagacity and wisdom which God had bestowed on Solomon was so great, that he exceeded the ancients; insomuch that he was no way inferior to the Egyptians, who are said to have been beyond all men in understanding; nay, indeed, it is evident that their sagacity was very much inferior to that of the king's. He also excelled and distinguished himself in wisdom above those who were most eminent among the Hebrews at that time for shrewdness… He also composed books of odes and songs a thousand and five, of parables and similitudes three thousand; for he spake a parable upon every sort of tree, from the hyssop to the cedar; and in like manner also about beasts, about all sorts of living creatures, whether upon the earth, or in the seas, or in the air; for he was not unacquainted with any of their natures, nor omitted inquiries about them, but described them all like a philosopher, and demonstrated his exquisite knowledge of their several properties."

the hyssop, likewise about beasts of burden, birds, reptiles, and fishes, all of which can bear certain magical powers of nature. Among later interpreters, Moses the Egyptian himself, in his commentaries on the Pentateuch, and most of the Talmudists have followed this.[279]

They call the other branch of this knowledge the *Merkavah*, which is concerned with the higher contemplations of divine and angelic virtues, sacred names, and seals.[280] It is a sort of symbolic theology in which letters, numbers, figures, things and names, and the apexes of elements, and lines, points, and accents, are all signs of the most profound things and great secrets.[281]

---

279 Here we have the Talmudic distinction between *ma'aseh bereshit*, the "work of creation" (or, as Maimonides interpreted it, the science of nature/Aristotelian physics/cosmology), and *ma'aseh merkavah*, the "work of the chariot" (the science of divinity/Aristotelian metaphysics). Agrippa's immediate source for this distinction is likely Giovanni Pico della Mirandola's *Oratio* and/or *Apologia*.

280 Lehrich, *The Language of Demons and Angels*, p. 98-146; Nowotny, "The Construction of Certain Seals and Characters in the Work of Agrippa of Nettesheim," p. 46-57.

281 Cf. Pico's *Conclusio* 28.33 in Farmer, *Syncretism and the West*, p. 358-359: "*Nullae sunt litterae in tota lege quae in formis, coniunctionibus, separationibus, tortuositate, directione, defectu, superabundantia, minoritate, maioritate, coronatione, clausura, apertura, et ordine, decem numerationum secreta non manifestent.*" ["There are no letters in the whole Law which in their forms, conjunctions, separations, crookedness, straightness, defect, excess, smallness, largeness, crowning, closure, openness, and order, do not reveal the secrets of the ten numerations" (i.e. *sephirot*)]. For the attribution of this passage

significativa. Hanc rursus bifariam secant, in Arithmantiam, videlicet quae notariacon vocatur, de angelicis virtutibus, nominibus, signaculisque, etiam daemonum ac animarum conditionibus tractans: atque in theomantiam, quae divinae maiestatis mysteria, emanationes, sacraque nomina, et pentacula scrutatur: quam qui norit, hunc aiunt admirandis pollere virtutibus, ita quod dum velit futura omnia praesciat, toti naturae imperet, in dae[359]mones et angelos ius habeat, et miracula faciat. Hac putant Moysen tot signa edidisse: virgam in colubrum, aquas in sanguinem vertisse: ranas, muscas, pediculos, locustas, bruchos, ignem cum grandine, vesicas et tabes Aegyptiis immisisse: primogenitum omne ab homine usque ad pecus interemisse: suosque deducentem, mare aperuisse, fontem de petra, coturnices de coelo produxisse: aquas amaras dulcorasse: fulgura et nubes per diem, columnam ignis per noctem, suis praemisse: vocem dei viventis ad populum, e coelis devocasse: arrogantes igne, murmurantes lepra, percussisse: male merentes subita strage, alios terrae hiatu absorptos affecisse: populum coelesti cibo pavisse: serpentes placasse: venenatos curasse: numerosam turbam ab infirmitate, vestes eorum a corrosione conservasse, et hostium victricem reddidisse.

---

to Menahem Recanati see Wirszubski, *Pico della Mirandola's Encounter with Jewish Mysticism*, p. 45.

This is again divided into two branches: 'arithmancy,' which is called *notarikon*, dealing with angelic virtues, names, and signs, as well as the conditions of demons and souls; and 'theomancy,' which investigates the mysteries of the divine majesty, emanations, sacred names, and pentacles: they say that whoever knows this is endowed with admirable powers, so that he can foresee all future things, command all of nature, have authority over demons and angels, and perform miracles. They believe that Moses performed all these signs: turning a rod into a serpent, turning waters into blood; sending frogs, flies, lice, locusts, and grasshoppers, fire with hail, boils, and plague upon the Egyptians; killing every firstborn from man to beast; parting the sea as he led his people; bringing forth water from the rock, quails from the sky; sweetening bitter waters; sending before his people lightning and clouds by day, a pillar of fire by night; calling down the voice of the living God from the heavens to the people; striking down the arrogant with fire, the murmurers with leprosy; afflicting the wicked with sudden destruction, and others being swallowed by the earth; feeding the people with heavenly food; appeasing serpents; healing those bitten by venomous ones; preserving a large crowd from illness, their clothes from wearing out, and making them victorious over their enemies.

Hac denique miraculorum arte et Iosue stare solem praecepisse, Eliam ignem in adversarios e coelo devocasse, puerum mortuum vita restituisse, Danielem leonum ora perstrinxisse, tres pueros in camino aestuantis incendii carminasse lusisse. Porro hac arte astruunt perfidi Iudaei etiam Christum tam admiranda saepe fecisse, Salomonem quoque hanc percalluisse, atque ex ea artem circa daemones, eorundemque vincula, et coniurationum modos, ac contra morbos, excantamenta tradidisse, ut autor est Iosephus.

By this miraculous art, Joshua is also said to have commanded the sun to stand still, Elijah to have called down fire from heaven upon his adversaries and to have restored a dead boy to life, Daniel to have closed the mouths of lions, and the three youths to have played unharmed in the blazing furnace.[282] Moreover, by this art, the perfidious Jews assert that Christ also often performed such marvels, that Solomon also mastered this art, and from it handed down knowledge about demons, their bonds, and modes of conjuration, as well as incantations against diseases, as Josephus reports.[283]

---

[282] Joshua 10:12-14; I Kings 18:36-38, II Kings 1:10-12, and I Kings 17:21-22; Daniel 6:21-22 and 3:23-27.

[283] Flavius Josephus, *Antiquities of the Jews*, 8.2.42: "God also enabled him to learn that skill which expels demons, which is a science useful and sanative to men. He composed such incantations also by which distempers are alleviated. And he left behind him the manner of using exorcisms, by which they drive away demons, so that they never return; and this method of cure is of great force unto this day; for I have seen a certain man of my own country, whose name was Eleazar, releasing people that were demoniacal in the presence of Vespasian, and his sons, and his captains, and the whole multitude of his soldiers. The manner of the cure was this: He put a ring that had a foot of one of those sorts mentioned by Solomon to the nostrils of the demoniac, after which he drew out the demon through his nostrils; and when the man fell down immediately, he abjured him to return into him no more, making still mention of Solomon, and reciting the incantations which he composed. And when Eleazar would persuade and demonstrate to the spectators that he had such a power, he set a little way off a cup or basin full of water, and commanded the demon, as he went

Verum ego Deum Moysi, caeterisque prophetis multa, quae continerentur sub cortice uerborum legis, prophano vulgo non communicanda mysteria retexuisse, ut non dubito, sic hanc quam iactant Hebraei cabalae artem, quam ego multo labore aliquando scrutatus sum, non nisi meram superstitionis rapsodiam, ac theurgicam quandam magiam agnosco: quod si (quod Iudaei iactant) a deo profecta ad vitae perfectionem, ad hominum salutem, ad dei cultum, ad intelligentiae ueritatem conduceret, profecto spiritus ille veritatis, qui repudiata synagoga venit nos docere omnem ueritatem, hanc usque in haec postrema tempora, suam non celasset ecclesiam: quae profecto omnia novit quae sunt dei, cuius benedictio, baptismus, caeteraque salutis sacramenta revelata, et perfecta sunt in omni lingua. Uniuscuiusque enim linguae par est et eadem virtus, modo par sit et eadem pietas: nec est aliud nomen in coelis, nec in terra, in quo oporteat nos salvos fieri, et in quo operemur virtutem, praeter unum nomen Iesu, in quo recapitulantur, et continentur omnia.

Hinc Iudaei in divinis nominibus peritissimi, parum aut nihil post Christum operari possunt, sicut prisci illorum patres.

---

out of the man, to overturn it, and thereby to let the spectators know that he had left the man; and when this was done, the skill and wisdom of Solomon was shown very manifestly: for which reason it is, that all men may know the vastness of Solomon's abilities, and how he was beloved of God…"

But as for myself, I do not doubt that the God of Moses and the other prophets revealed many mysteries hidden beneath the surface of the words of the law, which were not to be shared with the profane multitude. So for this art of the Cabala, which the Hebrews boast of, and which I have for some time explored with much effort, I recognize as nothing but a mere hodgepodge of superstition and a kind of theurgical magic. For if (as the Jews boast) it had been given by God for the perfection of life, the salvation of men, the worship of God, and the truth of understanding, then surely the Spirit of Truth, who came to teach us all truth after rejecting the synagogue, would not have concealed it from His Church up to these recent times: a Church that indeed knows all that is of God, whose blessing, baptism, and the other sacraments of salvation have been revealed and perfected in every language. For in each language there is equal and the same power, provided that there is equal and the same piety; nor is there any other name in heaven or on earth in which we must be saved, and in which we work virtue, except the one name of Jesus, in whom all things are gathered as one and contained.[284]

Hence, the Jews, who are very experienced with divine names, can accomplish little or nothing after Christ, unlike their ancient forefathers.

---

[284] Cf. Ephesians 1:10.

Quod autem experimur, et videmus huius artis (ut uocant) revolutionibus, saepe miras magnorum mysteriorum a sacris literis extorqueri sententias, totum hoc nihil aliud est, quam lusus quidam allegoriarum, quos otiosi homines, in singulis literis et punctis et numeris occupati, quod haec lingua, et scribendi ritus facile patiuntur, pro eorum arbitrio fingunt, atque refingunt: quae etsi nonnunquam magna sonent mysteria, nihil tamen probare, nec evincere queunt, quin iuxta verba Gregorii eadem facilitate contemnere liceat, qua asseruntur. Confinxit simili artificio pleraque Rabanus monachus, sed latinis characteribus et versibus, insertis variis imaginibus, qui quaque versus lecti, per quaelibet superficiei ac imaginum lineamenta sacrum aliquod denuntiant mysterium,

But what we experience and see in this 'art of revolution'[285] (as they call it), where miraculous interpretations of great mysteries are often extracted from the sacred letters, all this is nothing but a certain game of allegories, which idle men, obsessed with each letter, point, and number – things that this language and writing system easily allow – imagine and reimagine as they fancy. Even if these sometimes sound like great mysteries, they can prove or demonstrate nothing, for according to the words of Gregory, they can be dismissed with the same ease with which they are asserted. Rabanus the monk[286] fabricated many things through a similar contrivance, but with Latin letters and verses, inserting various images, which, when read in any direction, proclaim some sacred mystery

---

[285] I.e., "the science of the revolution of the alphabet," the very system of letter permutations that, thanks to the *Sefer Yetzirah*, Cabalists believed had been used by God to speak the world into creation. This was the same system that sat at the root of Abraham Abulafia's *ars combinandi,* a meditation system for provoking ecstatic and prophetic states. This lettrist tradition is distinct from the Lullian *ars combinatoria* used in the Latin West for mapping out the *dignitates Dei* – a system with which Agrippa was quite familiar, having written his own commentary on the Lullian art – though Pico della Mirandola had believed them to be related in some way as one branch of the *Cabala speculativa* (or the science of *shemot*/divine names). See Idel, "Ramon Lull and Ecstatic Kabbalah," p. 170-174 for a discussion of the similarities and differences between the Llullian and Abulafian arts, and how Pico interacted with both these systems.

[286] I.e., Rabanus Maurus (c. 780-856), a Carolingian Benedictine monk.

de pictae illic historiae repraesentativum: quae etiam ex prophanis literis extorque[360]ri posse nemo ignorat, qui Valeriae Probae ex Virgilii carminibus compositas de Christo centones legerit, quae omnia et eiusmodi sunt speculationes otiosorum hominum.

Quod autem ad miraculorum operationem attinet, neminem vestrum puto tam stolidae cervicis, qui de iis credat aliquam haberi artem vel scientiam. Est itaque nihil aliud haec Iudaeorum cabala, quam perniciosissima quaedam superstitio, qua verba, et nomina, et literas, sparsim in scriptura positas pro arbitrio suo colligunt, dividunt, transferunt: et alterum ex altero facientes, solvunt membra veritatis, sermones, inductiones et parabolas hinc inde ex propriis fictionibus construentes: aptare illis volunt eloquia dei, infamantes scripturas, et dicentes sua figmenta ex illis constare: calumniantur legem dei, et per impudenter extortas supputationes dictionum, syllabarum, literarum, numerorum tentant violentas et blasphemas perfidiae suae inferre probationes.

Praeterea iis nugis inflati, ineffabilia dei mysteria, et quae sunt supra scripturam arcana, sese invenire et scire iactant, per quae etiam prophetare, et uirtutes et miracula sese perficere, sine rubore, magnaque audacia mentiri non erubescunt.

through the lines and features of the surface and the images, representative of the story depicted there. No one who has read the centos of Valeria Proba, composed from the verses of Virgil about Christ, can deny that these things could also be extracted from profane literature.[287] All these and similar things are the speculations of idle men.

But as it pertains to the working of miracles, I do not think any of you are such stiff-necked fools as to believe that any art or science is involved in them. This Jewish Cabala, therefore, is nothing else but a most destructive superstition, by which they gather together, divvy up, and change words, names, and letters scattered throughout the scripture according to their own whims. By making one thing out of another, they dissolve the limbs of truth, constructing sayings, inductions, and parables here and there from their own fictions. These they seek to adapt to the oracles of God, defaming the scriptures, and claiming their fabrications to consist of them. They slander the law of God and, through impudently extorted computations of words, syllables, letters, and numbers, they attempt to impose violent and blasphemous proofs of their perfidy.

What is more, being puffed up with these trifles, they boast of discovering and knowing the ineffable mysteries of God and the secrets that are beyond scripture, through which they also claim to prophesy and perform miracles, lying without shame and with great audacity.

---

[287] I.e., Valeria Faltonia Proba (322-370), a Roman poet and author of the *Cento Vergilianus de laudibus Christi*.

Sed accidit illis, quod cani Aesopico, qui pane relicto, et umbram eius inhians, perdidit escam: sic perfidum hoc et durae cervicis hominum genus, semper in umbris scripturae occupatum, et circa illas vanitates sua artificiosa, sed superstitiosa cabala impetum faciens amittit panem vitae aeternae, et inanibus nominibus depastum perdit verbum veritatis. Ex hoc cabalisticae superstitionis Iudaico fermento prodierunt puto Ophitae, Gnostici, et Valentiniani haeretici, qui ipsi quoque cum discipulis suis Graecam quandam cabalam commentati sunt, omnia Christianae fidei mysteria pervertentes, et haeretica pravitate ad Graecas literas, et numeros protrahentes, ex illis construentes corpus, quod vocant veritatis, docentes, absque illis literarum et numerorum mysteriis non posse in evangelicis literis inveniri veritatem, quia variae sunt, et alicubi sibi repugnantes, plenaeque parabolis scriptae, ut videntes non videant, et audientes non audiant, et intelligentes non intelligant, sed caecis et errantibus iuxta suae caecitatis et erroris capacitatem propositas: latentem vero sub illis synceram veritatem solis perfectis, non per scripta, sed per vivae vocis successivam pronuntiationem esse creditam, atque hanc esse illam alphabetariam arithmanticam theologiam, quam Christus secreto manifestavit apostolis, et quam Paulus se loqui dicit non nisi inter perfectos. Cum enim haec altissima sint mysteria, ideo nec scripta esse, nec scribi, sed in silentio servari apud sapientes in abscondito secum illa custodientes. Sapiens autem apud eos nemo, nisi qui maxima haereseos monstra fabricare novit.

But they experience what happened to Aesop's dog, who, abandoning his bread, lost his meal while chasing after its shadow: thus this perfidious and stiff-necked race of men, always occupied with the shadows of Scripture and chasing after them with their artificial but superstitious Cabala, loses the bread of eternal life and, feeding on empty names, forfeits the word of truth. From this Jewish ferment of Cabalistic superstition, I think, arose the Ophites, Gnostics, and Valentinian heretics, who, with their disciples, devised a certain Greek Cabala, perverting all the mysteries of the Christian faith and, with heretical depravity, extending them to Greek letters and numbers, constructing from them a body which they call the truth, teaching that without the mysteries of these letters and numbers, the truth cannot be found in the gospel writings, because they are various, contradictory in places, and full of parables, written so that seeing they do not see, and hearing they do not hear, and understanding they do not understand, but are presented to the blind and erring according to the capacity of their blindness and error: while the hidden, sincere truth beneath them is believed to be entrusted only to the perfect, not through writings, but through the successive pronouncement of oral tradition, and that this is the alphabetic and arithmetic theology which Christ secretly revealed to the apostles, and which Paul says he speaks only among the perfect. Since these are the highest mysteries, they are therefore neither written nor to be written, but to be kept in silence by the wise, who guard them hidden within themselves. Among them, however, no one is considered wise except one who knows how to fabricate the greatest monstrosities of heresy.

DE PRAESTIGIIS

Sed redeamus ad magiam, cuius particula etiam est praestigiorum artificium, hoc est illusionum, quae secundum apparentiam tantum fiunt, quibus magi phantasmata edunt, multaque miracula circulatoriis [361] fraudibus ludunt, et somnia immittunt, quod non tam goeticis incantamentis, et imprecationibus, daemonumque fallaciis, quam etiam certis fumigiorum vaporibus, luminibus, phyltris, collyriis, alligationibus, et suspensionibus: praeterea annulis, imaginibus, speculis, similibusque magicae artis pharmaciis, et instrumentis, naturali caelestique virtute perpetratur. Multa et manuum prompta subtilitate et industria fiunt, cuiusmodi ab histrionibus et ioculatoribus quotidie fieri videmus, quos idcirco chirosophos, hoc est, manusapientes appellamus. Extant de hoc artificio libri praestigiorium Hermetis, et quorundam aliorum: legimus quoque Paseten quendam praestigiatorem refertissimum convivium hospitibus monstrare solitum, idque cum libuit rursus evanuisse, discumbentibus omnibus fame ac siti elusis. Numam Pompilium etiam istiusmodi praestigiis usum legimus. Sed et doctissimum Pythagoram id ridiculum aliquando factitasse, <ut quae collibuisset sanguine perscriberet in speculo, quo ad plenilunialem orbem obverso, stanti a tergo in disco lunae commonstrasse.>

ON TRICKERY

But let us return to magic, of which a part is also the art of trickery, that is, illusions, which are done only according to appearance, by which magicians produce phantasms, mimic many miracles by the deceptions of charlatans, and send dreams – not so much by goetic incantations, imprecations, and the lies of demons as by certain vapors of fumigations, lights, philters, eye salves, ligatures, and pendants: moreover, by rings, images, mirrors, and similar charms and instruments of magical art, it is accomplished by natural and celestial virtue. They also do many things with a quick subtlety and sleight of hand, of the sort we see performed daily by actors and jugglers, whom we therefore call chirosophists, that is, 'wise of hand.' There survive books on this art of tricks by Hermes and certain other men.[288] We also read of a certain trickster named Pasetes, who was accustomed to show a lavish feast to his guests, and when it pleased him, he made it disappear again, leaving all the diners fooled by hunger and thirst. We also read that Numa Pompilius used such tricks. But even the most learned Pythagoras is said to have engaged in this absurd practice at one time: he would write in blood whatever he wished on a mirror, and, turning it towards the full moon, he would show it to someone standing behind him, making it appear in the disk of the moon.

[288] E.g., Thabit ibn Qurra's *Liber prestigiorum* translated by Adelard of Bath in the 12th century.

Huc spectat etiam quicquid de hominum transformationibus legitur decantatum a poetis, creditum ab historicis, et a nonnullis Christianis theologis, insuper a sacris literis adfertum. Sic apparent homines asini vel equi, vel alia animalia oculis fascinatis, aut perturbato medio, idque arte naturali. Nonnunquam etiam haec fiunt a bonis et malis spiritibus, seu ad bonorum preces ab ipso deo, sicut in sacris literis legimus de Helisaeo propheta, obsesso ab exercitu regis vallantis Dothain: verum puris et apertis a deo oculis, ista non possunt illudere: sic mulier illa, quae a vulgo iumentum iudicabatur, Hilarioni non iumentum, sed quod erat mulier videbatur: ea igitur quae hoc modo secundum apparentiam fiunt praestigia dicuntur: quae autem fiunt arte permutantium aut transferentium, ut de Nabuchodonosor, aut messibus ad alios agros traductis, de his diximus superius: verum de hac praestigiorum arte sic ait Iamblichus: Quae praestigiati seu fascinati imaginantur, praeter imaginativa, nullam habent actionis et essentiae veritatem. Eisumodi nanque artificii finis est, non facere simpliciter, sed usque ad apparentiam imaginamenta porrigere, quorum mox nullum compareat vestigium.

This also relates to anything we read about the transformations of humans, celebrated by poets, believed by historians, and asserted by some Christian theologians, and even supported by sacred scripture. Thus, men appear as donkeys or horses, or other animals, when the eyes are enchanted or when the intervening air is disturbed, and this is done by natural art. Sometimes these things are also done by good and evil spirits, or by God Himself at the prayers of the righteous, as we read in the sacred scriptures about the prophet Elisha, besieged by the army of the king surrounding Dothan. Nevertheless, those with pure and open eyes given by God cannot be deceived by these things. Thus, that woman who was thought by the people to be a beast appeared to Hilarion not as a beast, but as a woman, as she truly was. Therefore, those things which are done in this way according to appearance are called tricks, while those that are done by the art of transformation or transfer, such as what happened to Nebuchadnezzar, or the crops being transferred to other fields, we have discussed above. But concerning this art of illusions, Iamblichus says: what those who are bewitched or fascinated envision, apart from imagination, has no truth of action or essence. For the purpose of such an artifice is not to do things simply, but to stretch images to the point of illusion, of which soon no trace remains.[289]

---

[289] Iamblichus, *De Mysteriis*, 25 (Taylor, *On the Mysteries*, p. 184): "But neither must you compare the most manifest surveys of the Gods with the imaginations artificially procured by enchantment. For the latter have neither the energy, nor the

Iam itaque ex his quae dicta sunt, patet non aliud esse magiam, quam complexum idololatriae, astrologiae, superstitiosaeque medicinae. Iamque etiam a magis magna haereticorum caterua in ecclesia orta est, qui sicut Iannes et Mambres restiterunt Moysi, sic illi restiterunt apostolicae veritati: horum princeps fuit Simon Samaritanus, qui Romae sub Claudio Caesare propter hanc artem statua donatus est, cum hac inscriptione: Simoni sancto deo. Eius blasphemias copiose narrant, Clemens, Eusebius, et Irenaeus. Ex hoc Simone tanquam ex haeresum omnium seminario, per multas successiones monstrosi Ophitae, turpes Gnostici, impii Valentiniani, Cerdoniani, Martionistae, Montaniani, et multi alii haeretici prodierunt, propter quaestum et inanem gloriam, mentientes adversus Deum, utilitatem nullam, [362] neque beneficia hominibus praestantes, sed decipientes, et in perniciem et in errorem mittentes, et qui credunt illis confundentur in iudicio Dei.

Verum de magicis scripsi ego iuvenis adhuc, libros tres amplo satis volumine, quos de Occulta philosophia nuncupavi, in quibus quicquid tunc per curiosam adolescentiam erratum est, nunc cautior hac palinodia recantatum volo: permultum enim temporis et rerum, in his vanitatibus olim contrivi.

---

essence, nor the truth of the things that are seen, but extend mere phantasms, as far as to appearances only."

Now, from what has been said, it is clear that magic is nothing other than a combination of idolatry, astrology, and superstitious medicine. And from the magicians a great crowd of heretics have arisen in the Church, who, just as Jannes and Jambres rose up against Moses, rose up against the apostolic truth. Their leader was Simon the Samaritan, who, under Emperor Claudius in Rome, was honored with a statue inscribed: "to Simon, the holy god." Clement, Eusebius, and Irenaeus extensively recount his blasphemies. From this Simon, as from the seedbed of all heresies, there arose through many generations the monstrous Ophites, the foul Gnostics, the impious Valentinians, the Cerdonians, the Marcionites, the Montanists, and many other heretics, who, out of greed and vain glory, lie against God, providing no benefit or utility to men, but deceiving them, leading them into ruin and error, and those who believe them will be confounded in God's judgment.

It is true that, while I was still a young man, I wrote about magic in three books of considerable volume, which I titled *On Occult Philosophy.* Whatever errors I then made in these on account of my curious youth, I now more cautiously wish to recant with this palinode: for I wasted much time and effort on these vanities in the past.

Tandem hoc profeci, quod sciam quibus rationibus oporteat alios ab hac pernicie dehortari. Quicunque enim non in veritate, nec in virtute dei, sed in elusione daemonum, secundum operationem malorum spirituum, divinare et prophetare praesumunt, et per vanitates magicas exorcismos, incantationes, amatoria, agogima, et caetera opera demoniaca, et idololatriae fraudes exercentes, praestigia et phantasmata ostentantes mox cessantia, miracula sese operari iactant: omnes hi cum Ianne et Mambre et Simone Mago aeternis ignibus cruciandi destinabuntur.

Occultae Philosophiae Henrici Cornelii Agrippae,
Finis Anno MDXXXIII,
Mense Iulio

In the end, I achieved this: I know by what means one should deter others from this peril. For whosoever presumes to divine and prophesy, not in truth nor in the power of God, but in the deception of demons, according to the operation of evil spirits, and whosoever boast of working miracles through magical vanities like exorcisms, incantations, love charms, binding spells, and other demonic works, and the frauds of idolatry which conjure up illusions and phantasms that quickly fade away: all these, together with Jannes and Jambres and Simon Magus, will be condemned to torment in eternal fires.[290]

End of Heinrich Cornelius Agrippa's
Occult Philosophy
July 1533

---

[290] II Timothy 3:8.

Bibliography

Agrippa, Heinrich Cornelius. *De occulta philosophia libri tres*. Edited by Vittoria Perrone Compagni. Leiden: Brill, 1992.

—. *De occulta philosophia libri tres*. 1510. MS Würzburg, Universitätsbibliothek, M.ch.q.50.

—. *Operum pars posterior*, Vol. 2. Lyon: Bering Brothers, c. 1600.

Ambrose. *De fide ad Gratianum Augustum*. Edited by Otto Faller. CSEL 78. Prague, Vienna, Leipzig: Hoelder-Tempsky-Freytag, 1897; reprint, London: Johnson, 1962.

Apuleius. *Metamorphoseon libri XI*. Edited by Rudolf Helm. Leipzig: Teubner, 1968.

Attrell, Dan, and David Porreca. *Picatrix: A Medieval Treatise on Astral Magic*. University Park: Penn State University Press, 2019.

Attrell, Dan, Brett Bartlett, and David Porreca. *Marsilio Ficino: On the Christian Religion*. Toronto: University of Toronto Press, 2022.

Augustine. *The City of God*. Translated by Marcus Dods. In *Nicene and Post-Nicene Fathers, First Series*, Vol. 2, edited by Philip Schaff. Buffalo, NY: Christian Literature Publishing Co., 1887.

Bacon, Roger. *Secretum Secretorum: Cum Glossis et Notulis*. Edited by Robert Steele. Oxford: Clarendon Press, 1920.

Black, Crofton. *Pico's Heptaplus and Biblical Hermeneutics*. Boston: Brill, 2006.

Blau, Joseph Leon. *The Christian Interpretation of the Cabala in the Renaissance*. New York: Columbia University Press, 1944.

Bohak, Gideon, and Charles Burnett. *Thābit ibn Qurra "On Talismans" and Ps.-Ptolemy "On Images 1-9". Together with the "Liber prestigiorum Thebidis" of Adelard of Bath*. Sismel: Edizioni del Galluzzo, 2021.

Burnett, C., "The Legend of the Three Hermes and Abu Ma'Shar's *'Kitab Al-Uluf'* in the Middle Ages." *Journal of the Warburg and Courtauld Institutes* 39, 1976: 231-234.

Campanelli, Maurizio. "Marsilio Ficino's Portrait of Hermes Trismegistus and Its Afterlife." *Intellectual History Review* 29, 1 (2019): 53-71.

Cicero, Marcus Tullius. *On Old Age; On Friendship; On Divination*. Translated by William A. Falconer. Loeb Classical Library. Cambridge, MA: Harvard University Press; London: William Heinemann Ltd., 1923.

Cicero, Marcus Tullius. *On Duties*. Translated by Walter Miller. Loeb Classical Library. Cambridge, MA: Harvard University Press; London: William Heinemann Ltd., 1913.

Cicero, Marcus Tullius. *On the Republic; On the Laws.* Translated by Clinton Walker Keyes. Loeb Classical Library. Cambridge, MA: Harvard University Press; London: William Heinemann Ltd., 1928.

Copenhaver, Brian. *Hermetica: The Greek Corpus Hermeticum and the Latin Asclepius in a New English Translation, with Notes and Introduction.* Cambridge: Cambridge University Press, 1992.

Copenhaver, Brian, and Michael J. B. Allen. *Gianfrancesco Pico della Mirandola: Life of Giovanni Pico della Mirandola and Giovanni Pico della Mirandola: Oration.* Cambridge: The I Tatti Renaissance Library, 2022.

Devereux, James A. "The Textual History of Ficino's De Amore." *Renaissance Quarterly* 28, 2, 1975: 173-182.

Dionysius the Areopagite. "Opera" in *Patrologia Graeca* 3. Edited by Jacques Paul Migne. Paris, 1857.

—. "The Celestial Hierarchy." In *The works of Dionysius the Areopagite*, Vol. 2. Translated and edited by John Parker. London, 1899.

Farmer, Stephen A. *Syncretism in the West: Pico's 900 Theses (1486): The Evolution of Traditional Religious and Philosophical Systems.* Binghamton: Arizona Center for Medieval and Renaissance Studies, 1998.

Ficino, Marsilio. *Commentary on Plato's Symposium on Love.* Translated by Sears Jayne. Dallas: Spring Publications, Inc., 1985.

—. *Epistolarum libri XII*. In *Opera omnia*, Vol. 1, 607-964. Basel: Henricpetri, 1576; reprint, Paris: Phénix, 2000.

—. *Platonic Theology*. Vol. 6, Books XVII–XVIII. Translated by Michael J. B. Allen, edited by James Hankins and William Bowen. *The I Tatti Renaissance Library*. Cambridge, MA: Harvard University Press, 2006.

Goodman, Martin, Sarah Goodman, G. Lloyd Jones, and Moshe Idel. *Johann Reuchlin: On the Art of the Kabbalah – De Arte Cabalistica*. Lincoln and London: University of Nebraska Press, 1993.

Hanegraaff, Wouter J. "Better than Magic: Cornelius Agrippa and Lazzarellian Hermetism." *Magic, Ritual, and Witchcraft* 4, 1, 2009: 1-25.

—. "Beyond the Yates Paradigm: The Study of Western Esotericism between Counterculture and New Complexity." *Aries: Journal for the Study of Western Esotericism* 1, 1, 2001: 5-37.

—. *Esotericism and the Academy: Rejected Knowledge in Western Culture*. Cambridge: Cambridge University Press, 2012.

—. "How Hermetic was Renaissance Hermetism?" *Aries* 15, 2, 2015: 179-209.

—. *Western Esotericism: A Guide for the Perplexed*. London: Bloomsbury Academic, 2013.

Hanegraaff, Wouter J., and Ruud M. Bouthoorn. *Lodovico Lazzarelli (1447-1500): The Hermetic Writings and Related Documents.* Tempe: Arizona Center for Medieval and Renaissance Studies, 2005.

Iamblichus. *On the Mysteries of the Egyptians, Chaldeans, and Assyrians.* Translated by Thomas Taylor. 2nd ed. London: Bertram Dobell and Reeves and Turner, 1895.

Idel, Moshe. *Kabbalah in Italy 1280-1510.* New Haven: Yale University Press, 2011.

—. Ramon Llull and Ecstatic Kabbalah: A Preliminary Observation." *Journal of the Warburg and Courtauld Institutes* 51, 1988: 170-174.

Josephus, Flavius. *The Works of Flavius Josephus.* Translated by William Whiston. Auburn and Buffalo: John E. Beardsley, 1895.

Jerome. *The Principal Works of St. Jerome.* Translated by William Henry Fremantle, George Lewis, and William Gibson Martley. In *Nicene and Post-Nicene Fathers, Second Series,* Vol. 6, edited by Philip Schaff and Henry Wace. Buffalo, NY: Christian Literature Publishing Co., 1893.

Lehrich, Christopher I., *The Language of Demons and Angels: Cornelius Agrippa's Occult Philosophy.* Brill: Leiden, 2003.

Matton, Sylvain. "D'un rayonnement des grammairiens latins ou le *De radiis* n'est pas d'al-Kindi." *Archives d'Histoire Doctrinale et Littéraire du Moyen Âge* 89, 1, 2023: 443-456.

McGaw, Jessie Brewer. *Heptaplus or Discourse on the Seven Days of Creation.* New York: Philosophical Library, 1977.

Maimonides, Moses. *The Guide for the Perplexed.* Translated by Michael Friedländer. New York: E. P. Dutton, 1904.

—. *The Guide of the Perplexed*, 2 vols. Translated by Shlomo Pines. Chicago and London: University of Chicago Press, 1963.

Manzalaoui, Mahmoud. *Secretum Secretorum: Nine English Versions.* Oxford: Published for the Early English Text Society by Oxford University Press, 1977.

Nauert, Charles G. *Agrippa and the Crisis of Renaissance Thought.* Urbana: University of Illinois Press, 1965.

Nowotny, Karl Anton. "The Construction of Certain Seals and Characters in the Work of Agrippa of Nettesheim." *Journal of the Warburg and Courtauld Institutes* 12 (1949): 46-57.

Ockenström, Lauri, and Vajra Regan. "The Hermetic Origins of the Liber sigillorum of Techel." *The Journal of Medieval Latin* 33 (2023): 173-266.

Ovid. *Ex Ponto*. Translated by Arthur Leslie Wheeler. Cambridge, MA: Harvard University Press, 1939.

Perrone Compagni, Vittoria. *Ermetismo e Cristianesimo in Agrippa: Il "De triplici ratione cognoscendi Deum"*. Florence: Polistampa, 2005.

—. "Heinrich Cornelius Agrippa von Nettesheim." In *The Stanford Encyclopedia of Philosophy*, edited by Edward Zalta. https://plato.stanford.edu/archives/spr2017/entries/agrippa-nettesheim/.

Philostratus. *The Life of Apollonius of Tyana*. Translated by F. C. Conybeare. Loeb Classical Library. Cambridge, MA: Harvard University Press, 1912.

Pico della Mirandola, Gianfrancesco. *De studio humanae et divinae philosophiae*. In *Opera omnia*, Vol. 2, 3-39. Basel: Henricpetri, 1573.

Pico della Mirandola, Giovanni. *On the Dignity of Man, On Being and the One, Heptaplus*. Translated by Charles G. Wallis, Paul J. W. Miller, and Douglas Carmichael. Indianapolis: Hackett, 1998 [1965].

—. *Apologia* in *Omnia quae extant opera*. Venice: Hieronymus Scotum, 1557, 13^{v}-40^{r}.

—. *Commentary on a Poem of Platonic Love*. Translated by Douglas Carmichael. Lanham: University Press of America, 1986.

Plato. *Plato in Twelve Volumes*. Vol. 8. Translated by Walter Rangeley Maitland Lamb. Cambridge: Harvard University Press; London: William Heinemann Ltd., 1955.

Pliny the Elder. *Natural History*. Translated by H. Rackham. Loeb Classical Library. 10 vols. Cambridge, MA: Harvard University Press; London: William Heinemann Ltd., 1938-1962.

Plutarch. *Plutarch's Morals*. Translated from the Greek by several hands. Revised by William W. Goodwin. Vol. 4. Boston: Little, Brown, and Company; Cambridge: Press of John Wilson and Son, 1874.

Porta, Giambattista della. *Natural Magick*. London: Thomas Young and Samuel Speed, 1658.

Pseudo-Apuleius (Hermes Trismegistus). *Asclepius*. Edited by Matteo Stefani. *Corpus Christianorum Continuatio Mediaevalis*, vol. 143. Turnhout: Brepols, 2019.

Regan, Vajra. "The *De consecratione lapidum*: A Previously Unknown Thirteenth-Century Version of the *Liber Almandal Salomonis*, Newly Introduced with a Critical Edition and Translation." *The Journal of Medieval Latin* 28, 2018: 277-333.

Reuchlin, Johannes. *De verbo mirifico*. Basel: Johann Amerbach, 1494.

Riccio, Paolo. *In cabalistarum seu allegorizantium eruditionem isagogae*. Augsburg: Johann Miller, 1515.

—. *Portae lucis: haec est porta Tetragrammaton, iusti intrabunt per eam* (*R. Josephi Gecatilia*). Augsburg: Johann Miller, 1516.

Secret, François. *Les Kabbalistes Chrétiens de la Renaissance.* Paris: Dunod, 1963.

van Bladel, K. "Sources of the Legend of Hermes in Arabic" in *Hermetism from Antiquity to the Renaissance.* Edited by Paolo Lucentini, I. Parri, and Vittoria Perrone Compagni. Turnhout: Brepols, 2003: 285-293.

—. *The Arabic Hermes: From Pagan Sage to Prophet of Science*, Oxford: Oxford University Press, 2009.

Van der Poel, Marc. *Cornelius Agrippa, the Humanist Theologian and His Declamations.* Leiden: Brill, 1997.

Virgil. *Eclogae.* In *Opera.* Edited by R. A. B. Mynors. Oxford: Clarendon Press, 1980.

Von Stuckrad, Kocku. "Christian Kabbalah and Anti-Jewish Polemics: Pico in Context." In *Polemical Encounters: Esoteric Discourse and Its Others*, by Olav Hammer and Kocku von Stuckrad. Boston: Brill, 2007.

Wirszubski, Chaim. *Pico della Mirandola's Encounter with Jewish Mysticism.* Cambridge: Harvard University Press, 1989.

Yates, Frances. *Giordano Bruno and the Hermetic Tradition.* Chicago: University of Chicago Press, 1964.

Zika, Charles. "Reuchlin and Erasmus: Humanism and Occult Philosophy." *Journal of Religious History* 9, 3, 1977: 223-246.

—. "Reuchlin's De Verbo Mirifico and the Magic Debate of the Late Fifteenth Century." *Journal of the Warburg and Courtauld Institutes* 39, 1976: 104-138.

Zambelli, Paola. *Albertus Magnus: Speculum Astronomiae.* Dordrecht: Kluwer Academic Publishers, 1992.